Unity as Prophetic Witness

Unity as Prophetic Witness

W. A. Visser 't Hooft and the Shaping of Ecumenical Theology

MICHAEL KINNAMON

FORTRESS PRESS
MINNEAPOLIS

UNITY AS PROPHETIC WITNESS
W. A. Visser 't Hooft and the Shaping of Ecumenical Theology

Every reasonable effort has been made to trace copyright holders and obtain permission to reproduce the excerpts from *The Renewal of the Church* (1956) and *No Other Name* (1963). If they come forward, the publisher will be pleased to make the necessary arrangements at the first opportunity.

Cover image: Visser 't Hooft at his desk ca. 1953 copyright © World Council of Churches. Reproduced by permission.
Cover design: Alisha Lofgren

Print ISBN: 978-1-5064-3018-8
eBook ISBN: 978-1-5064-3019-5

The paper used in this publication meets the minimum requirements of American National Standard for Information Sciences — Permanence of Paper for Printed Library Materials, ANSI Z329.48-1984.

Manufactured in the U.S.A.

Contents

Acknowledgments

This book is an opportunity, for which I am thankful, to acknowledge the senior colleagues on the staff of the World Council of Churches who, in the early 1980s, took time to share with me their understanding of, and passion for, the ecumenical movement. At the risk of overlooking persons important to my ecumenical education, I want to name Paul Abrecht, Samuel Amirtham, Marie Assaad, Huibert van Beek, Ans van der Bent, John Bluck, Ion Bria, Gwen Cashmore, Emilio Castro, Samuel Kobia, Ninan Koshy, William Lazareth, Philip Potter, Konrad Raiser, Todor Sabev, Stanley Samartha, George Tsetsis, Bärbel von Wartenberg (Potter), and Hans-Ruedi Weber. It is an extraordinary group of Christian leaders with whom I was privileged to serve.

Introduction

It was in the late summer of 1980 that I first entered the Ecumenical Center in Geneva, home to my new employer, the World Council of Churches. Arranged along one side of the expansive foyer were glass display cases filled with memorabilia of the council's first general secretary, Willem Adolf Visser 't Hooft. There were diplomas for honorary degrees from such schools as Princeton, Oxford, Toronto, Aberdeen, Harvard, and Geneva. There were medals and citations: the Grand Cross of the Order of Merit from the West German government, the Legion of Honor of France, the Cross of the Great Commander of the Holy Sepulchre from the (Orthodox) Ecumenical Patriarch, Denmark's Sonning Prize for contributions to European culture, among many others. There were letters of tribute from religious and secular officials on the occasion of his upcoming eightieth birthday, copies of various *festschrifts* compiled in his honor, and his picture on the cover of *Time* magazine. There was even a trading card from a set of "Great Christian Leaders."[1]

I was later to learn that, even then, the elderly general secretary was viewed by many as a relic of an earlier era; but bishops and theologians around the world knew his name, and, as the memorabilia display made clear, he was widely respected for the seminal contribution he had made to the ecumenical movement. Today, however, a generation after his death, Visser 't Hooft seems to have been all but forgotten. Older colleagues may know the name, but my experience tells me that even fewer of them are familiar with any of his sixteen books and hundreds of articles and essays. There is no doubt that a study of the man and his writings can tell us much about the shaping of ecumenical theology. I believe that new attention to his work can also provide insight for the contemporary church—its unity, mission, and renewal.

ECUMENICAL LEADER AND THEOLOGIAN

The term *ecumenical movement* designates those activities and organizations aimed at promoting common service and witness—as well as theological reconciliation—among Christian churches and, ultimately, at helping them to manifest their unity in Christ. *Ecumenism*, as the work of the movement is called, is expressed in countless local settings where Christians of different church traditions come together for various forms of cooperation and prayer. And it is expressed nationally and globally through such things as councils of churches, interdenominational relief organizations, and theological dialogues between still-separated churches. The most visible expression of ecumenism is the World Council of Churches (WCC), which resulted from the confluence of two streams of ecumenical activity: Life and Work, that part of the movement concerned with fostering common Christian response to such things as war, poverty, oppression, and natural calamity; and Faith and Order, that part concerned with overcoming doctrinal barriers to visible unity of the church (e.g., disagreements over sacraments, ministry, and church authority). The WCC was inaugurated on the heels of the Second World War, but the movement traces its roots to the nineteenth century, and its symbolic beginning is often identified with a great mission conference held in Edinburgh in 1910.[2]

There is no official *ecumenical theology* since the movement is, by definition, that place where churches with often-differing theological perspectives engage one another. The mere existence of such a "place," however, implies certain assumptions about the church. And over the past century, a number of ideas about the nature and mission of the church, and the God who calls and commissions it, have gained wide support as a result of ecumenical dialogue.

W. A. "Wim" Visser 't Hooft was the most influential, most indispensable, leader of the ecumenical movement in the twentieth century—a dominant presence and theological influence from the 1930s through the 1960s, still offering his written thoughts on the history and intellectual basis of the movement until his death in 1985. In the words of one longtime colleague, without Visser 't Hooft's "combination of gifts the WCC might never have existed. No other person possessed the acumen, imagination, statesmanship, experience, daring, energy and languages necessary to bring it into being."[3] The historian Martin Marty called him a "Dag Hammarskjöld of spiritual internationalism."[4]

Visser 't Hooft's greatest contribution was through the WCC, which he served as general secretary from its inception until his retirement in 1966. But he was closely associated with nearly every major ecumenical initiative of the century: the YMCA, the Student Christian Movement and the World Student Christian Federation, and both Life and Work and Faith and Order. I am the editor of an anthology of texts drawn from all of the major streams of ecumenism.[5] I could have included a writing from Visser 't Hooft in nearly every chapter, a statement I can make about no one else.

Most significantly, it was Visser 't Hooft, more than any other figure in the movement, who sought to integrate these disparate priorities—doctrinal reconciliation, common work for peace and justice, shared service to refugees and others in need, a cooperative approach to mission and evangelism, renewal of the church through education and the full inclusion of laity, women, and youth—in a compelling vision of the church and its engagement with wider society. Robert Mackie, WCC associate general secretary during the Visser 't Hooft years, says it was "Wim's ability to draw the different elements of the ecumenical movement together so that a coherent unity of purpose began to emerge that was his special gift."[6]

All of this makes a study of the WCC's first general secretary essential when discussing the shaping of ecumenical thought. His published work summarizes, with theological sophistication, the assumptions that drove the movement during what many historians regard as its heyday: the formation of the WCC (1948) and national councils around the world; the creation of numerous united churches, such as the Church of South India (1947) and the US-based United Church of Christ (1957); the entry into the movement of churches from newly independent countries in Asia and Africa; and the Second Vatican Council (1962–65), which moved the Roman Catholic Church from the periphery to the center of ecumenical activity.

It is interesting that Visser 't Hooft did not claim to be a theologian; in fact, he frequently disavowed the title, including in his *Memoirs*: "My own writings on theological matters are not original contributions to theological thought, but interpretations across confessional and linguistic frontiers of thoughts which I have picked up from theological path-finders."[7] A general secretary, he said, has too many irons in the fire to give sufficient attention to theological reflection. He was, at least in his own mind, simply a bridge between theological schools, a disseminator of insights learned from various churches and cultures.

There is no doubt that Visser 't Hooft *was* heavily indebted to other thinkers (who isn't?), especially Karl Barth. To say only this, however, would be to sell him short. Despite the administrative demands of his positions, he was well read in biblical studies, church history, and theology, and, as even he acknowledged in his *Memoirs*, he gave considerable place to theology in his public presentations. (When he invited me to his room in the Ecumenical Center, it was to his "study," not his "office.") He insisted that he could not make a budget without theologizing.[8]

The eminent Dutch theologian Hendrikus Berkhof goes further: "[Visser 't Hooft] was an independent thinker who took what he found to be true in the work of others and assembled it to form his own distinctive pattern. The other facet of his originality, undoubtedly the most important and influential one, was his capacity to use his insights as building materials for the construction of a new ecumenical theology transcending confessional and continental boundaries."[9] I cannot think of an instance where he appeals to Barth, or any other theologian, as the primary authority for a theological argument. The principal appeal is always to Scripture, which he treats with the well-informed nuance of a theologian.[10]

Speaking to the Third World Conference on Faith and Order (Lund, 1952), Visser 't Hooft called on the gathered scholars "to speak adequately about that intermediate situation in which, while having a real unity, we have not that greater unity which we believe the Lord desires us to have. In other words we need a theology of the abnormal situation in which we are today."[11] This, it seems to me, is the task he also saw for himself. Visser 't Hooft often contended that Christians lack the theological vocabulary for this "in-between time"—no longer completely divided, yet not fully united, recognizing the given oneness we already have in Christ, yet actively longing for the fuller expression of unity promised to us. Several of his books, especially *The Pressure of Our Common Calling*, try to provide a theological framework or vocabulary for understanding "how unity works" and for understanding the community peculiar to a council of churches, some of whose members don't recognize others as churches.

PERSONAL INFLUENCE

I knew Dr. Visser 't Hooft during my years on the staff of the World Council in the early 1980s, years when he was already debilitated by emphysema and nearing the end of his life. Despite this illness that limited his speaking and made even breathing difficult, he often drove to the Ecumenical Center for afternoon tea, where I took every possible opportunity to sit at his table. On several occasions, my wife and I prepared an evening meal that we ate with him in his home, with its Rembrandt etchings on the walls and wool "table rugs," typical of Dutch homes, on the smaller tables. (After one such meal, not long before I left the council, I expended all of his energy in order to tape an interview—that I later inadvertently recorded over!) And it was my pleasure to take part in monthly theological salons in his living room. Participants, usually senior colleagues from the WCC, would arrive by 7:00 p.m., pause for a glass of wine at 8:00 p.m., and leave by 9:00 p.m., when the emphysema forced our host to retire.

I consider it a great privilege to have known the man I invariably called Dr. Visser 't Hooft in this way, but I must admit that interacting with him was not always easy. Colleagues who knew him far longer and better than I have written of his "sometimes abrasive and aggressive style," his "short temper" and "acid tongue."[12] Robert Bilheimer, the behind-the-scenes organizer of early WCC assemblies, says that Visser 't Hooft "had little gift for putting up with what appeared to be the foolishness of others. His irritation rose, his rudeness obtruded, his anger flashed when his own discernment ran ahead of our ability to keep up with it."[13] I recall one dinner conversation, when I was complaining of something or other that some church had done. "The church is God's," said Dr. Visser 't Hooft. "You obviously don't trust enough in God." Another time he asked me, "Do you read your New Testament every day in Greek?" When I admitted that I didn't, he responded, "Then do not pretend to be a theologian." There was almost no small talk during our dinners together.

But what I learned from those conversations! Visser 't Hooft was the great keeper of ecumenical memory and interpreter of ecumenical trends. His mind, sharp to the end, was filled with descriptions and analyses of Life and Work conferences or the ecumenical importance of Bonhoeffer or the conflict over apartheid or contacts with ecumenical forerunners in the Roman Catholic Church. Misconceptions I had about ecumenism—for example, that steps toward unity involve theological "compromise," or that unity is in any way synonymous with cooperation—were blown away while listening to him over tea or dinner or a glass of wine.

And since that time, I have drawn repeatedly on his insights, especially during my tenure as general secretary of the National Council of Churches in the United States. It was Visser 't Hooft who helped me understand how the ecumenical movement can be both a forum where conflicting perspectives meet in dialogue and a renewal effort that boldly declares the gospel's partisanship on behalf of the excluded and oppressed. More than anyone else, Visser 't Hooft helped me to grasp the ecclesiological significance of life together in the fellowship of a council of churches. Perhaps his greatest gift to me was the clarity of his priorities: Christ, church, ecumenical movement, WCC, in that order. Despite his intimate identification with the WCC, Visser 't Hooft was anything but a defender of the council as institution. Indeed, he repeatedly insisted that conciliar bodies must see themselves as provisional steps toward deeper communion as the *church*. If a council is regarded as a service organization whose aim is its own continuation, then it actually hinders the work of ecumenism—becoming, in his words, "a narcotic rather than a stimulant."[14] Our focus should always be on the church, called into being by God's self-revelation in Jesus Christ, and its participation in God's liberating, reconciling mission to the world.

I know from experience that the ecumenical movement, without doubt one of the major developments in the past century of Christian history, is often perceived as a series of documents and consultations—perhaps life-changing for those who took part, but rather lifeless for those who didn't. At its core, however, is a vision of the church that was and is embodied in persons, in networks of relationships. Visser 't Hooft hoped that his *Memoirs* would "show that [ecumenism] is not just another piece of ecclesiastical machinery, but a movement in which human relations and creative ideas play the decisive role."[15]

My hope is that *this* book will generate fresh interest in ecumenism by enabling a new generation to experience it through the life and work of one of its greatest practitioners. Visser 't Hooft, as I have already suggested, was a complex man, one who most certainly cannot be reduced to his institutional role. He had, for example, an extraordinary breadth of intellectual interests. His book *Rembrandt and the Gospel*, written in German, was translated into several languages and well received by art historians. When asked by *The Christian Century* to name the books that shaped him, the novels of Dostoevsky were at the top of the list.[16] I recall that he was full of questions about the interdisciplinary field of my PhD study: religion and literature. At the same time, in WCC settings his singleness of focus on matters of the church was legendary, and he could be impatient when conversations digressed.

Visser 't Hooft's description of Cardinal Willebrands, a key leader in the Catholic Church's embrace of ecumenism, describes another dialectic in his own character: "He was at once a progressive ecumenist looking for ways of making a real advance towards unity and a realist who knew that, in order to have results, an ecumenical policy . . . must be the art of the possible and not a castle built in the air."[17] He had a distaste for detailed administration, apparently fearing that a concentration on procedure could get in the way of a proper focus on ideas and relationships;[18] yet I am incredibly impressed with his ability to keep the WCC on course when there was no precedent for the role of general secretary. The accuracy of his instincts enabled him to grasp the essential point in the midst of competing concerns and perspectives, to "raise with clarity and economy just the right issues."[19] Bilheimer calls him "a genuinely prophetic church policy-maker and administrator,"[20] a combination so rare it is practically oxymoronic.

His driven personality could give the impression of arrogance. For example, the American Methodist theologian and ecumenical leader Albert Outler claimed that Visser 't Hooft "fancies himself something of a Protestant pope."[21] I recall the evening when he told me, with evident pride, that his bibliography now listed a thousand items. But in his book *The Genesis and Formation of the World Council of Churches*, he never overemphasizes his role. He tells nothing of his reaction to being named general secretary. He says nothing of his part in formulating the famous Stuttgart Declaration (to which we will return later in this book) or in expanding the Basis Statement of the WCC. He quotes from only one of his speeches, his report to the Council's First Assembly, explaining that it was presented on behalf of the WCC's Provisional Committee. The story he tells is focused on the role of others, to whom, he believed, we are all indebted.

Visser 't Hooft often cited the results of ecumenical conferences and dialogues, urging recognition of the advances made through the movement. He was clear, however, that this was a celebration of God's unifying Spirit, not a cause for human triumphalism. In the immediate aftermath of Vatican II, when ecumenical influence was at its zenith, Visser 't Hooft insisted that

Christians should be ashamed of their continuing divisions, not proud of their incomplete efforts. The question, he wrote at the time, is whether the churches will be like a horse that gallops up to a hurdle and then shirks the jump.[22]

In one sense, he was remarkably consistent (as we shall see in later chapters); his theological framework and basic message remained the same from the early 1930s until his death. At the same time, he was able to take account of, and to some extent assimilate, the dramatically new developments in ecumenical thinking stemming from such things as the demise of Christendom and the growth of liberation movements—as long as they did not violate what he took to be the core message of the gospel. His emphatically Christocentric perspective could make interfaith relations problematic, but even here his position was by no means one of simple opposition.

A WORD FOR OUR ERA?

This complex man, so important to the shaping of the movement for Christian unity, was himself decisively shaped by the Christian confrontation with National Socialism. Of the thirty-eight chapters in his *Memoirs*, fifteen are devoted to the German church struggle of the 1930s and the churches' response during World War II. The times—dominated as they were by a deadly, idolatrous ideology—cried out for a bold, united counter-witness from the church. But Visser 't Hooft saw that the church, divided and compromised by the powers it was called to expose, was in no way up to the challenge. It desperately needed to overcome its enervating fragmentation through a renewed focus on the gift and promise of Christ. The Orthodox theologian Alexandros Papaderos has rightly called Visser 't Hooft "the most persistent 'gadfly' of world Christianity in the twentieth century,"[23] using his post at the WCC to encourage, reproach, and instruct the churches to realize their essential communion and to fulfill their calling. No one, according to Lesslie Newbigin, could work under Visser 't Hooft's leadership and then revert to "a cozy ecclesiastical domesticity."[24] He insisted, and insisted that others join him in his insistence, that the churches *together* fulfill their prophetic role in society.

As I write this book, the church, perhaps especially in the United States and Europe, is again confronted with seemingly insuperable challenges: growing nationalism and an accompanying fear of "others"; social fragmentation, including an ever-greater disparity between rich and poor; the threat of terrorism and a reliance on military responses to it; increasing threat to the environment. I do not mean to overstate the parallels, but I also do not want to refrain from noting certain similarities. Then as now, parts of the church give apology for militarism and xenophobia, while other parts lament their own weakness in opposing them. Then as now, the church is split by fissures of race and class and political perspective that run through the culture. Then as now, many Christians see their faith as a retreat from the issues and problems of the day, not a basis from which to engage them.

Visser 't Hooft conceived of the emerging ecumenical movement as a means for addressing such ecclesial weakness. He saw it as a movement of the Holy Spirit in which the parts of the body gain strength through contact with one another. He envisioned the day when much of the church, at least, would be able to bear concerted, biblically grounded witness to God's redemptive incarnation and to God's will for justice and peace. We know, however, that this movement for renewal, following a period of astonishing growth and vitality, has, over the past half century, lost energy and direction—is itself in need of renewal.[25]

Does Visser 't Hooft, a man who had such impact on the church of his era, have a word for ours? Can an examination of his theology, including where it now seems problematic, give clarity to our reflections about the nature and purpose of the church? I agree with documents prepared for the WCC's Tenth Assembly in 2013: "It would be misleading to call for a new vision for the ecumenical movement." After all, the core elements of the vision that emerged over the past hundred years—the unity and renewal of the one church and its participation in God's mission of renewing creation—are firmly rooted in Scripture. But "a fresh articulation of the ecumenical vision"[26] is certainly called for. Can an examination of Visser 't Hooft's thought help with this task?

THE SHAPE AND PURPOSE OF THIS BOOK

It is surprising that little has been written about Visser 't Hooft's life and theological thought in Dutch, French, German, or English—languages in which he wrote. There is an informative booklet on the WCC's first general secretary by the council's longtime librarian, Ans van der Bent, and a fine examination of Visser 't Hooft's theology of renewal, titled *The Future of the Church*, by François Gérard. The latter volume was published, however, in 1974, after which Visser 't Hooft lived eleven years and wrote four more books. A book in German by Jan Schubert, *Willem Adolph Visser 't Hooft (1900–1985): Ökumene und Europa*, was published as I was completing my own research in 2017, but it focuses on Visser 't Hooft's understanding of, and contribution to, European unity—political, social, and cultural. An invaluable resource is his own *Memoirs*, although all such works of self-interpretation must be approached with a critical eye.

The following pages are intended to introduce English readers directly to the work of Visser 't Hooft, to let his own voice speak to a new generation. This is especially true of chapter 2, which contains representative excerpts from his writings. That chapter is preceded by one that traces the course of his life, with special attention to his development as a theologian. This book is not a biography,[27] but it is important to set Visser 't Hooft's thought in historical context. The last two chapters examine key themes in his theology, identify major criticisms of his work, and suggest his possible relevance for the contemporary ecumenical movement.

Notes

1. A more extensive list of honors and degrees is in Ans J. van der Bent, *W. A. Visser 't Hooft: 1900–1985; Fisherman of the Ecumenical Movement* (Geneva: WCC Publications, 2000), 22–23.

2. For a full discussion of the term, see W. A. Visser 't Hooft, "The Word 'Ecumenical'—Its History and Use," in *A History of the Ecumenical Movement 1517–1948*, ed. Ruth Rouse and Stephen Charles Neill, 2nd ed. (Philadelphia: Westminster, 1967), 735–40.

3. Quoted in Ans J. van der Bent, "Visser 't Hooft, Willem Adolf," in *Dictionary of the Ecumenical Movement*, ed. Nicolas Lossky et al. (Geneva: WCC Publications, 2002), 1197.

4. The quotation is in prefatory comments to an article by Geiko Müller-Fahrenholz, "No Communion without Compassion: Visser 't Hooft," *Christian Century*, February 15, 1984, 166.

5. Michael Kinnamon, ed., *The Ecumenical Movement: An Anthology of Key Texts and Voices*, 2nd ed. (Geneva: WCC Publications, 2016).

6. Robert C. Mackie, "W. A. Visser 't Hooft: An Appreciation," in *The Sufficiency of God*, ed. Robert C. Mackie and Charles C. West (Philadelphia: Westminster, 1963), 8.

7. W. A. Visser 't Hooft, *Memoirs* (London: SCM, 1973), 351.

8. This observation comes from Visser 't Hooft's longtime associate, Robert S. Bilheimer, *Breakthrough: The Emergence of the Ecumenical Tradition* (Grand Rapids: Eerdmans, 1989), 74.

9. Hendrikus Berkhof, "Visser 't Hooft as Ecumenical Theologian," *Ecumenical Review* 38, no. 2 (1986): 203.

10. Bilheimer makes the same point in *Breakthrough*, 74, 82.

11. W. A. Visser 't Hooft, "Faith and Order and the Second Assembly of the World Council of Churches," in *The Third World Conference on Faith and Order*, ed. Oliver S. Tompkins (London: SCM, 1953), 135.

12. See van der Bent, *W. A. Visser 't Hooft*, 44; Bilheimer, *Breakthrough*, 74.

13. Bilheimer, *Breakthrough*, 74.

14. Visser 't Hooft, "Faith and Order and the Second Assembly," 130.

15. Visser 't Hooft, *Memoirs*, ix.

16. Material in this paragraph comes from van der Bent, *W. A. Visser 't Hooft*, 48–49, 25.

17. Visser 't Hooft, *Memoirs*, 329.

18. See Mackie, "An Appreciation," 14, 9. This observation is also made by Paul Abrecht, longtime director of the WCC office on Church and Society, in his review of Visser 't Hooft's *Memoirs*. See *Ecumenical Review* 40, nos. 3–4 (1988): 541.

19. Philip Potter, "But Still It Moves: A Review of the *Memoirs* of W. A. Visser 't Hooft," *Ecumenical Review* 25, no. 3 (1973): 377.

20. Bilheimer, *Breakthrough*, 75.

21. Bob Parrott, *Albert C. Outler: The Gifted Dilettante* (Anderson, IN: Bristol Books, 1999), 134; see also 316–17.

22. See Augustin Cardinal Bea and Willem A. Visser 't Hooft, *Peace among Christians*, trans. Judith Moser (New York: Association Press, 1967), 183–84.

23. Alexandros Papaderos, "The 'Gadfly' on Trial: The 'Political' Commitment of the World Council of Churches," in *Voices of Unity*, ed. Ans J. van der Bent (Geneva: WCC, 1981), 79.

24. Lesslie Newbigin, *Unfinished Agenda: An Autobiography* (Grand Rapids: Eerdmans, 1985), 215.

25. See Michael Kinnamon, *Can A Renewal Movement Be Renewed? Questions for the Future of Ecumenism* (Grand Rapids: Eerdmans, 2014), esp. chs. 1, 14.

26. These quotations are from "Ecumenism in the 21st Century" and "Ecumenical Covenant on Theological Education," both of which can be found in Mélisande Lorke and Dietrich Werner, eds., *Ecumenical Visions for the 21st Century* (Geneva: WCC Publications, 2013).

27. For a brief overview of Visser 't Hooft's life, see van der Bent, *W. A. Visser 't Hooft*, and the entry on him, also by van der Bent, in Lossky, *Dictionary of the Ecumenical Movement*.

1.

The Shaping of an Ecumenical Theologian

THE INFLUENCE OF BARTH

Given my experience with him, it is difficult for me to picture Willem Visser 't Hooft as anything other than an old man—*the* grand old man of the ecumenical movement. There was a time, however, when Visser 't Hooft was the youngest of ecumenical leaders. Indeed, the primary reservation to his selection in 1937 as general secretary of the World Council of Churches, then in process of formation, was his youth.[1] It is a reminder of how central he was to the movement for six decades.

The man who became such a leading figure in the global church was born into a prominent, stable, and cultured Dutch family—his father a lawyer, his grandfather the presiding judge of the district tribunal in Haarlem. The year of his birth, 1900, seems appropriate in that he was a friend to many of the century's leaders and participant in some of its momentous events. In order to honor the memory of a beloved aunt, Visser 't Hooft's father added her family name, Visser, to his own, 't Hooft. The resulting name, which also seems curiously appropriate, means "head fisherman." The young Visser 't Hooft attended a "classical" secondary school where, in addition to

Latin and Greek, he learned French, German, and English, languages in which he later communicated with equal proficiency. He also took private lessons in Hebrew.

His parents belonged to the Remonstrant Church, a community that had followed Jacobus Arminius in his resistance to certain teachings of Calvin and, by the start of the twentieth century, was dominated by liberal theology. Visser 't Hooft recalls in his *Memoirs* that the local pastor, who had a considerable influence on him, had worked out an understanding of religion that owed much to the philosophy of Hegel. It was, he writes, "religion in a strongly intellectualized form," with little emphasis on the scriptural witness to God's incarnation in human history. "I was on the way to becoming a syncretist, who considered all varieties of religious experience as equally true and equally false."[2] The danger of syncretism was to remain a concern throughout his career.

Two factors moved him in another direction. The first, and more experiential, was his participation in the Dutch Student Christian Movement, where "personal encounter with Jesus was the centre of everything." This call to commit his life to Christ was reinforced by a three-month stay at Woodbrooke, a Quaker center in England. What he experienced there was "the integration of conviction and life" and the exposure to a socially relevant gospel in a community where everyone was accepted, regardless of background.[3] According to Robert Bilheimer, a close associate of Visser 't Hooft's at the WCC, the general secretary's favorite biblical passage was 2 Corinthians 4:6: "For it is the God who said, 'Let light shine out of darkness,' who has shone in our hearts to give the light of the knowledge of the glory of God in the face of Jesus Christ." Christ *in our hearts*. It is an indication of the abiding influence of these early encounters.[4]

A second factor, more intellectual, was his reading of Karl Barth's *The Epistle to the Romans*, which had a life-changing impact not only on Visser 't Hooft but on many of his contemporaries. Barth's theological position, often called *dialectical* or *neoorthodox*, was a direct challenge to liberal theology, and it provided the student Visser 't Hooft with an intellectual basis for his new-found Christian commitment. "This was a man who proclaimed the death of all the little, comfortable gods and spoke again of the Living God of the Bible. It was as if all the different elements in my religious development could now fall into place. This was the message for which I had been waiting."[5] In his *Memoirs*, Visser 't Hooft denies being a "Barthian"[6]—in part, perhaps, because Barth issued scathing criticisms of early ecumenical conferences. He did, however, publish a pamphlet-length *Introduction á Karl Barth* in French (1931) and, in the *Memoirs*, expresses gratitude to Barth "for giving me ground under my feet" and for providing theological substance to the emerging movement.[7]

A good example of what Visser 't Hooft took from Barth can be seen in the latter's communication to the Second World Conference on Faith and Order (Edinburgh, 1937), published in English as *The Church and the Churches*. Barth argues passionately that the current multiplicity of denominations compromises the church's witness to the gospel, undermines its resistance to Europe's "new paganisms," and, most importantly, is a sinful denial of the New Testament, which "speaks of a variety of communities, of gifts, and of persons *within* the one Church." He calls such division "unthinkable" and declares that Christians "must not allow ourselves to acquiesce in its reality."[8]

In Barth's view, however, the effort to achieve a united church should not be seen as a quest for ecclesial unity itself and certainly not as a response to sociological imperatives. Rather, it must be "identical with the quest for Jesus Christ as the concrete Head and Lord of the Church."[9] *He is* its unity. Only to the degree that the churches put their trust in him, that they confess Christ and live in obedience to his teaching, will they be one.

This helps account for Barth's mistrust of most ecumenical initiatives. The ecumenical movement, he insists in his communication to Faith and Order, cannot be a step-by-step process of assimilating divergent theological perspectives. It must have no hint of doctrinal compromise in a mistaken attempt to camouflage differences. It is not to be confused with cooperation or emotional harmony—"to prescribe doses of love, patience, and tolerance is futile."[10] The union of the churches must be prayerfully discovered, not manufactured, because in Christ the church is *already* one "and does not await any desires, capacities, or labors of ours for its unification."[11] Human agreements achieved through dialogue can be received with gratitude, but they are signs of the oneness Christ gives and nothing more.

Barth goes so far in this text as to declare that "the union of the churches is too great a matter to be the result of a movement"[12]—words, wrote Visser 't Hooft, that "practically amounted to a denial of the ecumenical movement's *raison d'être*."[13] The great theologian later revised his estimate of ecumenical endeavor, delivering an address at the WCC's first assembly and participating actively in the drafting of a background paper on the theme for the second assembly. But he never provided a theological answer to the questions: How does unity grow? What moves the ecumenical movement? When Visser 't Hooft took on this task in his 1957 Taylor Lectures at Yale Divinity School, published as *The Pressure of Our Common Calling*, he was drawing more on the work of such theological giants as Dietrich Bonhoeffer and William Temple than on that of Karl Barth.

Still, Visser 't Hooft's frequent assertion that ecumenism "is either a Christocentric movement or it is nothing at all,"[14] his refusal to accept the papering over of differences, and his repeated denial that cooperation or conciliar fellowship are adequate expressions of our given unity in Christ clearly echo Barth. And some parts of his corpus, such as these sentences from *The Wretchedness and Greatness of the Church* (1944), could have come from Barth's own pen: "For the Church, the whole Church, is to be found wherever His Word and His Spirit are at work. . . . Unity is thus really the work of Christ and not a product of our own goodwill. . . . It is not agreement between the churches. . . . To believe in the Church, One and Holy, is not to believe that this Church will come in some way and in some place; it is to believe that it *is* and seeks to manifest itself among us."[15]

ENCOUNTER WITH THE SOCIAL GOSPEL

In 1924, having completed his theological examinations at the University of Leiden, Visser 't Hooft accepted a position on the staff of the World Alliance of YMCAs in Geneva. The central office was dominated by American Christians, most of them supporters of the social gospel, a theological movement that tended to link salvation with social transformation. Much of his work, however, was with boys' groups in Scandinavia and Germany, which meant that he was in regular contact with two contrasting theological worlds. For the Americans, World War I, which had been fought far from US soil, was "the war to end all wars." Its end, along with the creation of the League of Nations, were seen as signs that the kingdom of God, with its promise of peace, could be advanced by human endeavor. For the Germans, these four years of devastating conflict had left their nation, and their prewar ideals, in ruins. German Christians may have eagerly prayed "thy kingdom come," but an optimistic view of *human* activity seemed absurd.[16]

Visser 't Hooft's own experience as a European, and his reading of dialectical theology, with its emphasis on human sinfulness, placed him theologically on the side of the Germans. In his view, the "spirit of Geneva" that pervaded the international organizations had a "greater affinity with Rousseau than with Calvin."[17] At the same time, he admired the can-do enthusiasm that motivated his American colleagues to devote their lives to the cause of peace. And thus began the bridge building that would characterize his career. "I tried to convince the Germans that faith in the Kingdom of God as God's gift should not lead to a passive attitude with regard to the great issues of social justice and world peace, and I tried to convince the adherents of the social gospel that the Kingdom of God was something more and different from a world without war and exploitation."[18]

During his time with the Netherland's Student Organization, some of it as chairman of the group's relief committee, Visser 't Hooft had participated in several European-based ecumenical conferences; but his first exposure to global ecumenism came when the YMCA named him as a delegate to The Universal

Christian Conference on Life and Work (Stockholm, 1925), where he was the youngest participant. The tension Visser 't Hooft tried to bridge at the YMCA surfaced in dramatic fashion on the conference's first day. The Anglican Bishop of Winchester, in his opening sermon, spoke of "the establishment of the sovereignty of Jesus Christ" and the setting up of the kingdom of God on earth. Response came quickly from Bishop Ihmels of Saxony: "Nothing could be more mistaken or more disastrous than to suppose that we mortal men have to build up God's Kingdom in the world."[19] A conference that was designed to avoid theological discussion—its unofficial slogan was "doctrine divides, but service unites"—thus came to be dominated by a specifically theological issue. Visser 't Hooft's qualms about both positions are set forth in his *Memoirs*: "The German theologians used their eschatology too easily as a justification for a complete separation between Christianity and political or social life. The American 'social gospel' enthusiasts [and British sympathizers] were building castles in the air which had little relation to the hard realities of history."[20]

It was not surprising, therefore, that Visser 't Hooft chose to write his doctoral dissertation, published in 1928, on the background of the social gospel in America. We can see the influence of Barth in Visser 't Hooft's insistence that an authentic Christian social ethic "must be based on a faith in a personal God, who has the unqualified right to claim [our] full allegiance, because He is the sovereign Lord of all life. It is only before a God who is different from us, because He is Holy and we are sinful, that man begins to realize his calling."[21] As he reads the literature of the social gospel, this confession of a sovereign, transcendent Creator has been replaced by an understanding of God as imminent in nature and humanity. "Their God is more akin to the impersonal God of pantheism than to the dynamic God of Christian theism."[22] In the latter, God and humanity are radically separated by the inescapable—and, to Visser 't Hooft, undeniable—reality of human brokenness, connected only as a result of God's gracious self-revelation. In the former, there is less talk of a qualitative difference between divine and human, and more of "a happy comradeship in the common undertaking of building a fairer and brighter world."[23] This romantic view of human nature, he argues, shows the theological weakness of the movement. He is appreciative of efforts to ground the gospel in various cultures, but not when descriptions of the coming reign of God offered by American theologians look suspiciously like the spread of American-style democracy.[24]

But if Visser 't Hooft leaned toward the Germans in their doctrines of God and human nature, he leaned toward American Christianity in "its sense of responsibility for all of life, its challenge to those who are satisfied with things as they are, its moral courage."[25] The Americans' denunciation of social injustice, he argues, is a necessary corrective to the social-ethical complacency characteristic of much continental theology. The lynchpin of his argument, however, is that the social gospel advocates could have achieved their goals, and more, if their social mission had been firmly rooted in "the deepest and most abiding elements of the Christian faith."[26] Instead of accepting the tension between the existing social order and the kingdom of God, they maintained that the latter is a category of human history in process of gradual realization. This is understandable given the way Christians have often used this tension as an excuse for withdrawing from historical struggles, but it is still misguided because it is the great biblical witness to the transcendent, personal, sovereign God, imminent only as the incarnate Word, that is "the strongest possible motive for the transformation of the world." Christians who seek to confess and obey this God have a common calling "to represent a Kingdom not of this world in this world."[27] A purely futurist understanding of the kingdom makes Christ a potential king rather than our Lord here and now, but Jesus becomes a mere social reformer if the future (eschatological) character of the kingdom is lost.[28]

This bridge-building conviction remained central to Visser 't Hooft's thought. A good example is his address to the WCC's Fourth Assembly (Uppsala, 1968), an excerpt from which is included in chapter 2. He began the speech, forty years after completion of his doctoral dissertation, by recalling the tension at Stockholm between what he now calls "vertical" and "horizontal" interpretations of the gospel. In contrast to the ethos of the late 1960s, he insisted that there can be no horizontal advance toward human justice without the vertical, God-centered orientation, but then emphasized the other side of the tension in what may be his most widely quoted sentence: "It must become clear that church members who deny in fact their responsibility for the needy in any part of the world are just as much guilty of heresy as those who deny this or that article of faith."[29] He later wrote that if he had known the sentence would become so popular he would have added a complementary one: "And church members who deny that God has reconciled man to himself in Christ are just as much guilty of heresy as those who refuse to be involved in the struggle for justice and freedom for all men and who do nothing to help their brethren in need."[30] The health of the ecumenical movement, he told the assembly, depends on holding with equal firmness these two convictions: the vertical and the horizontal, the priority of God's sovereign grace and the necessity of humanity's ethical response.

The eminent Czech religious and political leader Josef Hromadka has suggested that Visser 't Hooft was shielded by his early experience and study "against the easy optimism of the modern Christian mind, which was prevalent in those days in the Anglo-Saxon, primarily the American, world, and at the same time against the dangers of an abstract, self-sufficient, self-righteous academic theology, unrelated to the filth and dust of ordinary life."[31] Seeing both sides of this coin became crucial when the financial crisis of 1929 undercut any notion of a steadily improving international order, and the emergence of Mussolini and then Hitler in the early 1930s undercut any notion that Christians could responsibly remain aloof from political developments. The first generation of ecumenical leaders saw the church as a spiritual support for the League of Nations and other forms of peace-building internationalism. Visser 't Hooft was beginning to see the supranational Christian community as an alternative to the malignant internationalism of totalitarians.

Any reader of Visser 't Hooft's books will likely be left with the impression that he found hundreds of ways to convey the same basic message! A more sympathetic reading will emphasize his consistency; by the time he was thirty, he already held many, if not most, of his key theological convictions, convictions that provided a basis and structure for his thought over the next fifty-five years. There were times, of course, when this made him resistant to new developments in ecumenism; more often, though, he was able to see issues clearly and assimilate new insights quickly because of his well-worked-out theological framework.[32]

LEARNING FROM STUDENTS

The same year he received his doctorate (1928), Visser 't Hooft joined the staff of the World Student Christian Federation (WSCF), becoming general secretary in 1931. His responsibilities included serving as editor of *The Student World*, which he turned into a leading forum for international ecumenism and through which he dealt directly with leading theologians of the era.[33]

His experience with the Student Christian Movement and the YMCA, as well as the WSCF, gave Visser 't Hooft an appreciation for the contributions of young people that informed his career and his ecclesiology. Philip Potter, third general secretary of the WCC, maintained that Visser 't Hooft gave greater impetus than any other leader to the role of youth in the ecumenical church.[34] Youth, as he saw it, have an essential impatience that challenges the status quo in the churches and the movement. Visser 't Hooft did not speak of students and others in the younger generation as "the church of tomorrow"; rather, he sought to enlist them *now* in the great struggles of the era.[35] He also did not try to coax ecumenical participation by pretending it is always fun or easy; the times required that "we should be more single-hearted in our devotion and more radical in our obedience" to the gospel.[36] The totalitarianisms around them must be confronted with the total claim of Christ (he *alone* is Lord of heaven and earth), and calls to national identity must be countered with the solidarity of the worldwide church.[37] Many students responded enthusiastically to such a demanding, and relevant, message.

As Visser 't Hooft notes in his *Memoirs*, an important aspect of the Federation's life in the 1930s was a renewed concern for the study of Scripture. Barth's commentary on Romans had been a turning point for Visser 't Hooft, convincing him that it was possible to take the results of historical criticism seriously while also seeing in the Bible the authoritative word of God. He still struggled, however, to find a unifying message within the bewildering welter of biblical voices.[38]

A breakthrough came in 1937 when the WSCF, under Visser 't Hooft's leadership, convened an international conference devoted exclusively to the Bible. He wrote about the conference this way in *Student World*: "As we struggled together to understand the Bible 'new light broke forth from the Word' and thus [the conference] became an experience of renewal of life." How did this happen? The key, he writes, "is that we did not take for granted that we knew the Bible, but worked hard for a new understanding of the Bible as a whole for our life as a whole. . . . The Bible becomes silent when we try to force it to answer our questions. It speaks when we come to it as eager seekers for the truth of God."[39] Scholars often speak of a tension between reading the Bible "piously" and reading it "critically," when the real question, as he saw it, is whether we read it "egocentrically" or "theocentrically."

The impact of this on his subsequent work is readily discernible. Nearly all of his later books have a chapter or more in which, using historical-critical scholarship, he explores pertinent biblical themes. The Bible, he writes in *The Kingship of Christ* (1948), provides the basic insights concerning God's design for human beings and society as a whole. Bolstering theological arguments with a single "proof text," however, usually prevents its readers from hearing the authentic scriptural word and is a denial of the unity and historicity of revelation.[40]

It would be folly [for example] to seek to force the remarkable social laws of Deuteronomy upon our modern nations. But it is by no means foolish to ask what lies behind these laws, what conception of man, of his relations to his neighbor and to God's creation, how all this is fulfilled in Christ and how it may guide us in our understanding of what obedience to the Lord means today in our society. At this point the thorough historical study of the Bible is not an enemy but an ally of Biblical theology and ethics, for it helps us to discover the true meaning of the Biblical conceptions, to enter much more deeply into the strange, rich world of the Bible.[41]

Visser 't Hooft was adamant that the Bible must be considered as a coherent whole. To regard it as a collection of disparate theologies is to deny its role as foundation for Christian unity. He certainly did not contend, however, that all of its passages are equally authoritative. His later book on the "racial problem," for example, does not try to explain those biblical texts that justify discrimination against those who are different. Instead, he affirms that the inner truth of Scripture, the gospel, opposes it.[42]

All of this helps explain Visser 't Hooft's fascination with Rembrandt. In one of his lectures on the artist, collected as *Rembrandt and the Gospel*, he argues that Rembrandt "lived with his Bible." In his mature years, the painter did not "exploit" the Bible, writes Visser 't Hooft, but found a visual style that allowed it to speak.[43] For Rembrandt, and Visser 't Hooft, "the mystery of Revelation does not consist in the glorification of man, but in the complete abasement of God."[44] Or, to say it another way, the majesty of God, hidden in the world, is only revealed to faith. Rembrandt's paintings do not attempt to excite our admiration for the power or beauty of the incarnate One. They are simply the painter's artistic confession, rooted in Scripture, that invite a response of faith.

THE GERMAN CHURCH STRUGGLE

If, during the 1930s, students were Visser 't Hooft's primary constituency and the Bible increasingly his inspiration, the struggle of the church against modern forms of idolatry was his dominant theme. The conference of the International Missionary Council, meeting in Jerusalem in 1928, had emphasized the threat of secularism. But "before long," writes Visser 't Hooft, "I came to see that secularism was too negative a concept to explain the spiritual situation of the time."[45] Fascism, National Socialism, and Marxism were nothing less than "false religions," demanding ultimate devotion to nation, race, or party—and should be responded to accordingly.[46]

In this regard, Visser 't Hooft was strongly influenced by the struggle of the Confessing Church in Germany against the so-called German Christian Movement, the network of state-supported churches that welcomed the leadership of Hitler and the ideology of Nazism. "Guiding Principles of the Faith Movement of German Christians," published in 1932, called for the union of German evangelical (i.e., Protestant) churches around the understanding that "race, folk and nation [are] orders of existence granted and entrusted to us by God. God's law for us is that we look to the preservation of these orders." Christian faith knows about love toward those who are helpless, said leaders of the movement, "but we also demand that the nation be protected against the unfit and inferior. . . . Holy Scripture is also able to speak of a holy wrath and a refusal of love." What we want is "an evangelical church that is rooted in our nationhood. We repudiate the spirit of world-citizenship." The church must be "in the forefront of the crucial battle for the existence of our people."[47]

In 1933, a mass meeting of German Christians in the Berlin Sports Palace passed a resolution calling for the discharge of ministers unwilling to cooperate with National Socialism, the removal of all Christians with "alien blood" to a Jewish Christian church, the removal of anything "un-Germanic" from the church service and confession, the freeing of the gospel from its "Oriental distortions," and reformulation of the idea of *diaconia* to mean service to fellow Aryans.[48] The effect of this in congregations was chilling, including altars draped with the swastika and children baptized in the three-fold name of nation, race, and Führer.

Six months after the Berlin gathering, delegates from Lutheran, Reformed, and United churches met in Barmen for the "free synod" of the German Evangelical Church, a courageous counter-witness to the majority movement. Some of these delegates had been part of a centrist group, seeking to give allegiance both to Christ and the state. By the time of the Barmen synod, however, "both-and" had given way to "either-or." We see this clearly in the famous "Barmen Declaration," the primary drafter of which was Karl Barth. The first of its six theses lays the groundwork for all that followed: "Jesus Christ, as he is attested for us in Holy Scripture, is the one Word of God which we have to hear and which we have to trust and obey in life and in death. We reject the false doctrine [that] the church could and would have to acknowledge as a source of its proclamation, apart from and besides this one Word of God, still other events and powers, figures and truths, as God's revelation."[49]

As this suggests, the delegates at Barmen realized that they were involved not simply in a struggle for control of the church but in a struggle over what the church *believes*. The most appropriate response to the situation, therefore, was not a resolution aimed at fostering political action but a declaration—a confession—aimed at clarifying the core of the Christian faith. Anglo-Saxon reaction to Barmen tended to celebrate it as a defense of religious freedom (i.e., that the church should be free from government interference), but leaders of the Confessing Church disputed this interpretation. Barmen, wrote Barth, is "not about freedom, but about the necessary bondage of the conscience" to the truth of the gospel.[50]

In several presentations of this period, Dietrich Bonhoeffer argued, often quite stridently, that the Confessing Church confronts the emerging ecumenical movement with essential challenges: On what grounds does it stand? What is the basis of genuine unity? And which side will it support in this struggle to define the church in Germany? It is not enough, wrote Bonhoeffer in a paper from 1935, for churches to be together on the basis of generalized good will. They need to name without equivocation the truth that binds them to one another. He condemned the "romantic liberal idea" that truth is in unity, unless Christians also insist that unity must be in truth. He added, however, that the church has too often separated on the basis of some theological abstraction. The church must confess in the concrete, staking out its claims to truth against this or that particular distortion[51]—for example, the German Christian Movement of the 1930s or, a generation later, the apartheid-supporting churches in South Africa.

There is no doubt that all of this shaped Visser 't Hooft decisively, in ways that will become apparent throughout this book. One of the leaders of the Confessing Church, Martin Fischer, has written of how Visser 't Hooft gave courage to him and his colleagues, "participated as few other foreigners in the give and take of theologically responsible action in Germany," and called the formation of the Confessing Church "the great ecumenical event of our time"[52]—a judgment since echoed by others.

Visser 't Hooft's major writing project from this period was his book of 1937, *None Other Gods*—the title itself, taken from the King James translation of the first commandment in Deuteronomy 5—indicating his intent to bring Christian faith to bear on the great heresies of the era.[53] The book also confirms his indebtedness to Barth. Christians must choose which God they will serve! The German church struggle shows the disastrous effects of trying to live with a "double loyalty." When the church claims fidelity to both Christ and nation, it has no prophetic word for its society, and thus becomes superfluous.[54] The choice, to say it another way, is not between religion and nonreligion (secularism). The choice is between religion and God—the holy Creator known to humanity most completely in God's self-disclosure, Jesus Christ. "For religion is a human affair: it has to do with *our* thoughts and feelings."[55] God may well be opposed to the Christian religion if (when) it begins to be self-centered. And that is why it would be preposterous, writes Visser 't Hooft, to try to convince others that our religion is superior, of benefit to the whole world.[56] We proclaim not Christianity but God, the Father of our Lord Jesus Christ, the sovereign One who relativizes all of our attempts to be religious.

In *None Other Gods*, Visser 't Hooft vigorously rejects what he sees as "a widespread and deep-rooted skepticism with regard to all truth, wherever it comes from."[57] Such relativism will not stand the test of radical evil. If we can't say "*this* is true," then we won't be able to say "*that* is false" with conviction. The problem is that others have reacted to this widespread uncertainty about truth by giving allegiance to the authoritarianisms (e.g., Nazism) that Visser 't Hooft identifies as false religions. His answer: Christians should be "intolerant concerning the things of God and tolerant concerning the things of man"[58]—that is, they should accept human differences while proclaiming, with unshakable confidence, the revealed truth on which Christianity is founded. Apart from such a stance, relativism will hide under a banner of tolerance, allowing intolerable things to flourish. False gods must be confronted with *the* good news.

It is when we think about this in light of the church that the discussion becomes explicitly ecumenical. Nineteenth-century liberal theology had generally devalued the church, regarding it as simply another human institution, an external added to the internal core of Christian faith.[59] Visser 't Hooft reflects a growing ecumenical conviction when he asserts in *None Other Gods* that the church is called to be nothing less than a visible embodiment of the gospel. The church, he writes, "is not an appendix to the Christian life but rather one of its constitutive and indispensable elements." Far from being a mere association of like-minded persons, the church is "the inevitable form which God's work takes in the world." To belong to the community of the church is to belong to "a fellowship which transcends all frontiers of nation or race or class"[60] and, thus, challenges head-on, by its very nature, the claims of the German Christian Movement and other such idolatries.

Of course, it is a great understatement to say that the church, timid and divided, has generally failed to live up to its calling! And, therefore, "the main task of the Christian Community, and the greatest service which it can render to the world, is to *be* the Christian Community"[61]—a position he reiterated in his chapter for *The Church and Its Function in Society*, a preparatory volume for the great Oxford Conference on church and society of 1937. We *believe* in the church God wills, even as the churches remain entangled in the world of nations, races, and classes. The ecumenical movement—by holding up a vision of the one, universal church—provides the criterion for the renewal of the now-separated ecclesial bodies. The movement, he writes, may even be a "down payment" on the united church that is to come.[62]

When thinking about how the swirling currents of the 1930s shaped Visser 't Hooft's theology, it is important to keep in mind that the Confessing Church, and its Barmen Declaration, had the immediate effect of promoting church division. The professed goal of the Nazi-supported movement was to create a German Protestant Church, united in confession and structure. The Barmen synod declared, to the contrary, that where the "destructive errors" of the German Christians hold sway, "the church . . . ceases to be the church." It's not that the Christians at Barmen were withdrawing from other followers of Christ; they were convinced that these others had already separated themselves by their false confession. Do not be fooled by talk of unity! The German Christian program, in its absorption of Nazi ideology as an alternative source of revelation, had gone well beyond the limits of legitimate diversity in the body of Christ.[63]

Life and Work, that part of the ecumenical movement that seeks to apply Christian ethics to the social problems of modern life, quickly identified itself with the Barmen Declaration, insisting, as early as 1934, that the Confessing Church was the sole legitimate representative of Protestant Christianity in Germany. Since this church was defending central Christian principles, there could be no neutrality in the conflict. By contrast, Faith and Order, that part of the movement that seeks to overcome traditionally divisive theological questions, refused to take sides in the struggle, regarding the Confessing Church as but one party within German Protestantism. The leaders of Faith and Order were certainly not pro-Nazi, but they contended that Faith and Order is a forum for dialogue among diverse, even troublingly diverse, Christian convictions.[64] This is a tension that runs throughout modern ecumenism.

Visser 't Hooft was part of the leadership team of both seminal ecumenical conferences in 1937: Oxford, the second in the Life and Work series (the first being Stockholm), and Edinburgh, the second world gathering of Faith and Order. There is no doubt, however, that his heart was in the former, the unofficial motto of which was "let the church be the church!" One reason was his suspicion that Faith and Order produced verbal agreements before real differences were thoroughly faced.[65] This idea that the churches need to understand one another in depth as a prelude to substantial agreement, a characteristic of his mature writing, was already present in his book of 1933, *Anglo-Catholicism and Orthodoxy*, where he warned against "official politeness" that avoids confronting deep differences.[66] The bigger reason, however, was his conviction that Faith and Order was too cautious and ecclesiastical. The church must be willing to enter the historical combat. It must be willing to take sides when it believes the gospel is at stake—even when doing so risks being divided or co-opted. Barth also recognized this when, years later, he condemned the church for its "habit of coming to the scene too late, of entering the fray only when its opinions no longer involve any risk and can no longer exert any particular influence."[67]

The whole German church struggle, as historians have called it, convinced Visser 't Hooft, if he didn't already know it, that theology is inherently political. To praise the living God is to challenge the human-centeredness of every culture and political system. To confess belief in God as creator, redeemer, and sustainer of life is to undercut the pretensions of every dominant ideology. To affirm the Christian doctrines of creation and incarnation is to declare that life in *this* world is precious to God, and that the church is, therefore, appropriately engaged in social transformation.

The problem is that the church often fails to draw—or, at least, make clear—the implications of its confession. "Hitler had no objections to Christians who confessed that Jesus is Lord," Arthur Cochrane points out in his study of the German church in this period, "but he was enraged when they confessed that Jesus is Lord and Hitler is not."[68] To say "yes" to the gospel is to say "no" to that which opposes or distorts it. And this no, which Barmen certainly declared, is unavoidably political.

ECUMENISM IN A TIME OF WAR

Just prior to the world conferences in Oxford and Edinburgh, a pivotal meeting of church leaders and officers of various ecumenical organizations was held in London aimed at recommending the future shape of the ecumenical movement. It was here that a specific proposal emerged for a world council of churches, a body through which the churches themselves would take responsibility for the work of Christian unity. The meeting also recommended that Visser 't Hooft be invited to become the principal staff member of this new—really, unprece-dented—entity.[69] In the words of Ans van der Bent, Visser 't Hooft's "personal knowledge of all important sectors of Christianity, his direct contacts with numerous church leaders and theologians, his intimate knowledge of the Faith and Order and Life and Work movements, of the International Missionary Council and movements for peace, his outspoken theological curiosity and his devotion to solving practical problems, his mastery of four languages and his organizational competence, his gift as an orator and his talents in writing, made him the indisputable candidate."[70]

It is telling that the thirty-seven-year-old Visser 't Hooft expressed specific reservations. He would not be willing to accept such a position unless its charter made clear that this was a *council* of *churches*, not simply a federation of religious bodies, and unless it included a department of interchurch aid, "for there could not be ecumenical fellowship without practical solidarity."[71] This is typical Visser 't Hooft: insisting on the ecclesial character of the movement and also on holding together *koinonia* (fellowship) and *diaconia* (service).

Official inauguration of the council had to wait until after the Second World War, but the new general secretary began his work with the World Council of Churches in Process of Formation in January of 1939, work dominated for the next six years by the threat, and then the reality, of war. From his headquarters in neutral Switzerland, Visser 't Hooft maintained valuable contacts with resistance groups in Germany and the Netherlands, feeding information to religious and government leaders in Great Britain and the United States, and keeping lines of communication open all over Europe.[72] These contacts were obviously of value to the resistance, but Visser 't Hooft also believed that the allies had much to learn from those in Germany and German-occupied areas, because "where Christians suffer, ecumenism grows stronger."[73] In addition, he and his colleagues provided much needed assistance to refugees, including Jews smuggled out of occupied France—a foreshadowing of work done on a much larger scale by the postwar WCC. During these years, Visser 't Hooft later wrote, the ecumenical task was spiritually easy since "the marching orders were so very clear and the basic unity of the defenders of the faith was so deeply felt."[74] The war gave the ecumenical movement the opportunity to prove that it was rooted in the gospel and was not simply the byproduct of political internationalism.

It was also a test case of whether newly formed ecumenical bonds were durable. With this in mind, Visser 't Hooft emphasized, especially in a document titled "The Church as an Ecumenical Society in Time of War," three crucial principles.[75] First, the fellowship of prayer, based on the injunction in Matthew 5 to love and pray for even those regarded as enemies and persecutors, must not be broken. The report from the Oxford conference had challenged any tendency to "pray against" others in the body of Christ and included this sentence in its "Message": "If war breaks out, then preeminently the Church must manifestly be the Church, still united as the one Body of Christ, though the nations wherein it is planted fight one another, consciously offering the same prayers that God's Name may be hallowed, His Kingdom come, and His Will be done in both, or all, the warring nations."[76] The general secretary called this "a charter for the ecumenical movement" and incorporated parts of it into the letter inviting churches to join the new WCC.[77] Visser 't Hooft's conviction is a challenge to churches in any era: Solidarity as members of the *Una Sancta*, the one body of Christ, should finally be stronger than the bonds of nationality, including (perhaps especially) in times of war. Ecumenism is not a peacetime luxury, but a wartime necessity, reminding the churches of their real identity.[78]

Second, this war—any war—must not be interpreted as a holy crusade. Already at Oxford, the church representatives had said together that war as a method of settling disputes is incompatible with the teachings and example of Jesus Christ. "No justification of war must be allowed to conceal or minimize this fact."[79] The WCC's First Assembly (Amsterdam, 1948) was even more succinct: "War is contrary to the will of God."[80] It may be that violence is, in the last resort, a necessary evil (neither Visser 't Hooft nor the movement as a whole espoused pacifism); but Christians should never go to war in the name of God. God's will is for peace. War always represents a sinful failure to live as God intends.[81]

Third, churches must prepare for eventual peace and reconciliation by maintaining communication across the military divide. In the document referred to above, Visser 't Hooft writes that "constant efforts should be made in time of war, as well as immediately after the war, to ascertain from brother Christians in the opposing camp what terms of peace may create a lasting peace."[82] A powerful expression of this principle is the "Stuttgart Declaration" (1946) in which postwar leaders of the German Evangelical Church said, "we accuse ourselves for not witnessing more courageously, for not praying more faithfully, for not believing more joyously, and for not loving more ardently."[83] This statement of repentance, facilitated by Visser 't Hooft and a small delegation of colleagues from Allied countries, helped bring German Protestants back into the ecumenical fold and, in his opinion, helped create the spiritual condition necessary to inaugurate the WCC in 1948. Division may be a short-term necessity when the gospel is fundamentally violated, but no door is irrevocably shut on those who claim the name of Jesus. In his *Memoirs*, Visser 't Hooft points to "Barmen" and "Stuttgart" as the most important and enduring documents to come out of German Christianity in the 1930s and 1940s,[84] an indication of their importance in shaping his own theological position.

His great frustration from this period, expressed at several points in his *Memoirs*, was the failure of the churches to speak with one voice, either in the years leading up to the conflict or during the war itself. One problem was that the council, still "in process of formation," had no clear membership, structure, or procedures for public witness. The bigger issue, however, was that some church leaders wanted the WCC to be as neutral as possible in order to enhance its capacity for postwar reconciliation, while others wanted the churches to render unambiguous witness against National Socialism and its military aggression.[85]

Visser 't Hooft, despite his commitment to eventual reconciliation, was clearly in the latter camp. No, the war against Nazi Germany should not be seen as a crusade; but the ecumenical church dare not remain silent or inactive, and certainly not neutral, when attack from totalitarian nations threatens the continent. The church must give definitive guidance to its members or risk "living in the clouds," irrelevant to the monumental struggles of the era. Visser 't Hooft believed that Reinhold Niebuhr hit the nail on the head when he argued that "the revulsion against moral over-simplifications in the last war [when churches generally identified with the interests of their nations] now tempts people to abstain from moral discriminations which are justified and essential in the present situation."[86]

There are places in his *Memoirs* where Visser 't Hooft rails against the "astounding insensitiveness" of church leaders, politicians, and students, especially in the US and Great Britain, to the menace posed by Hitler's regime. Elsewhere, however, his position is more nuanced. In a paper titled "The Ecumenical Church and the International Situation," circulated to friends and colleagues in the spring of 1940, Visser 't Hooft argues that there are, in fact, two wars: one a conflict between nations, having its roots in a history of power politics, the other "a spiritual conflict concerning the nature of the state and its right to impose an anti-Christian ideology."[87] The church, he writes, cannot bless certain nations while damning others, and it certainly cannot give its blessing to war per se. It could and should declare, however, "that the anti-Christian forces had to be resisted, and that those who did so without ulterior motives, without hatred and with the humility of men who knew themselves to be sinners, would be fulfilling a terrible but none the less real duty to God and man."[88] This, needless to say, is walking a very fine line: insisting on the necessity of taking sides while also trying to prepare the ground for the seeds of a constructive postwar peace.

This brief discussion of Visser 't Hooft's wartime activities and tensions is a reminder that the ecumenical movement cannot be comprehended without grasping how it was, in its initial phase, a response to a deep crisis, political and spiritual, in Western culture—a crisis manifest most visibly and tragically in two world wars. The four years of carnage we call World War I were, in effect, a Christian civil war—Protestant Britain, Roman Catholic France, and Orthodox Russia arrayed against Protestant Germany, Roman Catholic Austria, and Orthodox Bulgaria—with no mechanism or platform for bringing the churches together for dialogue and possible common witness. Ecumenism was not only a way of dealing with this crisis but a recognition that the churches were implicated in it. In *The Wretchedness and Greatness of the Church*, a short book published in January of 1944, Visser 't Hooft argues that in their weakness the churches failed to fill "the great spiritual void of the masses" and, thus, were at least partially responsible for the rise of Nazism and similar idolatries.[89] The need for renewal of the church, already a theme in Visser 't Hooft's writing, would become even more prominent in his later books—and, through him, in the movement.

This discussion underscores as well Visser 't Hooft's ability to read the signs of the times, often in the face of stiff opposition. Van der Bent claims that the council's staff grew to depend on the general secretary's discernment of historical trends affecting the churches and his vision of the ecumenical future. It was this capacity for discernment, according to Bilheimer, that kept the WCC, pulled as it always is by conflicting forces, on a fairly even keel during his years of leadership.[90]

THE THEOLOGY OF CONCILIAR ECUMENISM

The inaugural assembly of the World Council was finally held with great celebration in Amsterdam in 1948. For Visser 't Hooft, this meant, among many other things, giving increased attention to the theology of conciliar ecumenism. What is the ecclesiological significance of a council of churches? What does it mean to say, as the WCC does in its "Basis," that the council is a "fellowship of churches"?

These questions are made especially difficult by the fact that councils of still-divided churches are a new thing in the history of Christianity.[91] Prior to the beginning of the ecumenical movement in the early twentieth century, there were organizations of Christians from different communions dedicated to particular tasks (e.g., Bible societies and the YMCA). But when churches commit themselves to one another for common service, witness, study, and prayer, something new is coming into existence—less divided than in the past, but still far short of visible unity. Visser 't Hooft put it this way in a presentation to the WCC's Central Committee in 1963: "Our churches have not yet developed the categories of thought which can adequately describe [the ecumenical] experience. . . . We try to define ecumenical realities in the thought-forms of a pre-ecumenical age."[92]

Visser 't Hooft had already begun to fill this theological lacuna in his chapter for *The Church and Its Function in Society*, a background volume for the 1937 Oxford conference. This gathering of Christians, he writes, cannot speak for the churches, *and yet* the churches must be open to the possibility that God will speak through it.[93] This anticipates the paradoxical language he would later use in connection with the WCC: the council cannot speak with authority given the divided state of its members, and yet the council dare not refrain from speaking when God uses it for common witness and reconciliation.[94]

Visser 't Hooft's fullest statement of the theology of conciliar ecumenism came in a paper prepared for discussion at the Amsterdam assembly. By this time, it was becoming evident that church leaders from the various confessional traditions held quite different assumptions about the significance of the council. Some regarded it as an adequate expression of Christian unity, within which the churches recognized one another as members of the one body of Christ. Others saw it as an agency for practical cooperation and study, within which members maintained their own ecclesiological convictions.[95] Visser 't Hooft, displaying his preference for paradox, refuses either to claim too much for the WCC or to sell it short. The World Council must not minimize the disunity of its members or pretend that it represents the *Una Sancta* (the one church), "but it may and it must claim that it is the body in which and through which, when it pleases God, a foretaste of the *Una Sancta* is given."[96]

A substantial excerpt from this paper, written for the assembly in 1948, is included in the next chapter of this book, and commentary on Visser 't Hooft's conciliar theology can be found in chapter 3. Thus, I will not say more about it now, except to note that many of Visser 't Hooft's ideas, and much of his language, were incorporated into what is known as the "Toronto Statement," a document drafted by the WCC's Central Committee in 1950 and still one of the council's two most important attempts at self-definition.[97] It is a good indication of how Visser 't Hooft, who consciously reflected and disseminated concepts developed in ecumenical conferences, also often shaped the positions taken in those gatherings.

A personal word at this point may be appropriate. In recent years, I have written extensively on the theology behind councils of churches[98] and was one of the drafters of the document, "Towards a Common Understanding and Vision of the World Council of Churches," adopted by the WCC Central Committee in 1997. In all of this, Visser 't Hooft was, without doubt, my major informant. It was he, far more than anyone else, who provided intellectual foundation for this new conciliar phenomenon. We can question whether councils of churches, as Visser 't Hooft conceived them, are still viable vehicles for carrying the vision of the ecumenical movement, but his insights remain important even for such questioning.

The other theological priority for these early years of the council was to develop a shared understanding of the church's engagement with the world that would allow it to weigh in constructively on the ideological and political conflicts of the era.[99] Visser 't Hooft set forth his own theology of church and world in a series of lectures, delivered at Princeton Theological Seminary in 1947 and published as *The Kingship of Christ*. Protestant Christianity, he laments, has often reduced salvation to an individual affair that leaves the world in the hands of secular powers, as if "the church has no word for the world but only for individuals who are to be saved out of the world."[100] A biblical understanding, however, assures us that both the world and the church belong to Christ, whose incarnation "is the center of *all* history." The difference is that the church knows of Christ's kingdom, knows that the victory has been won, even though the old age has not yet disappeared.[101]

To put it another way, the church is "the pioneer, the advance guard of the Kingdom of God."[102] It is not an end in itself but is central to Christ's continuing work of world re-creation. It is the place where, through the Holy Spirit, the coming age is actively present—especially when it refuses to be separated by social barriers but shows the unity of all classes, races, and nations in Christ. The kingship of Christ does not mean that the church dominates the world (the mistake of medieval Christianity); rather, it serves the world in the name of Christ, a service that often puts it in conflict with political powers.[103]

In the judgment of Robert Bilheimer, this theology of Christ's kingship in and over the world and the church "was the foundation of ecumenical thought in the WCC"[104]—at least in its early years under Visser 't Hooft's leadership. It resolved the tension identified in his doctoral thesis by providing "the basis for a social gospel which is truly gospel." There is no need to choose, he writes, between a priestly witness that announces the forgiveness of sins but ignores the world and a prophetic witness that declares justice while overlooking grace. "We have a priestly and prophetic king. . . . The issue is not whether we will succeed in establishing his Kingdom; the question is whether we live right now as his grateful subjects expecting that what is already given us *in spe* (in hope), will come to us *in re* (in fact). Such an eschatology is not an opiate. It is a call to active service."[105]

One place where this theology found concrete expression in the early years of the WCC was in the struggle against apartheid, the policy of systematic segregation of the races in South Africa. Visser 't Hooft spent five weeks in South Africa in 1952,[106] after which he wrote a short book titled *The Ecumenical Movement and the Racial Problem*. Ecumenical conferences, he notes, have been denouncing race-based discrimination as a denial of the teaching of Jesus since the 1920s, even as they have admitted that the churches have often reflected and sanctioned racist practices. Visser 't Hooft's position is clear and consistent: The church is a divine creation, a foretaste of the "new humanity," not a human creation to be fashioned according to prevailing prejudices. In this new humanity, all racial barriers have fallen. Thus, racism in the church is a violation of its very nature and undercuts its witness to the fundamental unity of God's human family.[107] The South African situation is also a reminder of why the church must be a universal fellowship, refusing to accommodate local contexts that institutionalize racial or ethnic discrimination—a lesson he learned originally from the German church experience.

An indication of the tensions inherent in such a position is that ten African churches, undoubtedly encouraged by the council's public witness, became members of the WCC at its assembly in 1961, even as three apartheid-supporting churches were withdrawing. Visser 't Hooft's *Memoirs* tells the powerful story of the 1960 Cottesloe conference, at which an attempt was made to identify common convictions through dialogue involving representatives of all the South African churches. It is a testament to what he calls "the ecumenical method" that broad agreement was achieved on a number of points, including that there is no justification for excluding nonwhite citizens from participating in government and that "no one who believes in Christ may be excluded from any church on the grounds of his color or race." It is a testament to the power of entrenched political interests that the agreements were repudiated once the representatives returned home.[108]

The preceding discussion points to a tension that preoccupied Visser 't Hooft throughout his years as general secretary. He names this tension several times in his *Memoirs* (and other writings), including in the following passage:

> We found ourselves often in a real dilemma. For as a body called into being to create fellowship between the churches we should give a high priority to the concern to maintain fraternal relations between the churches. But we had in the history of the ecumenical movement learned together that it was the duty of the churches to speak out, and to speak out together, when the very foundations of the international order were shaken. Some said to us: if you continue to make statements on very controversial international issues, the World Council will disintegrate. Others replied: the World Council will become completely irrelevant if it has not the courage to take a stand on the great issues of international life.[109]

I certainly wrestled with this dilemma as general secretary of the National Council of Churches (NCC), and in such moments it was Visser 't Hooft's insistently theological approach that I found most helpful and compelling. Yes, the achievement of fellowship is the ultimate purpose of any council because unity is of the gospel. Christians cannot turn their backs on one another, certainly not because they live on different sides of the Iron Curtain. But Christian fellowship, as he put it, has *content*. Another part of a council's mandate is to affirm shared convictions—rooted in Scripture, arrived at through dialogue—and apply them, though often with trepidation, to concrete situations.[110] The rupture of church relations, as in South Africa, is always a cause for regret, and yet it is the church's right and duty to witness to the gospel. This spiritual tension said Visser 't Hooft repeatedly, is part of the situation in which God has placed us.[111]

THE AGENDA OF A GENERAL SECRETARY

It is not possible, or consistent with the intent of this chapter, to summarize Visser 't Hooft's activities during his years as general secretary of the WCC. Reference to the council's Third Assembly (New Delhi, 1961), however, will give some indication of the factors shaping ecumenical thought in this period.

This assembly, held in India, was the first outside Europe or North America, and, thus, was an important step in the effort to become a truly global fellowship of churches, with all the challenges that implies.[112] It was in 1933 that Visser 't Hooft first traveled to Asia, a continent with which he felt particular connection because of Holland's colonial presence in Indonesia. Already in his doctoral dissertation, he had affirmed that "all nations go through their own struggle to find the concrete form in which the eternal Word spoken to them must be put."[113] This insight—so obvious today, but far less so then—was reinforced at the meeting of Asian Student Christian Movements: "For we saw before our eyes that Christianity was not indissolubly linked to one culture and one part of the world. Christ belonged to all men."[114] His growing concern for syncretism in the European churches (Christianity being confused with ideological movements) made him particularly aware of how these churches had often become agents of cultural colonialism, rather than witnesses to the universal gospel of God's love.

Later trips left him shocked to find how "uncritically and

unimaginatively" Western forms of theology and church life had been transplanted to Asia.[115] The gospel, he argued in various presentations, must be interpreted in categories relevant to the Asian, and other, contexts—not in order to separate Asian Christians from other followers of Christ, but in order to clarify the meaning of the unifying gospel in distinctive cultures. The confusion of Christian theology with Nazi ideology in the 1930s served as a warning to other settings and led him to champion a dialogue of mutual correction and an appreciation for the supremacy of the Bible as the norm for evaluating all theologies.[116]

This assembly also saw the merger of the World Council of Churches with the International Missionary Council, a sign that effective, faithful mission demands a more unified church and that authentic unity requires active missionary commitment. Visser 't Hooft's passion for mission is especially clear in his address to the meeting of the WCC's new Commission on World Mission and Evangelism, two years after the assembly in New Delhi. Mission and evangelistic witness, he argued to the commission, are the decisive tests of faith. They reveal whether a church actually believes in the "happenedness" of the mighty acts of God in Christ, for only those who have been deeply penetrated by the faith that God's incarnation in Jesus is the center of all history will have the endurance for the missionary task. In the same way, mission discloses whether a church really believes in the universality of the gospel. It is relatively easy to affirm that Christ is *our* Savior and, therefore, to export *our* culturally conditioned brand of Christianity. But a true missionary church confesses that Christ is Savior of all and that the word of God cannot be imprisoned in any cultural expression.[117]

It is commonplace to say that "evangelical" churches have been little involved in modern ecumenism because they fear that the movement risks compromising essentials of the faith and blunting the missionary impulse. But if the hallmarks of evangelicalism are a personal relationship with Jesus, a strong affirmation of scriptural authority, and a commitment to evangelistic proclamation of the lordship of Christ, then Visser 't Hooft, greatest of the twentieth-century ecumenical leaders, deserves the label. He would likely have faulted evangelicals for devaluing the historical church and for being overly individualistic, but his insistence on the nonnegotiable uniqueness of Christian faith marks him as a kindred spirit.[118]

Two reports to the assembly—from the Department on the Laity and the Department on Cooperation of Men and Women in Church, Family, and Society—may not have received headline attention, but they were of central importance to Visser 't Hooft. Already in his paper for the Amsterdam Assembly in 1948, he had worried that the need for official representation from churches dominated by ordained men would leave little room for the often-creative and prophetic voices of laypersons, women, and youth.[119] He subsequently made sure this concern was visible in the structure of the council.

In several of his writings, Visser 't Hooft observes that the lifeblood of modern ecumenism flowed from the mission fields, the Sunday School movement, the YMCA and YWCA, the various Bible societies, and the Student Christian Movement—all of which featured lay leadership. He notes, in one of his last books, that his own professional mentors included more laypersons—including such eminent figures as John R. Mott and J. H. Oldham—than clergy or theologians.[120] Even before the World Council was officially formed, the Ecumenical Institute at Chateau de Bossey was opened with the express purpose of renewing the church through the nurture of lay vocations. Bossey, as it is known, was a product of Visser 't Hooft's vision for the WCC. We can also see his direct influence in the strong statements on the laity found in the reports of the first three assemblies, including the New Delhi assembly, which called the penetration of the world by lay witness "an essential part of God's plan for [the] church."[121] Bilheimer was not overstating the case when he wrote that "the most original aspect of ecumenical thought concerning the church's witness was its stress on the laity"[122]—at least as long as Visser 't Hooft was general secretary.

In his *Memoirs*, the Dutchman credits his wife, Jetty, with opening his eyes to how women are often prevented, by a culture in which maleness is the norm, from making their true contribution to church and society. "She convinced me that this was indeed one of the deepest unsolved problems of humanity"[123]–which is why he supported the creation of the department on the cooperation of women and men and was instrumental in recruiting its first director, a leader of wartime relief efforts in France, Madeleine Barot.

The New Delhi assembly was also where the Orthodox churches of Russia, Romania, Bulgaria, and Poland were accepted as members of the WCC. When the churches in Georgia and Serbia subsequently joined, nearly all of Eastern Orthodoxy was included in the council—a testimony to Visser 't Hooft's skill as an ecumenical diplomat. (Under his leadership, the WCC grew from 147 denominations in 40 countries to nearly 300 in 90.) This development made the council's agenda both more profound and more complicated since it heightened awareness of the theological differences between Eastern and Western Christianity and of the political tensions between Eastern and Western Europe.[124]

In his *Memoirs*, Visser 't Hooft suggests three reasons why the Orthodox felt at least somewhat comfortable in the WCC. First, the Toronto Statement made clear that different ecclesiological understandings were welcome in this fellowship of churches. Second, several key Orthodox leaders, friends of the general secretary, gave consistent support. And third, the council had demonstrated practical solidarity through its interchurch aid and service to refugees.[125] To this should be added Visser 't Hooft's theological sensitivity, especially his proposed rewording of the WCC's Basis to make it more explicitly Trinitarian—a key concern of the Orthodox.

Having mentioned the new member churches from Eastern Europe, it is important to add a word about the Cold War, the name given to the constant state of generally nonviolent hostility that existed between the United States and the Soviet Union, and their allies, after the Second World War. Visser 't Hooft notes in his historical overview of the era that there were two "lines of least resistance" the WCC could have adopted: either to identify with one of the power blocs (almost certainly the West, given the composition of WCC membership) or to remain silent with regard to contentious Cold War issues. Instead, the council sought to hammer out common convictions that would bring the light of the gospel to bear on contemporary crises.[126] In the words of the New Delhi assembly report (echoed by Visser 't Hooft in his *Memoirs*), the WCC "must stand for Christian values which by their nature apply to all sides of controversial disputes. . . . The churches must not be identified with any ideology; they must be in the world but not of it, for they can only stand for Christ."[127] This can be seen, for example, in the way the assembly named war as humanity's common enemy and pressed for comprehensive nuclear disarmament as an essential contribution to universally beneficial peace.[128]

Finally, New Delhi was the first WCC assembly with Roman Catholic observers, a harbinger of the ecumenical breakthrough that took place at the Second Vatican Council, the seminal gathering of Roman Catholic bishops that began the following year. Visser 't Hooft had been a frequent critic of Catholic resistance to things ecumenical, but his attitude warmed quickly, especially through his relationship with Cardinal Augustin Bea, first president of the Vatican Secretariat for Promoting Christian Unity. A book published at the close of Vatican II, *Peace among Christians*, is a record of their growing mutual respect. By the time he wrote his *Memoirs* (1973), Visser 't Hooft could declare, "I often found myself in far deeper agreement with those Roman Catholic theologians who sought to reinterpret the faith in modern terms, but did so on the basis of biblical theology, than with men of my own confession who were merely defending the formulations of the past or who were more concerned about adaptation to the modern world than about faithfulness to the original message."[129]

One issue that did not figure prominently on the assembly's agenda—somewhat surprisingly, given its Asian setting—was the diversity of religions and the need for improved relations among them. The report from the section on "Witness" simply observed that churches have little understanding of the wisdom and love God has given to people of other faiths, and called for increased interfaith conversation.[130]

By the time of Visser 't Hooft's retirement, only five years later, this call was greatly amplified, and he addressed its theological implications in a significant essay, published in *The Ecumenical Review* and reprinted in *Peace among Christians*: "Pluralism—Temptation or Opportunity." "It is only in our days," he writes, "that the churches [in North Atlantic countries] have come to face the issue of pluralism in its sharper form, namely, as the appearance on their own doorstep of a multitude of other conceptions of life, religious positions, or ideologies which claim the same rights as churches."[131] Confronted with this new situation, the churches must avoid four temptations: (1) the temptation of returning to Christendom, pretending that Christians can recover past hegemony; (2) the temptation of introversion, abandoning the church's prophetic ministry in society by focusing on personal salvation and the church's internal life; (3) the temptation of relativism, giving up the claim to have received truth that is universally valid; and (4) the temptation of syncretism, seeking to avoid religious strife by attempting to create a common religion.[132]

Visser 't Hooft's position is again clear and consistent: Christians "cannot possibly advocate pluralism as an ideal. [Christianity's] *raison d'être* is to bring all men to Christ; its universalism implies hope that pluralism will not have the last word."[133] It would be unrealistic, however, to expect that every knee will bow to Christ the Lord in the near future. In the meantime, pluralism provides the church with an opportunity to *be the church*, to live according to its own inherent principles rather than as a "cult maintained for the sake of social cohesion" or a chaplain to Western culture. It is an invitation for Christians to give account of the hope within them by entering into mutually honest and respectful dialogue with adherents of other faith traditions, dialogue understood as a battle for truth in which the only weapons are spiritual. And pluralism is also a spur to Christian unity, since a church preoccupied with old, internal divisions will be "unable to play its role in the coming great conflict of religions and cultures."[134] We will return to the issue of religious pluralism in later chapters.

It is not inaccurate to call Visser 't Hooft an ecumenical activist. He was not a hands-on administrator as general secretary, but his schedule was filled with activities aimed at producing practical results. He was constantly attempting to identify the best practices in the churches and to encourage their duplication in other communities.[135] One person who knew him observed that Visser 't Hooft "moved quickly, spoke quickly, thought quickly and never seemed to tire."[136]

In the midst of all this activity, however, he maintained a commitment to study and scholarship. It was during his years as general secretary, with its mind-boggling agenda, that he produced lecture series that resulted in arguably his most mature theological works: *The Renewal of the Church*, in which he lays out the case for the difficult-to-achieve interplay between unity and renewal; *The Pressure of Our Common Calling*, a biblically grounded exploration of what unity means at different points on the ecumenical journey; and *No Other Name*, in which he returns to the themes of syncretism and "Christian universalism," now with an eye toward other religions.

Since an excerpt from each of these books is included in chapter 2, and all of them are commented on in chapter 3, I will not elaborate now. I do want to underscore, however, that these theological reflections, far from being a distraction from his work at the World Council, were a great enhancement of it. Visser 't Hooft, like the council as a whole, faced a perpetual dilemma: the WCC was respected to the extent that it pioneered new forms of witness, but any suggestion that it was imposing ideas or actions on the churches would be met with stiff resistance.[137] Visser 't Hooft managed this balancing act, I am convinced, because of the well-thought-out wisdom of his own theological vision. At his best, he advocated policies and actions, even if they were politically inexpedient, because they reflected a consistent, biblically based understanding of the church and its engagement with the world. He believed that he had been called to be general secretary, not simply because the churches trusted his ability to broker theological discussion, but also because they trusted his theological judgments. His published ideas helped frame discussions in the council and invited dialogue.

NEW THOUGHTS FROM AN AGING THEOLOGIAN

During his nearly twenty years of retirement, despite increasingly poor health (the result of heavy smoking), Visser 't Hooft wrote constantly, starting with his *Memoirs* (1973). One task he set for himself was preservation of ecumenical memory, as in his book *The Genesis and Formation of the World Council of Churches* (1982). Another was reflection on the continuing viability of ecumenical structures.

It seems clear in retrospect that the ecumenical movement achieved greatest flower at a time when the idea of human unity was extolled, and longed for, in the aftermath of World War II—an idea expressed, for example, in the establishment of the United Nations and the drafting of a Universal Declaration on Human Rights. In this "modern" era, large structures, such as the World Council, were appreciated as a means for bringing people together. By the time of Visser 't Hooft's retirement, however, plurality—of cultures, religions, church traditions—was increasingly affirmed, and there was a growing backlash against centralized organizations. In this climate, the "official" ecumenical movement, with its once-heralded structures, began to lose its luster. Moreover, the newness of the "ecumenical revolution"[138] had begun to wear off, at least for those churches involved in it since the 1920s. "For my generation," lamented Visser 't Hooft in 1974, "the ecumenical movement had all the attraction of something unexpected and extraordinary. For the present generation, it is simply part of the church's design."[139]

He addressed this institutional crisis in several places, including a lengthy chapter for the second volume of *A History of the Ecumenical Movement*, and in a short, provocatively titled book, *Has the Ecumenical Movement a Future?* The answer to institutionalism, he argues, is to emphasize the vision not the organization, the goal not the means.[140] It is right, even necessary, for each new generation to revise inherited structures, to adapt them to present tasks; but it would be foolish to cast aside the ecumenical gains of the past half century.[141] This is not simply a matter of institutional continuity. "The ecumenical structures which were worked out in the 1930s and 1940s are not sacrosanct."[142] There is, however, a deeper continuity of vision and commitment that must not be lost. It is vital for ecumenically minded Christians to understand the potential and the limitations of what they have inherited in order to move creatively into the future.[143]

This same tension—change and continuity—can be seen in his repeated discussion of the relationship between church and world. Historians note that a major shift in the movement can be seen with the Geneva conference on church and society in 1966 and the WCC's Fourth Assembly in Uppsala, Sweden, two years later.[144] These were politically turbulent years when participants at ecumenical gatherings came increasingly from the Global South and argued that social and economic justice requires not just revision but dramatic, systemic change. As it is sometimes put, a theology of "Christian realism," in which churches seek to contribute to relative justice in a sinful world, gave way at the global level to "eschatological realism," in which churches seek to live in anticipation of God's intended shalom (humanity's true reality). The task of the churches, including when they work ecumenically, is to bring the values of God's reign to bear on economic, social, and political life, to embody and confess the eschatological demands of Christian faith as an alternative to the contemporary powers and principalities. In practice this meant a shift from attempting to influence those with power to participating in the struggles of those without it, symbolized most visibly in the WCC's controversial Program to Combat Racism.[145]

The council's longtime director of Church and Society, Paul Abrecht, has contended that Visser 't Hooft was opposed to this "new orientation." According to Abrecht, the optimistic faith in revolution and fervent dismissal of experts must have seemed to the retired leader like a return to the theological simplicity he railed against in his dissertation and worked to overcome as general secretary.[146]

There is surely truth in this observation, but I think it is only partially correct. The final pages of both the *Memoirs* and *Has the Ecumenical Movement a Future?* are a vigorous protest against caricaturing the ecumenical past. The movement has *never* been solely concerned with the internal life of the church.

It has *always* stressed that the church is accountable to God for the world. When the WCC actively confronts racism, it is not departing from its historic mandate but applying it to current challenges. When it links the unity of the church and the unity of humankind, it is not changing course but giving needed emphasis to their intersection. "So," he writes, "I welcome the new orientation in principle"[147]—though not always in practice. The ecumenical movement can easily become a tool of political ideologies if it ever loses its Christ-centered identity. To say it another way, the ecumenical church makes a contribution to the world only when its prophetic witness is that given it in Scripture. All human goals must be evaluated in light of the word it has received about God's kingdom. It must always ask: "Which development, which emancipation, which revolution is in line with God's design?"[148]

This question is explored from a particular angle in *The Fatherhood of God in an Age of Emancipation* (1982). Visser 't Hooft makes clear that he is in favor of feminism and other contemporary movements for emancipation; indeed, the oppression of women, to focus on that issue, is of urgent concern. The churches must stand for the liberation of women and men from everything that prevents them from living as responsible human beings, including the alienation caused by social structures. But Christians also know, he argues, that such emancipation is not the final goal. Oppression won't cease if sexism is overcome, because the deepest source of bondage is the sin that infects every heart. Beyond that, emancipation without commitment to the One Jesus teaches us to call "Father," the One whose forgiveness truly sets us free, often leads people to embrace new forms of enslavement—as happened in 1930s Germany.[149]

In addition to its content, the book provides insight into Visser 't Hooft's methodology. First, and above all, he grounds his thought in Scripture. When dealing, for example, with the question of whether God can be called "Mother," he insists that Christians must "ask themselves whether the revelation of God received from the Bible *permits* us to speak of the motherhood of God."[150] He cites various theologians who have wrestled with this question, but warns of the danger that such work will become "theological speculation rather than an interpretation of the revelation given to us." His conclusion: The fatherhood of God is open to "correction, enrichment, and completion" from other biblical symbols, including mother, but Christians appropriately call God Father because that is how Jesus, as recorded in Scripture, taught us to pray.[151]

Second, Visser 't Hooft has, in the words of Berkhof, "intense interest in history . . . geared wholly to clarifying the position we are constrained to adopt in the present."[152] This book, as one might expect, includes reflection on what the Bible means by freedom and makes considerable use of ecumenical documents, especially in the discussion of liberation from "ecclesiastical paternalism." The bulk of it, however, is an examination of emancipation in European history, from the ancient Greeks to thinkers of the twentieth century. The lessons he draws, positive and negative, by no means have for him the authority of Scripture, but they certainly inform his argument.

Third, Visser 't Hooft is at least somewhat aware of his own social location and how it influences his thinking. He acknowledges, for example, that he belongs to a generation shaped by patriarchalism. This worldview, he writes, was repeatedly challenged by his own international travels and ecumenical contacts[153]—although Philip Potter, in an important review of *Memoirs*, suggests that Visser 't Hooft could never fully shake off his "European Christendom triumphalism" heritage. "Visser 't Hooft was born and brought up in the comfortable, middle-class world of a neutral yet imperialist country. There is a touch of self-confidence and complacency which runs right through [his career] which is only rarely shaken."[154]

Fourth, this book is typical of Visser 't Hooft's method in the way it sets up a tension—in this case, between emancipation movements as a panacea and as a dangerous descent into anarchy—and then offers a middle way.[155] His works are full of such dialectics (not a foreign strategy for continental Protestants of his era) that he seeks to resolve, though not until the tension has been thoroughly explored.

In his final book, *Teachers and the Teaching Authorities*, published posthumously, Visser 't Hooft turns to the thorny issue of authority and, more specifically, to the place of theologians in the life of the church. Who, he asks, has the authority to speak for the churches in ecumenical dialogue? Is the role of the participants, often theologians (*magistri*, teachers), to represent the position of their churches as determined by the *magisterium* (teaching authority, especially as exercised by bishops), or should they be free to explore possibilities for agreement that may go beyond traditional teachings? Readers of this chapter will not be surprised by his answer: "Theology has a task of its own. It must not only repeat and explain what has been formulated in the past, but also question critically whether the church's teaching and preaching are faithful to the revelation contained in the holy scriptures. It must relate the Christian gospel to new cultural situations and show that it meets new challenges. . . . our times demand that the prophetic dimension of the Christian witness be heard in the church."[156] Theologians are obviously not free to ignore the teachings of the magisterium, and they are constrained by the limits of biblical revelation. But when the church is functioning well, theologians are not merely "auxiliaries of the hierarchy." Through ecumenical dialogue—understood as a spiritual battle for truth, a journey of mutual discovery—theologians play an indispensable, creative role in the body of Christ.

Visser 't Hooft ends the book by naming three moments when, in his judgment, the magisterium called on theologians, even empowered theologians, to make such a contribution.[157] One was the Second Vatican Council, when bishops and their theological advisors collaborated in the drafting of groundbreaking documents, including the *Decree on Ecumenism*. Another was the Oxford conference on church and society, preparation for which included seven volumes of theological essays. And the third was, of course, the synod of the Confessing Church in Germany, where theologians defended the integrity of Christian faith by producing the Barmen Declaration. It is a fitting summary of the influences that shaped this shaper of ecumenical theology.

Notes

1. See Visser 't Hooft, *Memoirs*, 82. Another useful source for details of Visser 't Hooft's life is van der Bent, *W. A. Visser 't Hooft*, 4–24.

2. Visser 't Hooft, *Memoirs*, 5.

3. The two quotations in this paragraph are from Visser 't Hooft, *Memoirs*, 5, 9.

4. Bilheimer, *Breakthrough*, 82.

5. Visser 't Hooft, *Memoirs*, 16.

6. Visser 't Hooft, *Memoirs*, 37.

7. Visser 't Hooft, *Memoirs*, 37.

8. Karl Barth, *The Church and the Churches* (Grand Rapids: Eerdmans, 2005), 22–23; for the ideas in this paragraph, see also 11.

9. Barth, *The Church*, 13.

10. Barth, *The Church*, 25. See also Barth, *The Church*, 43; and W. A. Visser 't Hooft, "Karl Barth and the Ecumenical Movement," *Ecumenical Review* 32, no. 2 (1980): 131.

11. Barth, *The Church*, 33; for ideas in this paragraph, see also 28, 39.

12. Barth, *The Church*, 38.

13. Visser 't Hooft, "Karl Barth," 133.

14. W. A Visser 't Hooft, "The Calling of the World Council of Churches," *Ecumenical Review* 14, no. 2 (1962): 224; Bea and Visser 't Hooft, *Peace among Christians*, 186.

15. W. A. Visser 't Hooft, *The Wretchedness and Greatness of the Church*, trans. Dorothy Mackie and Hugh Martin (London: SCM, 1944), 54, 56, 61.

16. For a discussion of this dynamic, see Berkhof, "Visser 't Hooft as Ecumenical Theologian," 204–5.

17. Visser 't Hooft, *Memoirs*, 17.

18. Visser 't Hooft, *Memoirs*, 18.

19. Ruth Rouse and Stephen Charles Neil, eds., *A History of the Ecumenical Movement 1517–1948*, 2nd ed. (Philadelphia: Westminster, 1967), 547.

20. Visser 't Hooft, *Memoirs*, 26.

21. W. A. Visser 't Hooft, *The Background of the Social Gospel in America* (St. Louis: Bethany, 1966), 183. This is a reprint of the 1928 publication by H. D. Tjeenk Willink and Zoon.

22. Visser 't Hooft, *Background of the Social Gospel*, 180. Visser 't Hooft's view that the doctrine of divine immanence is central to understanding the social gospel is not widely affirmed by scholars of the social gospel movement, as is hinted at by Harold Lunger in an editor's preface to the reprint edition.

23. Visser 't Hooft, *Background of the Social Gospel*, 175.

24. Visser 't Hooft, *Memoirs*, 27.

25. Visser 't Hooft, *Background of the Social Gospel*, 185.

26. Visser 't Hooft, *Background of the Social Gospel*, 181.

27. Visser 't Hooft, *Background of the Social Gospel*, 182.

28. See W. A. Visser 't Hooft, *The Kingship of Christ* (New York: Harper, 1948), 82–83. This tension in Visser 't Hooft's thought is nicely summarized in François C. Gérard, *The Future of the Church: The Theology of Renewal of Willem Adolf Visser 't Hooft* (Pittsburg: Pickwick, 1974), 63–64.

29. W. A. Visser 't Hooft, "The Mandate of the Ecumenical Movement," in *The Uppsala Report 1968: Official Report of the Fourth Assembly of the World Council of Churches*, ed. Norman Goodall (Geneva: WCC, 1968), 320.

30. Visser 't Hooft, *Memoirs*, 363.

31. Josef L. Hromadka, "Biblical Theology in the Ecumenical Struggle," in Mackie and West, *Sufficiency of God*, 19.

32. Visser 't Hooft's close associate, Robert Mackie, writes about Visser 't Hooft's "unusually flexible mind." See Robert C. Mackie, "An Appreciation," 7–8. Evidence of Visser 't Hooft's willingness to change his mind in light of new experience is found at various places in his *Memoirs*, including his refusal to rule out violence in the face of grave injustice (292–93) and his admission that evangelism is not appropriate in all circumstances (pp. 302–3).

33. These included Reinhold Niebuhr, Emil Brunner, William Temple, Hendrik Kraemer, Henry Pitney Van Dusen, Toyohiko Kagawa, Stefan Zankov, and Yves Congar. See van der Bent, *W. A. Visser 't Hooft*, 7.

34. Philip Potter, "Youth and the Ecumenical Movement," in Mackie

and West, *Sufficiency of God*, 207.

35. See Potter, "Youth," 219, where he quotes from Visser 't Hooft's address to the Ecumenical Youth Assembly in 1960. See also W. A. Visser 't Hooft, "I Have Overcome the World," in *Christus Victor: The Report of the World Conference of Christian Youth*, ed. Denzil G. M. Patrick (Geneva: Conference Headquarters, 1939), 234.

36. This statement, made in the 1930s while Visser 't Hooft was still head of the World Student Christian Federation, is quoted in Potter, "Youth," 210.

37. See Visser 't Hooft, *Kingship of Christ*, 43; Potter, "Youth," 211.

38. See Visser 't Hooft, *Memoirs*, 48.

39. W. A. Visser 't Hooft, "Weakness and Strength of the Christian Community," *Student World* 30, no. 4 (1937): 352. It is also quoted in Visser 't Hooft, *Memoirs*, 49.

40. Visser 't Hooft, *Kingship of Christ*, 142–43.

41. Visser 't Hooft, *Kingship of Christ*, 145.

42. W. A. Visser 't Hooft, *The Ecumenical Movement and the Racial Problem* (Paris: UNESCO, 1954), 53–55.

43. W. A. Visser 't Hooft, *Rembrandt and the Gospel*, trans. Gregor K. Smith (New York: Meridian, 1960), 110, 19.

44. Visser 't Hooft, *Rembrandt*, 115; see also 58–59.

45. Visser 't Hooft, *Memoirs*, 41.

46. A discussion of this is in D. C. Mulder, "'None Other Gods'—'No Other Name,'" in *Ecumenical Review* 38, no. 2 (1986): 210–11.

47. Cited in Arthur C. Cochrane, *The Church's Confession under Hitler* (Philadelphia: Westminster, 1962), 222–23.

48. Cochrane, *Church's Confession*, 112. See also Michael Kinnamon, *Truth and Community: Diversity and Its Limits in the Ecumenical Movement* (Grand Rapids: Eerdmans, 1988), 60–62.

49. The Barmen Declaration is widely reprinted and available online.

50. Quoted in Keith Clements, *Ecumenical Dynamic* (Geneva: WCC Publications, 2013), 96. Chapter 6 of Clements's book is an excellent introduction to the ecumenical implications of the German church struggle. See also Visser 't Hooft, *Memoirs*, 74.

51. Dietrich Bonhoeffer, "The Confessing Church and the Ecumeni-

cal Movement," in *The Ecumenical Movement: An Anthology of Key Texts and Voices*, ed. Michael Kinnamon (Geneva: WCC Publications, 2016), 7–12. See also Clements, *Ecumenical Dynamic*, 101–2; W. A. Visser 't Hooft, "Dietrich Bonhoeffer and the Self-Understanding of the Ecumenical Movement," *Ecumenical Review* 28, no. 2 (1976): 198–203.

52.   Martin Fischer, "The Confessing Church and the Ecumenical Movement," in Mackie and West, *Sufficiency of God*, 138.

53.   Visser 't Hooft, *Memoirs*, 47.

54.   W. A. Visser 't Hooft, *None Other Gods* (New York: Harper, 1937), 76.

55.   Visser 't Hooft, *None Other Gods*, 28.

56.   Visser 't Hooft, *None Other Gods*, 38, 40.

57.   Visser 't Hooft, *None Other Gods*, 160.

58.   Visser 't Hooft, *None Other Gods*, 172.

59.   Visser 't Hooft touches on this in *Wretchedness and Greatness*, 29.

60.   Visser 't Hooft, *None Other Gods*, 71–72.

61.   Visser 't Hooft, *None Other Gods*, 70.

62.   W. A. Visser 't Hooft, "The Church as an Oecumenical Society," in *The Church and Its Function in Society*, by W. A. Visser 't Hooft and J. H. Oldham (London: George Allen & Unwin, 1937), 95, 97, 100.

63.   See Kinnamon, *Truth and Community*, ch. 4.

64.   See Clements, *Ecumenical Dynamic*, 100–101; W. A. Visser 't Hooft, *Has the Ecumenical Movement a Future?* (Belfast: Christian Journals, 1974), 16.

65.   Visser 't Hooft, *Memoirs*, 75.

66.   W. A. Visser 't Hooft, *Anglo-Catholicism and Orthodoxy* (London: SCM, 1933), 151.

67.   Karl Barth, *Against the Stream: Shorter Post-War Writings* (London: SCM, 1954), 47.

68.   Cochrane, *Church's Confession*, 211.

69.   See W. A. Visser 't Hooft, *The Genesis and Formation of the World Council of Churches* (Geneva: WCC, 1982), ch. 11; Visser 't Hooft, *Memoirs*, 76.

70. van der Bent, *W. A. Visser 't Hooft*, 8–9.

71. Visser 't Hooft, *Memoirs*, 80–81.

72. Some of this story is told in Visser 't Hooft, *Memoirs*, chs. 20–23.

73. Müller-Fahrenholz, "No Communion without Compassion," 167.

74. Visser 't Hooft, *Memoirs*, 196–97.

75. This is discussed in Visser 't Hooft, *Memoirs*, 110.

76. J. H. Oldham, *The Oxford Conference: Official Report* (Chicago: Willett, Clark, 1937), 47.

77. Visser 't Hooft, *Memoirs*, 73.

78. Visser 't Hooft, *Memoirs*, 129.

79. Oldham, *Oxford Conference*, 162.

80. W. A. Visser 't Hooft, "The Church and the International Disorder," in *Man's Disorder and God's Design*, ed. W. A. Visser 't Hooft (New York: Harper, 1948), 218.

81. For a discussion of this issue, see Kinnamon, *Can a Renewal Movement*, 24–25.

82. Visser 't Hooft, *Memoirs*, 110.

83. Quoted in Visser 't Hooft, *Memoirs*, 192.

84. See Visser 't Hooft, *Memoirs*, 190–94, 201.

85. See Visser 't Hooft, *Memoirs*, 134.

86. Quoted in Visser 't Hooft, *Memoirs*, 114.

87. Visser 't Hooft, *Memoirs*, 122,

88. Visser 't Hooft, *Memoirs*, 122.

89. This is discussed in Kinnamon, *Can a Renewal Movement*, ch. 3. See also Visser 't Hooft, *Wretchedness and Greatness*, 22.

90. van der Bent, *W. A. Visser 't Hooft*, 20; Bilheimer, *Breakthrough*, 74. A good example of Visser 't Hooft's capacity to discern and summarize trends is his chapter, "The General Ecumenical Development since 1948," in *The Ecumenical Advance: A History of the Ecumenical Movement*, ed. Harold E. Fey, vol. 2, 2nd ed. (Geneva: WCC, 1970), 3–26.

91. W. A. Visser 't Hooft, "The Significance of the World Council of Churches," in Visser 't Hooft, *Man's Disorder and God's Design*, 177.

92. An excerpt from this presentation is in Michael Kinnamon and Brian E. Cope, eds., *The Ecumenical Movement: An Anthology of Key Texts and Voices* (Grand Rapids: Eerdmans, 1997), 495.

93. Visser 't Hooft, "Church as an Oecumenical Society," 98–99.

94. Visser 't Hooft, "Significance of the World Council of Churches," 190.

95. See Visser 't Hooft, *Memoirs*, 217.

96. Visser 't Hooft, "Significance of the World Council of Churches," 187.

97. The Toronto Statement can be found in Kinnamon, *Ecumenical Movement*, 2nd ed., 418–22.

98. See, e.g., Diane Kessler and Michael Kinnamon, *Councils of Churches and the Ecumenical Vision* (Geneva: WCC Publications, 2000); Michael Kinnamon, *The Vision of the Ecumenical Movement: And How It Has Been Impoverished by Its Friends* (St. Louis: Chalice, 2003), ch. 7.

99. Visser 't Hooft, *Memoirs*, 216–17.

100. Visser 't Hooft, *Kingship of Christ*, 25.

101. Visser 't Hooft, *Kingship of Christ*, 119, 97.

102. Visser 't Hooft, *Kingship of Christ*, 119.

103. See Visser 't Hooft, *Kingship of Christ*, 95, 111, 131.

104. Bilheimer, *Breakthrough*, 91.

105. Visser 't Hooft, *Kingship of Christ*, 140.

106. Visser 't Hooft, *Memoirs*, ch. 34.

107. Visser 't Hooft, *Racial Problem*, 46, 48, 53, 54.

108. Visser 't Hooft, *Memoirs*, 286–87.

109. Visser 't Hooft, *Memoirs*, 307–8.

110. Visser 't Hooft, *Has the Ecumenical Movement a Future?*, 43.

111. Visser 't Hooft, *Memoirs*, 223.

112. Visser 't Hooft names some of those challenges in *Memoirs*, 317.

113. Visser 't Hooft, *Social Gospel*, 187.

114. Visser 't Hooft, *Memoirs*, 52.

115. Visser 't Hooft, *Memoirs*, 243.

116. Visser 't Hooft, *Memoirs*, 244. See also W. A. Visser 't Hooft, "Accommodation, True or False?," *South East Asia Journal of Theology* 8, no. 3 (1967): 9. A thoughtful commentary on Visser 't Hooft's approach to this issue is Lesslie Newbigin, "The Legacy of W. A. Visser 't Hooft," *International Bulletin of Missionary Research* 16, no. 2 (April 1992): 78–82.

117. W. A. Visser 't Hooft, "Missions as the Test of Faith," in *Witness in Six Continents: Records of the Meeting of the Commission on World Mission and Evangelism*, ed. Ronald K. Orchard (London: Edinburgh House, 1964), 23–24.

118. See W. A. Visser 't Hooft, "Our Ecumenical Task in the Light of History," *Ecumenical Review* 7, no. 4 (1955): 309–20.

119. Visser 't Hooft, "Significance of the World Council of Churches," 194.

120. W. A. Visser 't Hooft, *The Fatherhood of God in an Age of Emancipation* (Geneva: WCC, 1982), 72–73.

121. W. A. Visser 't Hooft, ed., *The New Delhi Report: The Third Assembly of the World Council of Churches* (New York: Association Press, 1962), 88.

122. Bilheimer, *Breakthrough*, 125. See also van der Bent, *W. A. Visser 't Hooft*, 35–36; Kinnamon, *Vision of the Ecumenical Movement*, 78–81.

123. Visser 't Hooft, *Memoirs*, 363.

124. Visser 't Hooft, *Memoirs*, 313.

125. Visser 't Hooft, *Memoirs*, 260–61. See also Ion Bria, "The Eastern Orthodox in the Ecumenical Movement," *Ecumenical Review* 38, no. 2 (1986): 216, 218.

126. Visser 't Hooft, "General Ecumenical Development," 22–23.

127. Visser 't Hooft, *New Delhi Report*, 265; for the fuller assembly discussion, see 265–68. See also Visser 't Hooft, *Memoirs*, 302.

128. Visser 't Hooft, *New Delhi Report*, 280.

129. Visser 't Hooft, *Memoirs*, 338.

130. W. A. Visser 't Hooft, *New Delhi Speaks* (London: SCM, 1962), 18.

131. Willem A. Visser 't Hooft, "Pluralism—Temptation or Opportunity," in Bea and Visser 't Hooft, *Peace among Christians*, 205–6.

132. Visser 't Hooft, "Pluralism," 213–26.

133. Visser 't Hooft, "Pluralism," 226.

134. This paragraph draws on Visser 't Hooft, "Pluralism," 224, 230–31, 233.

135. See, e.g., Visser 't Hooft, *Ecumenical Movement and the Racial Problem*, 26–29.

136. A. M. Chirgwin, *These I Have Known* (London: London Missionary Society, 1964), 37.

137. Visser 't Hooft, *Memoirs*, 345.

138. This is the title of a well-known study of ecumenism, including the role of Visser 't Hooft in the movement, by an observer at Vatican II, Robert McAfee Brown, *The Ecumenical Revolution* (New York: Doubleday, 1969).

139. Visser 't Hooft, *Has the Ecumenical Movement a Future?*, 40–41.

140. Visser 't Hooft, "General Ecumenical Development," 20.

141. Visser 't Hooft, *Has the Ecumenical Movement a Future?*, 53.

142. Visser 't Hooft, *Memoirs*, 368.

143. Visser 't Hooft, *Genesis and Formation*, viii.

144. "Uppsala '68 was a church historical event comparable in certain respects to the Second Vatican Council. This assembly changed the entire ecumenical movement." Jonas Jonson, *Wounded Visions: Unity, Justice, and Peace in the World Church after 1968*, trans. Norman A. Hjelm (Grand Rapids: Eerdmans, 2013), 34.

145. For a brief discussion, see the introduction to the chapter "Ecumenical Social Thought," in Kinnamon, *The Ecumenical Movement*, 2nd. ed., 183–84.

146. Paul Abrecht in a review of *Memoirs* in *Ecumenical Review* 40, nos. 3–4 (1988): 539–43.

147. Visser 't Hooft, *Memoirs*, 367.

148. Visser 't Hooft, *Memoirs*, 367. See also Visser 't Hooft, *Has the Ecumenical Movement a Future?*, 92. My own experience of a WCC assembly beset by political ideologies is described in Michael Kinnamon, ed., *Signs of the Spirit: Official Report of the Seventh Assembly* (Geneva: WCC Publications, 1991), 26.

149. Visser 't Hooft, *Fatherhood of God*, x, 149, 150.

150. Visser 't Hooft, *Fatherhood of God*, 128; italics added.

151. Visser 't Hooft, *Fatherhood of God*, 130–33.

152. Berkhof, "Visser 't Hooft as Ecumenical Theologian," 205.

153. Visser 't Hooft, *Fatherhood of God*, 3.

154. Potter, "But Still It Moves," 378–79.

155. See, e.g., Visser 't Hooft, *Fatherhood of God*, xi.

156. W. A. Visser 't Hooft, *Teachers and the Teaching Authorities* (Geneva: WCC Publications, 2000), 69.

157. Visser 't Hooft, *Teachers and the Teaching Authorities*, 76–77.

2.

The Writings of an Ecumenical Theologian

The six texts in this chapter, all coming from the twenty-year period at the core of Visser 't Hooft's career, are not arranged in chronological order. "The Ground of Our Unity" is put first because it is a fine, brief introduction to Visser 't Hooft's thought. Following it are chapters from two of his best-known books that focus on the key, and inseparable, themes of unity and renewal. The fourth entry, "The Mandate of the Ecumenical Movement," succinctly sets forth his understanding of the relationship between the church and the world. The fifth text, arguably the most important for grasping his theological vision, explains what he means by "Christocentric universalism," and explores its implications for ecumenical and interfaith relations. The last of these six texts, the first one chronologically, discusses the nature and purpose of a council of churches.

"The Ground of Our Unity"

*One of the major ecumenical events ever to take place on US soil
was the North American Conference on Faith and Order, which met
at Oberlin College in September of 1957. One purpose of the conference, which drew a confessionally diverse group of church leaders from
across the United States and Canada, was to urge ecumenical bodies in these countries to establish permanent programs for the study of
issues of faith and order. As general secretary of the World Council
of Churches, Visser 't Hooft was invited to deliver the sermon during
the conference's Sunday morning worship. The sermon, reprinted here,
touches on many ideas central to his theology of ecumenism.*

"The Ground of Our Unity," in The Nature of the Unity We Seek,
ed. Paul S. Minear (St. Louis: Bethany, 1958), 121–26.

Therefore, holy brethren, who share in a heavenly call, consider
Jesus, the apostle and high priest of our confession. (Hebrews
3:1, RSV)

We are assembled in order to confront our lives with the
Word of God and to receive his gifts of grace. But on this particular Sunday morning which comes in the midst of a conference of the churches on the unity of the Church of God, we are
not together as mere individuals, but as responsible churchmen.
Our Sunday worship is to throw light on our weekday struggle for truth. So let us ask what this passage of the Epistle to the
Hebrews means for our task.

Our theme is: the unity we seek. But is it so certain that "we," that is the members of all the churches here represented, really seek unity?

There are a number of Christians who do not seem to be too dissatisfied with the present situation of the Christian churches. They see no reason for radical changes and do not suffer from our divisions. We hear it said that the great diversity of denominations is really an asset in that every type of person can somewhere find something which will suit his special need. The underlying assumption is, of course, that the Church exists in order to satisfy one of the many desires of men, and that the Church is therefore, in the last analysis, an instrument which belongs to men and which they have a right to fashion according to their own will and insight.

As long as that conception of the Church is so widely held, there is little hope for any true advance in unity. Considerations of efficiency, of the need for a common witness and a common strategy may limit our ecclesiastical anarchy to some extent, but unity will never be achieved as long as we remain imprisoned in a human, all-too-human view of the nature of the Church. Ecumenical education may widen our horizons, but it will fail in its basic purpose, as long as the ecumenical seed is sown in the barren soil of man-centered church life. The ecumenical movement itself is in danger as long as its deepest intentions are not understood by the great mass of churchmen. There is therefore nothing more urgent than to ask what God's Word has to say about the nature of the Church and of its unity. We read again Hebrews 3:1, and note that the literal translation is: *partners* or *partakers* in a heavenly call.

In the Bible the point of departure is a call. It is a person-to-person call from God who is a living, speaking God to individual men and women. To hear that call, to discover that there is not only the silence of loneliness, the music of voices which we love and the noise of the crowd, but that we are addressed by one who as Creator and Redeemer is the true sovereign of our lives, is the first step on the road toward Christian faith.

The Epistle speaks of a *heavenly* call. That does not mean a call which concerns our future existence alone, but a call which comes from beyond our world, a transcendent call, a call which is characterized by ultimate, fully sovereign authority and which reminds us that our true citizenship is citizenship in that kingdom of God, the full manifestation of which we expect and for the coming of which we pray. The call comes to all those who have ears to hear. They are in the language of St. Paul the "called saints." As soon as we are called we find ourselves in the company of other men and women who have heard the same voice and have decided to respond to its invitation.

And this company is not a collection of individuals; it is a body of fellow pilgrims. Our text defines the holy brethren as those who share in a heavenly call, literally as those who are partners in the call; that is, who participate in what is in the last analysis one and the same call.

With our deep-rooted modem individualism we tend to think of calling or vocation first of all in terms of the specific mandate which God addresses to each particular person. Now the New Testament speaks very clearly about such specific callings. In fact the variety of ministries and gifts of grace which we find in the life of the early church has practically never been equalled in the life of the church in later periods. But these particular calls are never considered as private affairs. They are part of the overall call to the people of God. The cohesion and oneness of God's work among men is constantly brought out. We are partners in that we have heard one and the same comprehensive call. What you have heard and what I have heard comes from one and the same God who speaks to us in one and the same man, Jesus Christ. We have one and the same hope of our calling—the hope for one and the same kingdom. If God's call to us is one call, that must mean that God sees us as one people, one family. We may draw as many dividing lines as we can, we may organize specific confessions and denominations; in God's sight there is just the one body of those who have heard his call and respond to it. God's Church cannot be divided because its unity belongs to its very essence. It has been remarked that in the impressive, monotonous enumeration in Ephesians 4: one body, one Spirit, one hope, one faith, one baptism, one Lord—we do not find the expression: one Church. The reason is surely that the oneness of the Church is so obvious to the New Testament generation that it need not be explicitly stated.

This, then, is the true ground of our unity. This is the reason why we are not called to construct laboriously our unity out of a great many fragments which do not seem to fit together. This is why our search for unity is not in vain. What we are called to do is to manifest what is inherent in our common call, to liberate the Church of God from the man-made prisons in which we have sought to capture it, to make visible to ourselves and to the world that we are partners in one heavenly calling. This then is the first consequence which we must draw from our text: our unity is given in the will of God and in his plan. In that sense our unity is *real*, for what can be more real than that which exists in God? In another sense it is terribly unreal for we have obscured it by our divisions. Even though by the grace of God we are no longer as isolated from each other as we were and we have the World Council of Churches through which we can give expression to our sense of belonging together, we are far from showing the world that unique unity in faith, in life, in worship and order which is inherent in the Christian Gospel. Such unity does not exclude a great and rich variety, but it would exclude contradictions in essential affirmations of faith, separation at the Lord's table, competition except in the form of spiritual emulation.

It is a dangerous misunderstanding to think that the only alternative to disunity is a monolithic, centralized and imperialistic super-church, a sort of ecclesiastical leviathan. We are precisely called to manifest that wonderful combination of authority and freedom, of unity and diversity, of partnership in the call of God and variety in the gifts of grace which is described in 1 Cor., chapter 12. It would be a sorry defeatism to believe that that is merely an ecclesiastical castle in the air.

If we are really partners in one and the same call. Unity—visible, convincing unity—is not a matter that Christians can be for or against. It does not admit of neutrality. This is part of our Christian commitment. There is no place for neutrality. The pioneers of the ecumenical movement, men like Brent, Gardiner, Mott, Ainslie in this country were not the victims of some wild utopianism. They had rediscovered a basic biblical insight. "Dieu le veut." He who does not gather with the Lord—that is, he who does not work for the unity of the Church—scatters; that is, he is not on the side of the God who gathers his children together.

There will be no true advance in the ecumenical movement until this constraint, this pressure of our common calling, is felt by the whole membership of our churches. The finest systems of ecumenical education will be of no avail, unless it is preached and understood in our congregations that the Church is the Church of God and that he wills its unity. How can the very imperfect unity which we already have become the unity which we should have?

But how can we arrive at this unity? The answer is contained in our text. We are told to consider Jesus and to consider him as apostle and high priest. Is it strange that Jesus is called an apostle? Not if we remember that the verb *apostellein* is so often used by Jesus himself. In John 17 we read that Jesus prays: "As thou didst send me into the world, so I have sent them (the disciples) into the world." The apostle is God's special servant entrusted with a mission. And Jesus is in a very real sense the original apostle, as Hebrews 12 puts it: "the pioneer" whose life and death and resurrection are at the same time the beginning and the foundation of the mission to which God calls his people.

The fact that we are asked to consider Jesus as the one sent by God to perform a specific mission shows that the call we have heard is not simply a call to a new status. God did not call us to give us a claim to specific spiritual privileges. His call is a call to action, a mandate, an invitation to participate in the great mission entrusted to his people in the whole world. There is only one mission as there is one call and one Church. The mission consists in the ministry of reconciliation through which men are reconciled to God and with each other. It includes, of course, the witness to the ends of the earth among all who have not yet heard the call. For the very *raison d'être* of the Church lies in God's desire that his offer of reconciliation in Christ may be carried by his ambassadors to all nations, to all men. But mission refers to the total task of the Church and includes therefore the life which it exemplifies in its fellowship as it reconciles nations, races and classes, the disinterested service it renders to all in need, the witness through which it proclaims the Lordship of Christ over all realms of life and pronounces God's judgment on injustice, greed, lust for power. Since the mission is the response to the one call, it must be carried out in togetherness and fellowship. It is not simply that we waste our energies by failing to cooperate or to develop a common strategy. This goes deeper. We do not accomplish the full purpose of God unless we witness in unity, unless our whole approach to the world manifests the marvelous cohesion and harmony of God's plan, unless we demonstrate how God reconciles his own people among themselves. In the great encounter with the other religions which have found new vitality, in the conflict with totalitarianism, in the struggle against cheap caricatures of the Christian Gospel, our cause lacks convincing power as long as we do not prove that we live under the authority of the same Word of God and have received the same marching orders.

Unity grows as we realize that we share in one call and begin to fulfill our mission together. This means far more than cooperation between the churches—as-they-are. Churches can cooperate without being changed. They cannot participate in the total mission of the Church without their life being transformed. Once the common mission takes precedence over everything else, the whole center of attention is shifted, and the Church receives a new sense of proportion. Self-centered institutionalism is replaced by faithfulness to the divine plan, and the wonderful traffic of sharing of the gifts of grace begins to flow. Has that not been the most precious thing in the life of the ecumenical movement already, how the renewed obedience of some churches has helped other churches to rediscover the great common mission? How shallow, how poor would the ecumenical movement be today if it had not received the testimony of those churches which have found new life in the very moment of their greatest peril. We need unity in order that each of us, each of our churches, may be really surrounded by the great cloud of witnesses.

We have got to give attention to one further aspect of our text. We are not only to consider Jesus, the Apostle, but also Jesus, the High Priest. The ultimate reason why we are indestructibly linked together is the act by which Jesus performed once and for all the supreme sacrifice. The call which has come to us is an offer of reconciliation—not a possible reconciliation or a theory about reconciliation, but an effective, factual reconciliation. Our unity has its irremovable center in the cross. As we come nearer to that cross, we come nearer to each other. As we consider the High Priest who has shared our condition, tempted in every respect as we are, yet without sinning, we realize more deeply that our lack of unity is a denial of his work of salvation. At the Lord's table to which we are invited we will meet him as he shares with us his body, broken for us, and his blood, shed for us. We come as men and women who know only too well that they are not worthy to gather the crumbs under that table. We hear embarrassing questions. If this sacrament is the sacrament of unity *par excellence*, how can it be that we meet at this table and still remain separate in other ways? And have we the right to deny access to the Lord's table to any who believe sincerely that they will meet the Lord himself in this sacrament? But, thank God, at his table the Lord himself speaks the first and the last word. As he gives himself once again to us, he will convince us that he holds the initiative in our lives and that of our churches, that he continues to gather his disciples and that he will complete what he began.

"How Does Unity Grow?"

In 1957, Visser 't Hooft delivered the Taylor Lectures in Theology at the Yale Divinity School. These lectures—revised, with new material added, in light of comments from ecumenical colleagues—were published in 1959 as The Pressure of Our Common Calling. *This is perhaps Visser 't Hooft's best-known book, in part because it served as a working document for an international conference of the World Student Christian Federation in 1960, and because, while carefully defining unity, the book offers criteria for evaluating the ecumenical movement. The general secretary stresses in the preface to all of his books from this period that his thoughts are, in no sense, an official statement of the World Council of Churches.*

"How Does Unity Grow?," in The Pressure of Our Common Calling *(Garden City, NY: Doubleday, 1959), 13–28. Footnotes have been converted to endnotes.*

Dietrich Bonhoeffer, whose life and witness was so wholly identified with the ecumenical movement and who had thought deeply about its true meaning, wrote in 1932: "There is as yet no theology of the ecumenical movement," and he continued: "Each time when the Church of Christ in history has arrived at a new understanding of its own nature, it has produced a theology which expresses that understanding adequately . . . If the ecumenical movement is based on a new understanding of the Church of Christ it will produce a theology. If it does not succeed in doing so, this will mean that it is nothing else than a purely utilitarian organisation."[1]

What would Bonhoeffer say about the ecumenical situation twenty-five years later if he could be with us? I believe that he would say something like this: "It is true that there has been a certain amount of progress in clarifying the nature and the objectives of the ecumenical movement. In such documents as the Toronto Statement of 1950 on "The Church, the Churches and the World Council of Churches" and in the Evanston report on "Our Oneness in Christ and Our Disunity as Churches" we have answered a number of questions about the meaning of our ecumenical relationships. We know better than we knew before that the motivating force of the ecumenical movement is the rediscovery of the Church as the Church of God rooted in the work of Christ, the indispensable instrument for the fulfillment of the divine plan, existing essentially as one single people gathered by the Holy Spirit. But that does not yet mean that we have a theology of the ecumenical *movement*. For this common consensus on the *nature* of the Church is in danger of remaining an abstraction unless we succeed in relating it to the concrete realities of our interchurch relationships. We need a theology which will help us to bridge the gulf between our theory and our practice—a theology which answers the questions: What is it that makes the ecumenical movement move? How does unity grow?

This would not be an unfair judgment. We have a wealth of literature on the issues of church unity, but this deals nearly exclusively with the question: What are the true characteristics of a united Church? Now this is obviously a fundamental problem which must find a common answer if the ecumenical movement is to reach its ultimate purpose. But it is not the only ecumenical problem. We must not be so exclusively concerned with the goal that we have no energy or time left for the planning and mapping of the road which will lead to the goal. A theology of the ecumenical movement must deal with the meaning of our *present* relationships. It must give guidance for that in-between period when we can no longer remain wholly isolated from each other and realize that we must stay together, but when we are not yet able to enter into that full fellowship with each other which would express itself in living together as members of one visible body.

We need such a theology of the ecumenical movement because a Christian movement without theology is like a ship without a rudder. The choices which must be made, the decisions which have to be taken imply assumptions about the task of the ecumenical movement. One cannot even draw up a budget for the World Council of Churches without theologizing. And if one acts without any realization that theological issues are involved, one is likely to follow non-theological principles which are only a nice expression for worldy motives.

We also need a theology for the ecumenical movement in order to arrive at clear common criteria by which we can evaluate its work, its utterances. At the present moment we are in the dangerous situation that ecumenical activities are often judged from a great variety of different standpoints, each of which represents a specific interest or hobby. Some who are actively engaged in ecumenical activities are exclusively concerned with the practical service which the World Council renders; others consider that nothing counts except the discussion of questions of faith and order; others again ask only whether the ecumenical movement promotes evangelism and missions; some see no other point in the existence of the movement than its work for international peace; some ask only whether the ecumenical study work produces worthy theological results. Thus we are in danger of producing a number of unrelated ecumenical operations without a commonly accepted strategy in which first things come first. Now it is impossible to arrive at clear criteria unless we work out a coherent conception of the total task of the ecumenical movement, and we cannot see that task as a whole until we succeed in answering the basic questions about its raison d'être and about the implications which its existence has for the life of the churches.

This applies equally to the various bodies which together make up the ecumenical movement. For all of them the question how they can best serve the main purpose of the movement is vital; for all of them it is essential to discover how Christian unity grows. In this matter there is no fundamental difference between the tasks of the World Council of Churches, of the International Missionary Council, of the confessional alliances, and of the "independent" Christian lay movements.

But is there no danger that a theology of the ecumenical movement will divide rather than unite? That danger exists. It is conceivable that by defining such a theology we may cut ourselves off from those who will not or cannot accept it. For that reason we have to be very careful not to declare that any particular theology is *the* theology of the ecumenical movement until it has been fully considered by all concerned. That applies also to this book, which is no more than a contribution to the ecumenical discussion on the subject. There is, however, even greater danger in refusing to face these basic issues. For such a refusal could only mean, as Bonhoeffer said, that we are not engaged in a common spiritual enterprise with common assumptions as to its meaning, but rather in a purely utilitarian effort of practical co-operation.

The basic issues of the theology of the ecumenical movement are: What is the nature of the relation which the churches have together in that movement? Is it a purely organizational relationship or is it an expression of a real unity? If the latter is true, how is that unity related to the unity of which the New Testament speaks? And how can that unity which we have already grow toward that full unity which is, according to New Testament teaching, an indispensable characteristic of the Church of Christ?

The paradox that churches which do not only differ from each other in matters of faith and order but disagree with each other about important points of doctrine, and in many cases do not have sacramental fellowship, are, nevertheless, able to work together and even to witness together in specific matters had, of course, occupied the thoughts of the pioneers of the ecumenical movement. The 1920 Encyclical of the Patriarchate of Constantinople,[2] which was of great importance for the thinking of the ecumenical movement in its first stage, had said that closer relationship and fellowship (*koinonia*) between the Christian churches was not prevented by the doctrinal differences existing between them and that such understanding would be in the interest of the whole Christian body and could prepare and facilitate "the complete blessed union" of the churches. In the following years leaders of the Life and Work movement formulated a more explicit answer to the fundamental question. This answer is contained in a letter which the leaders of the Life and Work movement sent to Faith and Order in 1922. This is the important passage: "The Bishop of Winchester has rightly said: 'that in the region of moral and social questions we desire all Christians to begin at once to act as if they were one body in one visible fellowship. This can be done by all alike without any injury to theological principles.' As Dr. Kapler has said: 'Doctrine divides, but service unites.' We are concerned with service, and we believe that by serving the co-operation of the churches we shall break down prejudices and create a spirit of fellowship which will render the accomplishment of the aims of the Faith and Order movement less difficult to achieve."[3]

This theory of ecumenical action had first been formulated in 1918 in the report of the Church of England commission on "Christianity and Industrial Problems," a report submitted to the Archbishop of Canterbury. It had been taken over two years later in the report of the Lambeth Conference of Anglican bishops in a slightly stronger form: "We believe that there are no principles at stake which can rightly be held to hinder all denominations from beginning without delay to act as if they were wholly one body in the department of public, moral and social witness."[4]

In the following years this "as if" theory came to exert a widespread influence. Archbishop Nathan Söderblom used it again and again in order to explain and justify the Life and Work approach to Christian unity and stated as late as the year 1929 that "all" had "witnessed the correctness of this opinion."[5] Wilred Monod went so far as to describe the "as-if" method as the characteristic method of the Stockholm conference of 1925. He said: "We had recourse to the method advocated in psychology and spirituality: 'Act as if.' Go forward as if the Church of Christ here on earth were actually a united front."[6] At the Lausanne Conference Professor Balanos of Athens quoted the phrase with approvals.[7]

At the first world conference on Faith and Order in 1927 the phrase became almost a part of the official conference findings.

The report of the seventh section, which was submitted to that conference by Archbishop Söderblom, contained the following sentence: "In fulfilling the Master's law of love all Christians should act together as if they were one body in one visible fellowship without any injury to theological principles."[8] But this report was rejected and the new text written by Bishop Brent to replace it does not contain these or similar words.[9]

Now this widely accepted pragmatic approach (which curiously enough was not invented in the country which has so often been regarded as the country of pragmatism *par excellence*, but which came from the older churches) was in many ways a danger to the spiritual and theological health of the ecumenical movement. It is certainly true that Christians can speak and act on specific moral issues even if they are not at one about important matters of faith and order. And it is highly desirable that they should do so. It is also true that by so doing they may be drawn closer together. But such common action excluding the common consideration of the basis of action on such application of the Christian faith, and not attempting to agree as to the content of the Christian faith, is in no way comparable to the fellowship in Christ of which the New Testament speaks. For that fellowship is precisely a comprehensive fellowship which embraces faith and life, doctrine and service. To act together "as if" that fellowship had been established when, in reality, agreement is sought only in the realm of social principles is to create the wrong impression that a utilitarian relationship is an adequate response to the call which God addresses to His Church and to the need of the world. The answer is inadequate because it neglects the central ecumenical task of the Church, namely, to restore its unity in Christ. Co-operation is not unity. A consensus about social action combined with a moratorium on theological and doctrinal discussion leads easily to the conclusion that the churches have done enough when they have established co-operative relationships. But that is a false conclusion. For unity in Christ is unity in the deepest convictions and unity which embraces all of life. Those who accept co-operation as sufficient are in danger of retarding the growth of that true unity.

The "as if" answer is also inadequate because it fails to take account of the importance of theological agreement for action itself. Common action which is not based on common convictions cannot deal with the deepest needs of society. Action which is not controlled and purified by the eternal truth of the gospel can easily degenerate and become the defense of idealogical interests rather than of specifically Christian concerns. It is, therefore, impossible to separate faith from life, or theology from moral action. Dr. J. H. Oldham, whose keen and penetrating mind shaped the program and content of the second Life and Work Conference at Oxford in 1937, wrote just before that conference: "The chief need of the Church to-day to equip it to fulfil its mission to society is theology."[10] And Oxford, 1937, proved that, by putting the issue of thy Christian attitude to the state, to the nation, and to society in the framework of central Christian doctrine, the ecumenical movement gained in clarity, in spiritual authority, and in relevance to the modern world.

It is, therefore, not surprising that the "as if" method created grave misunderstanding of the nature of the ecumenical movement. Some went so far as to state that this kind of ecumenism did not arise from supernatural faith but from merely human considerations, and that, instead of being concerned with unity of belief, Life and Work was concerned only with "the moral attitude common to all the sects and underlying the variety and contrariety of their creeds."[11] This was, of course, an unfair judgment, for the great majority of the advocates of the "as if" method never meant to apply their method as a general theological principle. It was for them a provisional solution of a difficult practical problem. But the fact remains that they made it easy to interpret the ecumenical movement in terms of doctrinal relativism.

Were the pioneers, then, wholly wrong? In the perspective of all that we have learned since those early days we can see that they were in fact seeking to express an important truth which belongs to the heart of the ecumenical experience, but which need not be formulated in such a misleading way. They had themselves expressed their meaning much more adequately when they had given the Life and Work movement the title, *communio in serviendo ecumenica* (ecumenical communion in serving), for that title made it clear that in serving our Lord and in rendering service to the world, they were brought together in an ecumenical fellowship which, while far from being an adequate manifestation of the one Church of Christ, was, nevertheless, a real witness to the gathering work of Christ. Again the Encyclica of the Ecumenical, Patriarchate of 1920 had said: "We consider as the most important thing that love between the churches must be revived and strengthened so that they may no longer look upon each other as strangers and enemies, but as relatives and friends in Christ and as 'fellow heirs, members of the same body, and partakers of the promise in Christ Jesus through the gospel'" (Eph. 3:6). And this also implied that by living together the life of Christian agape, both in their relations with each other and in their relations with the world, the churches could begin to rediscover that unity which is rooted in the fact that Christ's work embraces them all. Archbishop Nathan Söderblom, speaking at the Lausanne Conference in 1927, applied Pascal's famous words to the ecumenical situation, "You would not seek me if you had not already found me," and said that the very seeking after a fuller joint expression of unity indicated that we had already at the bottom of our Christian experience such a unity. In other words, Söderblom and his colleagues were really seeking to give expression to the conviction that there existed a real unity and that that unity could become more explicit if the churches would seek to fulfill together the mission given to the Church by its Lord.

In 1937 when the Life and Work and Faith and Order movements held their second world conference, the time had come to formulate a clearer answer to the question of the nature of the ecumenical movement. Life and Work, at Oxford under Oldham's leadership, took its stand on the conviction that "the real crisis of the Church relates not to its social programme but to its faith."[12] The conference message (written by Archbishop William Temple) spoke boldly of "our unity in Christ" as "an experienced fact, not a theme of aspiration," and based on "the redeeming acts of the one Lord of the Church." And it was again Archbishop Temple who said in the opening sermon of the Faith and Order Conference at Edinburgh: "We could not seek union if we did not already possess unity. . . . It is because we are one in allegiance to one Lord that we seek and hope for the way of manifesting that unity in our witness to Him before the world."[13] In other words, we need no "as if"; we can say thankfully "because." The ecumenical task is not a hopeless task because Jesus Christ is gathering us together.

Some years later William Paton, who at that time served both the International Missionary Council and the World Council of Churches, struggled with the same problem of the unity already given and the unity to be achieved. In the so-called Paton memorandum of 1941, addressed to the churches and missions of India, he raised the question whether churches which desired to be united could not act in all possible matters in the same way as they should if there were a united Church in being. This formulation was much less open to criticism. For he explained his proposal in this way: "It is possible in view of the ascertained large measure of agreement between the churches, to proceed at this time of urgency to act in virtue of that agreement so far as it extends."[14] In other words, that unity which already exists must be allowed to have its full effect. It is not enough to discuss plans of reunion; we must also expose ourselves right now to those forces which make for unity, and that means living and acting together on the basis of the convictions which we already have in common.

Ecumenical history teaches us, therefore, that we must learn to distinguish between the unity which exists and the fuller unity which should characterize the Church of Christ and which it is our task to realize. There is the unity which holds us together right now and obliges us to go forward together. And there is the unity which is promised to us and which will be given to us in God's time if we respond obediently to His work of gathering. There is the unity of the road and there is the unity of the goal.

Thus, by the time when the plan to establish the World Council of Churches was formed, the fourteen signatories of the "Letter of Invitation" said: "It is not only or chiefly because it may be practical convenience and utility that we commend this scheme. Rather it is because the very nature of the Church demands that it shall make manifest to the world the unity in Christ of all who believe in Him. The full unity of the Church is something for which we must still work and pray. But there exists a unity in allegiance to our Lord for the manifestation of which we are responsible. We may not pretend that the existing unity among Christians is greater than in fact it is; but we should act upon it so far as it is already a reality."[15]

The basic problem of the ecumenical movement lies in that last phrase. There exists already a real unity. The churches would not have declared (as they did at the first assembly of the World Council of Churches) that they did intend to stay together if they were not aware of a real bond between them, the bond of their common faith in Jesus Christ as God and Savior, the bond of their common calling. The Amsterdam message describes that unity in these words: "We are divided from one another, but Christ has made us His own and He is not divided." In a resolution concerning the nature of the World Council, also adopted by the first assembly, it was said of the churches: "They find their unity in Him. They have not to create their unity; it is the gift of God." Again, when in 1950 an attempt was made to define the ecclesiological significance of the World Council in the Toronto statement on "The Church, the Churches and the World Council of Churches," it was underlined that "a very real unity has been discovered in ecumenical meetings which is, to all who collaborate in the World Council, the most precious element of its life."[16]

This already existing unity enables the World Council to be a channel for common witness and action of the churches in those matters in which they have come to a common mind. There are areas in which a substantial common witness has been given; there are others in which this has not been possible. But we may say that there is reason for deep gratitude that in the short period of its life, the World Council has been allowed to manifest such a large degree of unity among the churches.

It is, however, essential that we do not pretend that the existing unity is greater than, in fact, it is. We must not speak, as happens too often, as if the ecumenical movement can properly be called "the World Church." For that terminology gives the impression that what we have today in the World Council is the definite and sufficient answer to the problem of Christian unity. In fact the World Council is only the provisional solution of that problem, or, in the words of Bishop Lesslie Newbigin, "a transitory phase of the journey from disunity to unity."[17]

The unity which we have is real, but it is not to be identified with that unity which, according to the New Testament, belongs to the nature of the Church of Christ and existed in fact in the New Testament Church. This is so because the unity which we have in the World Council does not imply full sacramental communion between the churches. It is so because there exist differences in the realms of doctrine and witness which are not merely various expressions of our basic gospel, such as we find in the New Testament, but which contradict each other. It is so because we have our self-contained confessional and denominational structures, so that even churches which are willing to have full sacramental communion with each other, nevertheless, continue to live as separate entities and do not manifest unity at the decisive level of the local congregation or parish.

It must, of course, be added that there is a further respect in which our present unity is not comparable to the unity of the early Church. That unity included all who called upon the name of Christ. The unity we have in the ecumenical movement embraces many churches, but there are also a number of large churches which do not share in it. In other words, the ecumenical movement is far from being fully ecumenical.

Now it is, of course, true that the New Testament Church also had to cope with divisive tendencies, but these tendencies were never allowed to harden into self-sufficient organizational units. It seems to me that Professor John Knox, in his book on *The Early Church and The Coming Great Church*,[18] with its strong emphasis on the existence of these divisions has at the same time shown us that these divisions were never accepted and justified because the thought of a plurality of peoples of God was as unthinkable as that of a plurality of saviors. In a penetrating study on this subject,[19] Professor Oscar Cullman calls attention to the remarkable fact that the very real divisive tendencies in the early Church never led to a real break or to the creation of church bodies separated from each other. He gives four reasons for this: the general realization that the Church must be one; the energetic resistance against ecclesiastical parties; the readiness to make concessions whenever this could be done without giving up fundamental convictions; the bond of love as expressed in interchurch aid, particularly the aid for the poor of Jerusalem.

We cannot possibly maintain that the unity which we have today in the World Council has reached the point at which it corresponds to that picture. The realization that the Church must be one because of its very nature and mission has not penetrated into the whole life of our churches; we are not yet thoroughly ashamed of our many "parties"; there is little readiness to make a sacrifice for the cause of unity. Only with regard to interchurch aid is our record perhaps somewhat comparable to, that of the early church.

Our present unity in the ecumenical movement cannot be considered as the unity which the Church is meant to have, because the continued existence of separate churches which do not only show a great variety (such as should characterize the life of the body of Christ) but also real divergence and disagreement contradicts the central truth of the oneness of the Church of Christ. At present our ecumenical relationships manifest unity, but the visible expressions of our church life obscure that unity. The World Council of Churches is not the adequate answer to the problem of disunity. The adequate answer cannot be a council of churches which are not yet ready to be united. That answer must simply be the one Church of Christ.

So we must neither underestimate nor overestimate our present unity. It is a real point of departure; but it is only a point of departure. If we do not recognize and accept gratefully the great gift of God, which is the unity which we have already, we will never be able to receive the greater gift of the full unity which is in store for us. On the other hand, if we believe that we have already found the unity which the Church is meant to have, we deny that the word of God really means what it says about full unity in Christ. The two temptations of the ecumenical life prove to be the same as those of the Christian life in general: on the one hand, lack of gratitude for that which God does for us; on the other hand, anticipation of the fulfillment of God's promise.

The real issue, then, is how our present unity can *grow* toward the unity which is biblically normal. So far we have not given sufficient attention to that question. Thus the most substantial statement on the significance of the World Council, the Toronto statement of 1950 on "The Church, the Churches and the World Council of Churches," is drawn up to answer the question: What is the World Council of Churches? rather than the even more important question: How can the World Council of Churches help the churches in their growing together until they reach the fuller unity? This was inevitable at the time, for the World Council had first to explain what membership in the World Council did mean and did not mean for the member churches. But the time has now come to ask that second question and to concentrate on the issue of the *growth* of Christian unity. "Toronto" had stated that membership in the World Council does not imply the acceptance of a specific doctrine concerning the nature of Church unity. But it had also said: "The Council stands for church unity." In other words, the Council must, by its very nature, remain neutral with regard to the precise form which unity must take. That remains wholly a matter to be decided by the churches themselves. But the Council believes that there must be real and manifest unity, and that implies that it believes in the *growth* of unity and in its own obligation to further that growth. In this its purpose is not to magnify itself—on the contrary, the achievement of real unity would make the Council's existence superfluous—but to help the churches to live and witness as the one Church of Christ.

How does Christian unity grow? The answer is given in the key word of the classical passage on unity: Ephesians 4. That key word is: calling. The unity of the Church is the necessary corollary to its calling. The Church is the community of those who are called (1 Cor. 1:23). It can simply be described as "the called" (Jude 1). And the word *ekklesia* means the body of those who are called out.[20] Thus, in the New Testament, calling does not refer primarily to individual callings, or vocations, but to the common calling in Christ (Rom. 8:30, 2 Tim. 1:9). And it is this common calling which binds the Christians together in an indestructible fellowship. They are united because they "share in a heavenly call" (Heb. 3:1). And there is one body because it can be said of them: "You were called to the one hope that belongs to your call" (Eph. 4:4).

This calling is not a privilege to be enjoyed; it demands constantly renewed response. It must be confirmed, implemented (2 Pet. 1:10). Christians are exhorted to lead a life worthy of their calling (Eph. 4:1).

God unites those whom He calls. And the unity of the called is realized as they live up to their calling. Unity grows, therefore, as they become more deeply aware of and more obedient to their calling. In the same way, church unity grows whenever and wherever the churches expose themselves to the pressure of their common calling and live worthy of that common calling.

In the New Testament, unity is never static. Unity is always the result of the gathering, upbuilding, perfecting work of the Lord of the Church. He is the creator of all real unity. Unity grows when and where the Church puts itself wholly at His disposal. Unity is weakened when and where the Church seek its own ends and the parts do not "work properly" (Eph. 4:16), that is, where they do not fulfill their God-given calling. When this is true of the growth of such unity as existed in the New Testament Church, it is equally true of the growth of the unity which we have already among the churches in the ecumenical movement. There is no way for churches which are neither fully united nor completely separated to arrive at real, concrete, manifest unity except the way of common obedience to the common calling. The ecumenical task is to go forward together in making a common response to the one calling.

This must, of course, not be taken to mean that any church at any time is to be forced to participate in any action, in any common utterance which it considers to be in conflict with the truth and the will of God. To act on the unity which exists already, to work toward the growth of that unity does not imply that any pressure is brought upon the churches other than the pressure which is inherent in the common calling and to which every church must make its own free response.

But then there is no need for any human, organizational pressure once it is realized what the common calling really means and once the churches are, in fact, seeking to become worthy of that calling. It is only when the churches are introverted and self-centered or when they seek the glory of man rather than the glory of God that the question of unity is seen as a debatable issue. Once churches are again *in via*, once they remember their character as a pilgrim people which seek the eternal city, they are naturally concerned with their unity as they are with their calling.

Bishop Lesslie Newbigin has underlined that when Christians are engaged in the task of missionary obedience they are in the situation in which the Church is truly the Church and that, in that situation, the disunity which is easily taken for granted among churches which are not in a missionary situation becomes literally intolerable, because it is felt to contradict the whole nature of the apostolic mission at its heart.[21] This is profoundly true, but it must be applied to the total mission of the Church, which includes not only its missionary outreach in the technical sense of that word but all aspects of its calling.

Thus the theme of the ecumenical movement is not unity as an isolated goal; it is unity as the outcome of the common effort to express the integrity and the wholeness of the Church of Christ. It is unity through renewal. Nikolaus L. Zinzendorf, that ecumenical theologian *avant la lettre*, had seen this already: "All, fellowship [*gemeinschaft*] which is only based on agreement of opinions and forms without a change of heart, is a dangerous sect."[22]

The ecumenical movement does not owe its origin to a passion for unity alone. Its roots lie in a rediscovery of the nature and mission of the Church of Christ. Nothing less than that could have created the movement; nothing less than that can keep it going and growing. A theology of the ecumenical movement must, therefore, be concerned with the whole calling of the Church and seek to answer the question what implications that calling has for the relationships which the churches should have with each other in the ecumenical movement and for the tasks which they should undertake together.

What is the whole calling of the Church? It is to fulfill the mission with which it has been entrusted by Christ. "As thou didst send me into the world, so I have sent them into the world" (Jn. 17:18). That mission can neither be wholly identified with nor separated from the mission of Christ Himself. To identify it with the mission of Christ is to forget the uniqueness of His work and ministry, to separate it from the mission of Christ is to deny His continued presence in and with His Church. "The ministry of the Church is related to the ministry of Christ in such a way that in and through the ministry of the Church, it is always Christ Himself who is at work, nourishing, sustaining, ordering and governing His Church on earth."[23] It follows that "the pattern" of Jesus' ministry remains the pattern of the Church's ministry"[24] or that "the shape of His life is the shape of the Church's life."[25]

Notes

1. *Die Eiche*, 1932, p. 334; also in *Gesammelte Schriften*, Band I, München, 1958, p. 140.

2. *Documents of Christian Unity*. A selection, 1955, London, p. 17.

3. Söderblom, *The Church and Peace*, Burge Memorial Lecture, Oxford. 1929, p. 32. See also *A History of the Ecumenical Movement*, London, 1954, p. 572.

4. Report, Lambeth Conference, 1920, pp. 74–75. See Bell, *Christian Unity: The Anglican Position*, 1948, p. 156.

5. *The Church and Peace*, p. 32. See also *"Einigung der Christenheit,"* 1925. p. 218, and Söderblom's address at the Lausanne Faith and Order Conference. Official Report (German edition), p. 321.

6. Quoted in Congar, *Divided Christendom*, 1937, p. 118.

7. Report, Lausanne World Conference on Faith and Order (German edition), p. 506. He ascribed the words incorrectly to the Bishop of Manchester (William Temple).

8. Report, p. 397.

9. There is, however, nothing in the record of the conference to indicate that any delegate objected to the "as if" formula.

10. *The Church and Its Function in Society*, London, 1937, p. 163.

11. Congar, *Divided Christendom*, London, 1939, p. 120. See also Journet, *L'Unité de l'Eglise*, Paris, 1927, p. 83.

12. Oldham in *The Church and Its Function in Society*, London, 1937, p. 105.

13. Report, Faith and Order Conference, Edinburgh, 1937, London, 1938, p. 21.

14. *International Review of Missions*, 1941, p. 506.

15. *The World Council of Churches. Its Process of Formation*, 1946, pp. 172–73. The letter was drafted by Archbishop Temple.

16. Compare also "A Word to the Churches" from the third World Conference on Faith and Order, Lund, 1952: "As we have come to know one another better our eyes have been opened to the depth and pain of our separations and also to our fundamental unity. The measure of unity which it has been given to the

Churches to experience together must now find clearer manifestation. A faith in the one Church of Christ which is not implemented by *acts* of obedience is dead. There are truths about the nature of God and His Church which will remain for ever closed to us unless we act together in obedience to the unity which is already ours."

17. *The Household of God*, London, 1953, p. 21.

18. New York, 1955.

19. *Das Urchristentum und das ökumenische Problem. Kirchenblatt für die Reformierte Schweiz*, February 21, 1957.

20. *Significat ecclesia evocationem* (*Catechismus Romanus* 1:10:2).

21. *The Household of God*, London, 1953, p. 151.

22. Quoted by Wallau, *Die Einigung der Kirchen*, 1925, p. 267.

23. Torrance, *Royal Priesthood*, Edinburgh, 1955, p. 37. See also Schweizer, *Das Leben des Herrn in der Gemeinde und ihren Diensten*, 1946.

24. Paul Minear in *Work and Vocation*, New York, 1954.

25. Report of the third World Conference on Faith and Order, Lund, p. 22.

"Renewal and Unity"

This book, too, began as a series of lectures—in this case, the Dale Lectures, delivered at Mansfield College, Oxford, in 1955. In preparing them, Visser 't Hooft drew material from lectures he had given at the Facultad Evangelica in Buenos Aires three years earlier, an indication of how his writings evolved from presentations and subsequent discussions. A common theme of this period, as we have seen above, was "the nature of the unity we seek"; but "there has been little reflection," according to Visser 't Hooft, "on the nature of the renewal that we seek." This chapter from The Renewal of the Church, *shows him attempting to fill this gap, and to insist that unity and renewal go together.*

"Renewal and Unity," in The Renewal of the Church *(London: SCM, 1956), 117–24. Footnotes have been converted to endnotes.*

The history of the Church seems to teach us that there is a constant conflict between renewal and unity. There have been those in all ages for whom the whole emphasis in *Una Sancta* is on *Sancta* and there have been those to whom it is all important to maintain the Church's integrity as the *Una*. There have been those for whom the Church has no meaning unless it exemplifies the life of the new creation in constant renewal of life; there have been those to whom the Church as given in history is so precious that they look with suspicion upon any outbreak of new life which might affect the unity and peace of the Church. From the days of the Montanists, when Tertullian entered into conflict with the established hierarchy, till our own days, when groups break away from the historic churches to form sects exemplifying the new life of the spirit, the conflict has gone on in an almost monotonous fashion.

There are fanatics of renewal such as the Labadists in Holland in the seventeenth century who said that

> *Le mal est que le nom d'Église Réformée*
> *Fait croire qu'il suffit qu'on réforme en idée*

and proceeded to create a church in which the life of the whole as well as the life of each member was to manifest the total newness of the Church. And there are the fanatics of Unity as the 'integralists' (not only in the Roman but also in other churches) who believe that the slightest deviation from accepted traditions is an attack on the Church itself and (to use words of Father Congar)[1] 'for whom everything which has come into existence after a certain date finds itself *ipso facto* in a state of mortal sin and damnation'.

The story of the conflict between unity and renewal has been described more than once, but the very way in which it has been written shows how difficult it is to take the two viewpoints seriously at the same time. Gottfried Arnold, whose writings made such a deep impression on Goethe, called his history a *Non-partisan History of the Church and the Heresies* (1700) and pretended that his account of the heresies was really the first objective account of the great struggle between the Church and those who sought to change its doctrine or life. But the underlying presupposition of the whole work is that the institutional Church is always wrong, when it defends its unity and that true renewal of Christian life can only come through breaking away from all institutional religion. On the other hand R. A. Knox tells us in the preface of his book on *Enthusiasm* that at first he desired to write a trumpet blast against 'enthusiasm', but that as he pursued his studies, the men he had to write about became so human, that he became more concerned to find out why they thought as they did than to prove they were wrong. And his book is certainly unique in that a faithful member of a Church which according to his own statement is more institutional than all the other 'Christianities' shows penetrating insight into the thoughts and motivation of the so-called enthusiasts and even warns his fellow churchmen that the Church cannot live without enthusiasm. At the same time the basic presupposition of the book is that Christianity is 'a balance of doctrines, and not merely of doctrines but of emphases' (p. 580), and that this balance is given in the teaching of the Roman Catholic Church. In other words the criterion of judgment is whether the unity created by this balance is maintained or disturbed. And the very title *Enthusiasm* which refers to a human attitude, obscures the fact that in many of the movements here described there is another factor at work, namely the gospel itself with its explicit insistence on the new life and the new creation.

Now it is a striking fact that in the Bible renewal and unity are not seen as alternatives or as competing objectives. On the contrary they are considered as interdependent, as two aspects of the work of God in and for his people. Thus the 'gathering' of the people, the reconstitution of their unity, to which the prophets look forward is far more than their being reassembled in the same place. It has always the overtone of the beginning of new life. The people will be gathered when they return unto the Lord (Deut. 30.2–3), when they keep his commandments (Neh. 1.9). The unity of the people under the coming messianic king, who will be their one shepherd, will be a unity in the observation of the statutes of the Lord (Ezek. 37.24).

The well-known vision of Ezekiel concerning the dry bones provides a further illustration. He sees the bones coming together. They are again covered by sinews and flesh and skin. But that is not sufficient, for there is no breath in them (Ezek. 37.8). Unity by itself is nothing, may even mean death. It is only when the breath of God comes upon the bones that the whole house of Israel is truly gathered and united. Unity in the biblical sense is God-given unity which implies new life.

In the New Testament the togetherness of the two comes out even more clearly. In Romans 12 the call to the faithful to let their lives be transformed by the renewal of their mind is made specific and concrete in the description of the true unity through the interchange and interplay of the spiritual gifts. In Ephesians 2.15 the oneness of Jew and Gentile in the Church is described as the creation of one new man in place of two. And in this expression we have the strongest possible affirmation that renewal is to participate in the life of the new community, which finds its unity in Christ, and that the unity of that community is unity in the newness of life which Christ incarnates and communicates to those who believe in him.

The Gospel of John provides further evidence. In the high-priestly prayer our Lord prays (John 17.22–23) according to the translation of William Temple: 'And the glory which thou hast given to me I have given to them that they may be one as we are one—I in them and thou in me, that they may be perfected into one. . . .' The true unity is the consequence of the *doxa*, the glory, which is the quality of life of the new creation in Christ. The Lord prays that the plan of God may be brought to its final consummation and that consummation is the total newness of the faithful in perfect unity, a unity which consists in sharing in the glory of the new creation. Now it has often been suggested that this profound unity can only be understood as a spiritual and invisible unity. But that is to deny the very evidence of the text. For this perfect unity is, according to the words of the prayer, to convince the world that God has sent Christ and thus revealed his love for the world. As Temple observes: 'there is offered something for the world to see, namely the glory which the Father gave to the Son and the Son to the disciples'. The unity of which the New Testament speaks is at the same time the most deeply spiritual unity and the most tangible, incarnate unity.

Both unity and renewal are divine gifts. The Epistle to Titus (3.5), speaks of 'renewal of the Holy Spirit' and the Epistle to the Ephesians (4.3) of the 'unity of the Holy Spirit'. These parallel expressions mean that renewal and unity are both created by the Holy Spirit, the giver of life and the builder of the Church.

Why is it then that two intrinsic qualities of the Church which are so closely related to each other in the New Testament, appear to us as alternatives or even as mutually exclusive goals? I believe that the reason is that we have consciously or unconsciously secularized both notions. I take secularizing in its literal meaning of adaptation to this age as opposed to orientation toward the new age. It is our lack of a truly eschatological perspective which makes it so hard to take renewal as seriously as unity and unity as seriously as renewal.

We have already seen that renewal in the biblical sense is something quite different from renewal on the purely historical level. True renewal is not to be equated with adaptation to a changed situation, with a passing from lethargy to activism, with a change of structure or with new forms of expression. Far too often these signs of life, or (to use the phrase of R. A. Knox) these forms of enthusiasm, which may very well be mere signs of the vitality of natural man, have been taken or are taken as evidence, that a true reformation or renewal of the Church takes place. The criterion of renewal, it cannot be said too strongly, is the newness of the new creation. The real issue is whether the Church lives up to its calling to be the representative on earth of the new age which has begun in Christ.

In the same way we have to de-secularize our thinking about unity. We must not think of it in merely institutional terms. For institutional unity may be very worldly unity. Like newness, unity is rooted in the new age, in the unity which. characterizes the life of the Kingdom. This unity enters into our age through the Church and it is therefore by no means a 'Platonic' ideal or a merely invisible thing. But its source and criterion are not historical or sociological. We are truly one only when our unity reflects that unity which the Son has with the Father and which he gives to those who belong to him.

It is then only if we seek again to recapture the eschatological dimensions of the New Testament that we may hope to find a way out of the dilemma which the conflict of unity and renewal has created for us.

These are not merely theological considerations. They have a very practical bearing on the life of our churches as they participate together in the ecumenical movement. If we have rightly interpreted the biblical teaching, the ecumenical movement must be concerned with renewal as well as with unity. We think and talk too much about the ecumenical movement, as if it were only interested in the unity of the Church. As a matter of fact it has never concentrated exclusively on the reunion of the churches. The unofficial slogan of the Oxford Conference of 1937: 'let the Church be the Church' was in fact an expression of a deep and widespread awareness that the churches stood in need of a radical renewal. This conviction was all the stronger because it grew out of a return to biblical theology. Men and women of differing confessions who could not see their way to agreement on the form and order of the Church, were united in their new understanding of the Church as a peculiar people or (as Moffatt has it) 'the people who belong to him' (1 Peter 2.9) and which is therefore not to be conformed to this world, but to be constantly transformed by the renewal of its mind. Again the struggle of the Confessing churches in Germany, and in several occupied countries, helped many to understand that the unity which the churches must seek is not unity at any price, but on the contrary unity in deeper common understanding of the specific nature and mission of the Church. And this has found expression in the life of the world Council of Churches. The 'Call to the Churches' concerning its first assembly said: 'We have failed because we ourselves have been partakers in man's disorder. Our first and deepest need is not new organization, but the renewal, or rather the rebirth, of the actual churches. May God grant that we hear the call of the Spirit.' That is also why in the programme of the World Council there is a strong emphasis on those aspects of the life of the Church such as evangelism, the mission of the laity, the relations of men and women, in which the renewal of the Church must become manifest. And when 'Faith and Order', seeking to advance the cause of unity, deals with the 'social and cultural factors' which prove to be tenacious obstacles to unity, it is in fact challenging the churches to disentangle themselves from their alliances with the old world and to become churches of the new age.

In the same way recent ecumenical history has made us understand better that the gift of renewal like every spiritual gift is given 'for the common good' (1 Cor. 12.7), that is for the upbuilding of the whole body in its unity. It has always been true that renewal in one church tended to call forth renewal in other churches and that in this way a new sense of belonging together across confessional frontiers was created. But that process of sharing has been intensified and widened as the churches have been drawn out of their isolation into ecumenical relationships. The churches have now an opportunity of letting themselves be challenged by those signs of renewal which take place in other parts of the total fellowship. And as the sense of responsibility for each other and solidarity with each other grows, we learn at the same time that renewal is not necessarily renewal against those who are considered to be living in conformity to the world, but renewal for the sake of the whole.

But if it is now widely understood that unity and renewal belong together, that does not yet mean that it is clearly understood how they are related to each other and how, as we tried to show, both are essential aspects of that eschatological life which the Church is called to live. At this point we can only say that there are signs that the rediscovery of that neglected dimension of the Church's life is taking place. The Report on the main theme of the Evanston Assembly was, in spite of all criticisms directed against it, a document of very considerable ecumenical importance in that it showed so clearly what this rediscovery may mean for the whole life and message of the churches. The urgent question is whether the churches will come to realize that they can have neither renewal nor unity unless they accept to live the hopeful and expectant life, praying constantly for the gift of newness and unity, and unless in order to render their truest service to the world they are ready to be less at home in the world. 'Let the Church be the Church' means: let the Church be the pilgrim people of God tasting and demonstrating the powers of the age to come; let it truly believe that, in the words of the report to the Evanston Assembly, 'God acts from moment to moment and from generation to generation, re-creating the Church ever anew by the Spirit who indwells it, renewing its faithfulness, its purity, its self-sacrifice, its courage.'

Notes

1. Conclusion of 'Vraie and Fausse Réforme dans l'Église' as trans-
    lated in *Cross-currents*, 1951, 4.

"The Mandate of the Ecumenical Movement"

This plenary address was delivered to the Fourth Assembly of the World Council of Churches, held in Uppsala, Sweden, in 1968, two years after Visser 't Hooft retired from the position of general secretary. The ecumenical movement, he told the delegates, is in a paradoxical situation: on the one hand, it is a time of great ecumenical advance; on the other, it is a time when the movement is being called into question as never before. "And once again the basic issue is that of the relation between the Church and the world." This theme had been central to his thinking for more than forty years, and he here offers a summary of his mature reflection on it.

"The Mandate of the Ecumenical Movement," in The Uppsala Report 1968: Official Report of the Fourth Assembly of the World Council of Churches, *ed. Norman Goodall (Geneva: WCC, 1968), 316–23.*

WHERE DO WE STAND TODAY?

It seems to me that the present ecumenical situation can only be described in the paradoxical statement that the ecumenical movement has entered into a period of reaping an astonishingly rich harvest, but that precisely at this moment the movement is more seriously called in question than ever before. And once again the basic issue is that of the relation between the Church and the world.

I need not develop why we can speak of the success of the ecumenical movement. We need only to think of this Assembly in comparison to earlier ecumenical world conferences. Who would have dared to believe in 1925 or even in 1948 that by 1968 we would have reached the point at which practically all Eastern Orthodox Churches would bring their much-needed contribution, at which Africa, Asia and Latin America would have such a distinctive word to speak, and in which through a great network of close fraternal relationships the Roman Catholic Church, after having elaborated its own position concerning the central ecumenical issues, would enrich and stimulate our discussions so greatly? We are near the point when Söderblom's dream will come true: that all churches of Christendom can speak out together on the great problems of mankind. And as the various main streams of the ecumenical movement have joined together we have a greater opportunity than ever to act in the field of evangelism and mission, of faith and order, of life and work as one well coordinated world-wide Christian movement. But at this very moment there are many inside and outside our churches, particularly among the younger generation, who have their deep doubts about the relevance of the ecumenical movement and turn away from it with a sense of disappointment. So our very success is ambiguous. And once again it is the decisive issue of the relation between the Church and the world which claims the centre of the stage.

For we hear it said that the ecumenical movement as it has developed over the last forty or fifty years is unable to help the churches to perform that mission which they should perform in the world of our time. That world requires radical renewal. But how can churches speak convincingly of radical renewal, if they are not radically renewed themselves? That world needs a thorough transformation of its traditional structures, but do not the churches exemplify that traditional structures resist such transformation? That world must become a world-wide responsible society, but are the churches themselves living as a responsible society in which full solidarity in service and mission is practised and in which all members, including all laymen and women, are able to bear their full share of responsibility for the common life?

Or again, this world needs effective unity. But is the relationship which the churches have in the ecumenical movement more than a pale reflection of the unity they should have? And is the progress toward full unity not so slow that it reveals rather a fear of unity than a great and passionate conviction about the essential oneness of the people of God? And must we therefore not admit that the ecumenical movement has had its time, and that we have now entered into the "post-ecumenical" age in which Christians will have to make their contribution and render their service to the world through other, less cumbersome channels?

Such questions are being asked in many places, and we have every reason to take them seriously. It is inevitable that they lead also to a new discussion within our own ranks. Once again we have to face the old issue of the true relation between the Church and the world and between the vertical and horizontal dimensions of the Christian faith. My hope is that at this Assembly we will deal with it positively and ecumenically. Positively in the sense that we give a clear sense of orientation to our movement. Ecumenically in the sense that we will truly listen to each other and not write others off as brothers who are so weak in the faith that they do not deserve our attention. And also ecumenically in that the generations do not treat each other as strangers; that the older ones do not pretend that all the real questions have already been answered in ecumenical history and the younger ones do not claim that ecumenical history is a tale told, if not by an idiot, at least by a spokesman of the hopeless establishment. As a contribution to the discussion of these crucial questions I would now make the following four points:

1. NO HORIZONTAL ADVANCE WITHOUT VERTICAL ORIENTATION

I believe that, with regard to the great tension between the vertical interpretation of the Gospel as essentially concerned with God's saving action in the life of individuals, and the horizontal interpretation of it as mainly concerned with human relationships in the world, we must get out of that rather primitive oscillating movement of going from one extreme to the other, which is not worthy of a movement which by its nature seeks to embrace the truth of the Gospel in its fulness. A Christianity which has lost its vertical dimension has lost its salt and is not only insipid in itself, but useless for the world. But a Christianity which would use the vertical preoccupation as a means to escape from its responsibility for and in the common life of man is a denial of the incarnation of God's love for the world manifested in Christ.

The whole secret of the Christian faith is that it is man-centred because it is God-centred. We cannot speak of Christ as the man for others without speaking of him as the man who came from God and who lived for God.

This is a very practical truth. For on it depends the relevance of the Christian witness in the world. Let me illustrate this by referring to one of the most important problems on our agenda.

We are all deeply concerned over the problem of international social justice with its different aspects of the increasing danger of famine-conditions in large parts of the world, of the slow pace of development and of the growing tension between the affluent nations and those which live in conditions of poverty. We are profoundly disturbed by the fact that the attempts to deal with this most acute human problem are quite inadequate, so that, as Dr Prebitsch has said, the decade of development has become the decade of frustration over development.It is not that we do not know what should be done. The experts, including several who have participated in our World Conference on Church and Society and its follow-up meetings, have worked out specific plans which would go a very long way in meeting the need. But these plans are not being carried out.Why not? Because they require that much larger amounts be made available for this purpose and that much closer collaboration be achieved between all the nations concerned. And the governments are at present not able to promise more aid and to enter into more far-reaching agreements because there is no sufficiently strong and clear public opinion which would back them up in such a course of action. For public opinion in the West is today rather tired of the issues of development. There seem to be so many urgent tasks in our immediate environment. And the arguments used to "sell" development seem to have lost their force. The economic argument that development is good for the growth of trade is not very convincing when the Western world is so obviously able to make tremendous progress on the basis of its own inherent strength. The political argument that we cannot afford to let the tension between the rich and the poor parts of the world grow to the point of explosion carries little weight when a few great powers have the means to dominate the international political situation.And so we seem to be condemned to let the situation drift, and hand to our children a world in which there will be famine and despair and as an inevitable result even more violence than we have already known in our time.

What can the churches do about this? They can adopt resolutions and reports. But will that make much difference? The crisis is a crisis of motivation, of fundamental attitudes. The deep trouble lies underneath the political and economic level. The root of the matter is that at a time when history requires that humanity should live as a coherent responsible society men still refuse to accept responsibility for their fellow-beings.

Now we can, of course, seek to awaken a sense of solidarity with and sympathy for the needy. We do so with some success. And we must go on doing this. But that is not the radical operation which is needed. That does not lead to a changing of the structures of world-economy; that does not lead to a full acceptance of responsibility, so that the economically-weak in one part of the world are as a matter of course assisted by the economically-strong in other parts of the world, just as this happens in our modern welfare-states. No, what is needed is nothing less than a new conception of humanity.

New in relation to our present situation. Not new in an absolute sense. For as we look all over the place for the vision of humanity which we need, we are like the explorer who sought a new country and discovered his own country. For it is in our Holy Scriptures that the unity of mankind is proclaimed in the most definite manner.

The churches have not taken that proclamation seriously enough. They are largely responsible for the false impression that Christians are advocates of the Church and leave the advocacy of humanity to the philosophers, the humanists, the Marxists. But the fact is that the vision of the oneness of humanity is an original and essential part of the biblical revelation. Centuries before Alexander the Great's Oikoumene began to give Mediterranean man an idea of a wider human family, Israel had already recorded its insight that all men are made in the image of God, that they share a common task: to have dominion over the earth, that all were together included in the covenant of God's patience, made with Noah; that all are to be blessed in Abraham. And the Second Isaiah had already prophesied in one of his songs concerning the Servant of Jahveh that he would be "a covenant of humanity" and a light to the nations. (For it seems clear that in Isaiah 42:6 the word *am* really means "humanity"). This prophecy is fulfilled in Jesus Christ. He is the manifestation of God's love for the whole of mankind. He dies for all and inaugurates the new humanity as the second Adam. When it is said that God makes all things new this means above all that through Christ God re-creates humanity as a family united under his reign. Mankind is one, not in itself, not because of its own merits or qualities. Mankind is one as the object of God's love and saving action. Mankind is one because of its common calling. The vertical dimension of its unity determines the horizontal dimension.

So Christians have more reason than anyone else to be advocates of humanity. They are not humanitarians in the sentimental sense that it is nice to be nice to other people. They are not humanists in the aristocratic sense that learning and culture constitute a bond between the privileged few of all nations. They are on the side of *all* humanity because God is on that side and his Son died for it. So they do not get so easily discouraged when the service of mankind proves to be a much tougher task than was anticipated. They do not say: We will let you have economic justice if you fulfil my conditions. For it is their very *raison d'etre* as followers of Christ to ensure that his suffering brothers receive what they need.

It seems to me that no amount of resolution-making and moralising can help us in our present predicament if we do not first recover in theology, in our teaching, and in our preaching the clear biblical doctrine of the unity of mankind and so give our churches the strong foundation for a new approach to the whole question of world economic justice and to a better and more convincing motivation for development aid. It must become clear that church members who

deny in fact their responsibility for the needy in any part of the world are just as much guilty of heresy as those who deny this or that article of the faith. The unity of mankind is not a fine ideal in the clouds; it is part and parcel of God's own revelation. Here if anywhere the vertical, God-given, dimension is essential for any action on the horizontal, inter-human plane.

2. THE ECUMENICAL MOVEMENT AND THE CHURCHES NEED EACH OTHER

It is not difficult to understand why the question is raised whether the ecumenical movement should be so largely in the hands of the churches. Churches stand not only for the great common Christian tradition, but also for the many separate and historically conditioned traditions, not all of which have theological dignity. From a purely sociological standpoint churches must be classified as institutions which offer the most tenacious resistance to attempts at reformation and renewal. How then can an ecumenical movement which seeks to speak to the condition of our rapidly changing society and which would proclaim the need of renewal in all spheres of life lean so heavily on the churches? Should we not reverse the direction which the ecumenical movement took in the 1930's, give up the struggle to mobilize the churches for their new common tasks and follow the exhortations of the prophets of the "post-ecumenical" era in order to concentrate our attention exclusively on the urgent tasks in the world without wasting time on efforts to renew the Churches?

I feel the force of this question. In a sense we have asked for this reaction. For we have in all our churches and in the World Council talked so much about renewal and about the true mission of the Church, but we have made so little real progress toward the realization of that renewal and the true accomplishment of that mission, that the reaction is inevitable. Was it then a mistake to form a World Council of Churches and so to give the churches a central place in the ecumenical movement? I am convinced that it was not a mistake and that the 1937 decision holds good in 1968. In the ecumenical movement there has always been an important place for movements which are not dependent on the churches. They have pioneered, they must continue to challenge and stimulate us. But an ecumenical movement which would not be supported and carried by the churches would become a castle in the air. It would not be a movement representing the faith in the incarnation. It would deny one of the basic discoveries of ecumenical history that the *una Sancta* is not a beautiful ideal, but a God-given reality which demands concrete manifestation. It would not be more truly involved in the decisive spiritual, cultural, social battles of our time. It would be less, not more, concerned with the real world of human history. In order to act in society Christians must have identity with recognizable structures of common life. If the world, as Stockholm said, is too strong for a divided Church, it is surely too strong for Christians who do not seek to live as a people with a peculiar calling and thus fail to incarnate the mandate which they have received from their Lord. We do not have a chance to make a real impact on the great decisions which mankind has to take in the field of international economic justice, of peace and war, and so many other fields unless we use the tremendous spiritual potentiality still largely hidden in the Christian churches.

But it must be added immediately that the churches also need the ecumenical movement. For it is largely through that movement that the pressure for true renewal is exercised. God knows that they need that pressure. The Amsterdam Assembly spoke of the mutual correction which the churches are meant to receive from each other. We may gratefully say that in the course of the last twenty years there have been signs that this process of correction in which the World Council can play a decisive role, is actually in operation. The gifts of the Spirit are being shared. East and West, younger and older churches, and since Vatican II the Roman Catholic Church and the other churches, receive gifts from each other "for the upbuilding of the body". But still it is only a small beginning. At the present moment we need especially a far more intensive dialogue between the churches of the Eastern Orthodox and those of the Western tradition—a dialogue which requires much imagination and patience on both sides, but which can lead to a great enrichment and deepening of the ecumenical movement. If we really lived according to the pattern of 1 Corinthians 12, if we really had a common market for the *charismata*, we would not need to worry about lack of new life in our churches. The time has come for the churches to open their eyes and discover the unspeakable gift which God offers them in the new opportunities for living together as members of the one body which receives the many gifts from the one Spirit.

3. CHURCH UNITY IS IMPORTANT

It is natural that many inside and outside the churches wonder whether we in the ecumenical movement, do not attach an exaggerated importance to the question of church unity. Some have no interest in that question because they consider that the differences between the churches are disappearing anyway. They find Christians in other churches with whom they feel closer kinship than with many in their own church. Others feel that church unity might aggravate the institutionalist tendencies in church life and create even less flexible structures than we have today. I believe that we must hold on to the original conviction of the ecumenical movement, that it belongs to the very nature of the people of God to live as one reconciled and therefore united family, and that it belongs to its witness to present to the world the image of a new humanity which knows no walls of separation within its own life. Even the best cooperation and the most intensive dialogue are no substitutes for full fellowship in Christ.

But I wonder at the same time whether it is not largely our own fault that so many conceive of unity in terms of uniformity and centralization and are therefore afraid of it. Should we not have learned after these decades of common life in the ecumenical movement that the Holy Spirit has used very many different forms of church order for his work of inspiration, conversion and prophesy? And have we given sufficient attention to the indisputable fact that the earliest Church knew several quite distinct types of church order? My point is simply that there seems to be no really urgent reason to identify unity with acceptance of one and the same church order. Do we not discover in our increasingly pluralistic cultural situation that what is good for one continent or region is not necessarily good for another? And must we not draw the conclusion that there can be real fellowship in faith and in sacrament even when structures differ?

In any case it remains a central part of the mandate of the ecumenical movement to maintain, as New Delhi put it, that unity is both God's will and his gift to the Church; that it must be made visible in each place and that the faithful in each place must be united with the whole Christian fellowship in all places and all ages. I hope that Uppsala will not merely confirm this insight, but develop its implications so clearly that all churches may be encouraged to make a much greater effort for the promotion of true unity.

"The Rediscovery of Christocentric Universalism in the Ecumenical Movement"

Most of the material in No Other Name *came from the Hein Lectures, presented by Visser 't Hooft in 1962 at the theological seminaries of the American Lutheran Church in Columbus, Ohio; Dubuque, Iowa; and Saint Paul, Minnesota. In them, Visser 't Hooft attempted to provide clarity on the nature of syncretism, a topic dear to his heart, and the attitude the ecumenical movement should take toward it. "Christocentric universalism" is sometimes used as shorthand for Visser 't Hooft's vision of ecumenism, and this excerpt is his fullest statement of what he means by the term.*

"The Rediscovery of Christocentric Universalism in the Ecumenical Movement," in No Other Name *(London: SCM, 1963), 103–25. Footnotes have been converted to endnotes and renumbered.*

The ecumenical movement of our time is an attempt to realize this specific Christian universalism. The story of the development of that movement shows how it discovered progressively the different constituent elements of that universalism and their fundamental interdependence. That discovery has taken a long time and is still going on. Strong resistance has had to be overcome. A bird's eye view of the history of the ecumenical movement from this perspective will help us to see more clearly what has been achieved and how much remains to be done.

The World Missionary Conference of 1910 had the wide perspective of the total missionary task. Its chairman, John R.

Mott, will always be remembered as the man who not only proclaimed, but embodied in his life, the universal dimension of the gospel of Christ. Karl Barth wrote in 1911 about Mott: 'This is Mott's personality: something happens. And what happens is not just anything, but at once the ultimate and most important thing that can happen: man is judged by his aim and the aim is mankind.'[1] The Edinburgh Conference reflected this preoccupation with the world-wide evangelization of the whole world as the one urgent Christian task. So the Edinburgh Conference gave a clear witness to the world-embracing nature of the Christian faith. Nevertheless it did not give a complete witness concerning the nature of Christian universalism. For the resolution about the continuation of the Conference said specifically that this continuation was to follow the lines of the Conference itself 'which are interdenominational and do not involve the idea of organic and ecclesiastical union'. Because of the resistance in many missionary circles against any relationship that might lead to a unity in doctrine, this restriction was at the time inevitable. But by thus preventing all discussion on matters of faith and order the International Missionary Council (which grew out of the Edinburgh Conference) could not give a clear interpretation of the nature of Christian universalism which includes, as we have seen, the witness to the unity of the people of God. It is also remarkable that the Council did not adopt a specific basis, but simply said that 'it is recognized that the successful working of the International Missionary Council is entirely dependent on the gift from God of the spirit of fellowship, mutual understanding, and desire to co-operate'. In the official documents no explicit statement concerning the Christocentric character of Christian universalism was made. In the case of a missionary body this was less serious than it would have been elsewhere, because practically all missionary agencies took their stand on the foundation of a Christocentric faith. But it meant that the Council could not present a coherent conception of the nature of a specifically Christian universalism.

As the years went by, the themes which had been at first considered too dangerous, began to knock on the doors of the IMC. At the Tambaram meeting of 1938, with its strong emphasis on the Church, the issues of unity and the theological issues in general took a very prominent place. It was increasingly seen that the universalism of world evangelization needed to be based on the two other great components of Christian universalism: the common affirmation of the centrality of Christ and a common conception of the nature and task of the Church. Thus the Council was increasingly prepared to join with other parts of the ecumenical movement which had in their own way discovered the full implications of Christian universalism.

Almost immediately after the Edinburgh Conference of 1910 Bishop Brent, who had been deeply impressed by that conference, began to organize the 'Faith and Order' movement. He felt that there was need for a body which would specifically deal with the questions of visible unity. He shared the vision of Mott, but was convinced that Christianity would not and could not perform its universal mission as long as it remained so hopelessly divided. Now Faith and Order emphasized precisely those aspects of universalism which the missionary movement had not been able to emphasize. Brent and his associates realized that, as they sought to bring the churches together in conference to consider the question of visible unity, they had to answer the question what should be the nature and scope of that unity. They could not of course make an *a priori* choice between the differing conceptions of unity held by the various Christian traditions. But they could try to indicate what they believed to be the distinctive character of church unity as compared with secular concepts of unity. It is well known that they decided to address their invitation to churches 'which accept our Lord Jesus Christ as God and Saviour'.

This decision has often been interpreted as a device to exclude certain groups of churches. But its purpose was in the first place positive. It was a choice for Christocentric unity over against a vague and undefined unity, a choice for the unity given once for all in and by Jesus Christ as God incarnate. It was not a choice for an introverted orthodoxy. Bishop Brent, who was an active fighter for world peace, and took a great share in the struggle against the opium trade, had none of the characteristics of a narrow ecclesiastic.

The remarkable layman who translated the 'Faith and Order'

plan of Bishop Brent into reality, Robert Gardiner, explained again and again the real significance of the Basis. It was functional, for it had to do with the nature of the unity that was envisaged. Thus Gardiner said at one of the early Faith and Order meetings in 1915: 'The reason for the restriction of the Conference to those Communions throughout the world which confess our Lord Jesus Christ as God and Saviour must be made plain. Our attempt is not simply to promote kindly feeling or good fellowship, or even good works, but to reunite all Christians in the one living Body of the one Lord, both God and man, incarnate, crucified, buried, risen from the dead and ascended on high, living to-day, the Head over all things to the Church which is his Body, the fulness of him that filleth all in all.'[2] And in 1919 Gardiner wrote to Dr Siegmund Schultze: 'It seems to us that the conception of Christian unity held by those who accept that fact and doctrine (i.e. the Incarnation) must be totally different from that of those who regard our Lord only as a great religious teacher. Moreover, we believe that the only hope for the future of the world rests in that visible unity of Christians which shall manifest to the world God incarnate in the person of his Son, in Jesus Christ, manifesting himself in infinite love, that his new commandment that we should love one another even as he has loved us, may be the fundamental obligation of mankind in every relation, international, social and industrial.'[3]

These two statements show that when these early Faith and Order leaders spoke of Jesus Christ, God and Saviour, they meant the incarnation. It is not difficult to criticize their choice of words. But we can only be grateful for their insistence that the unity and universality with which the ecumenical movement must be concerned can only be the one that is created by Jesus Christ himself as the one in whom God reconciles the world to himself.

Just as the historic deed of the fathers of Edinburgh had been to give a clear, concrete witness to the objective of universalism—the proclamation of salvation in Christ to all men—so the fathers of Faith and Order gave a definite witness to its centre, the one Jesus Christ who is the author of both unity and universality.

Faith and Order continued to concentrate on this central

truth. The affirmation of Unity of the Edinburgh Conference of 1937 says: 'This unity does not consist in the agreement of our minds or the consent of our wills. It is founded in Jesus Christ himself, who lived, died and rose again to bring us to the Father and who through the Holy Spirit dwells in his Church. We are one because we are all the objects of the love and grace of God, and called by him to witness in all the world to his glorious Gospel.'

But Faith and Order's witness was also incomplete. By concerning itself exclusively with the issues of church unity it was in danger of forgetting the objective of that unity. It raised the question of the unity that is in Christ without setting that question sufficiently in the context of the universal work of Christ in and for mankind. It also needed to be inserted in a wider framework. Faith and Order understood this increasingly and thus became prepared for an integration with other parts of the ecumenical movement.

The 'Life and Work' movement, which became widely known through the Stockholm Conference of 1925, was due to the initiative of Archbishop Söderblom of Sweden. He had felt deeply about the impotence of the Church to stem the tide of hatred during the First World War. His was a burning desire to unite the different churches in the application of the Spirit and teaching of Christ to social, national and international relationships. Thus 'Life and Work' became a movement for 'practical Christianity' and excluded from its deliberations the issues of faith and order. Here then we have another form of Christian universalism, an attempt to proclaim the lordship of Christ in all realms of life. Although such claims as that Stockholm represented the 'Nicaea of ethics' went a good deal too far, it was no small thing that representatives of so many churches spoke out together for the validity of Christian principles for the whole life of society and of the world.

But here again there were elements of uncertainty in the witness. The basic concept of Stockholm remained unclear. It had been decided to exclude all doctrinal issues from the deliberations. Now in order to justify that decision arguments were used which seemed to imply a denial of the need for any common starting point or any common conviction concerning the nature of Christian unity. Thus the Executive Committee stated in 1922 that 'doctrine divides, but service unites'.[4] But is it not precisely the characteristic of Christian universalism that its centre is the one whom Christians confess to be the agent of unity, so that the affirmation (which is of course doctrinal) that he is the divine Saviour and the response to his call in service are both indispensable elements of Christian universalism? There were a number of prominent Stockholm delegates who considered it the greatest merit of the conference that it had discovered a unity which was not based on any specific common affirmation of faith, but on a common life, and thus made Stockholm appear as a victory for the type of ecumenism which was so broad that it had neither a clear centre nor recognizable frontiers.

It must be added that some Stockholm leaders confused the picture by organizing immediately after the Stockholm Conference a movement called the 'Universal Religious Peace Conference' which stated that it did not want to mix the religions, but did in fact move toward syncretism by publishing a book of devotions taken from the scriptures of all religions.

It is probable that the aggressive Encyclical '*Mortalium Animos*' of 1928, in which the Vatican described the ecumenical movement as a body of complete relativists who considered that 'all religions are more or less good and praiseworthy', was at least partly based on impressions from such sources. That was of course a caricature and showed that the Vatican had not really studied the conference documents. Those documents make it clear that Söderblom and the vast majority of the delegates took their stand on a Christocentric foundation. The Message of the Conference had made this clear when it said: 'The nearer we draw to the Crucified, the nearer we come to one another. . . . In the Crucified and Risen Lord alone lies the world's hope.' Stockholm gave in fact a clearer Christian witness than its unsatisfactory underlying theory seemed to imply.

In the twelve years between the Life and Work Conferences of Stockholm and of Oxford a great change took place in the theological climate. The emergence of a new biblical theology, the influence of Karl Barth, the challenge of totalitarianism and the new emphasis on the Church as an inherent part of the

Christian message, made it inevitable that the 1937 conference should think of unity in new terms.

Once again a layman became the central figure in the ecumenical movement. For it was Dr J. H. Oldham who in the thirties laid the foundations, not only of the Oxford Conference of 1937, but also of the World Council of Churches. His great passion was to make the Christian faith relevant to the modern world. He spent a great deal of his time and energy on discovering what laymen in different spheres of life were thinking. One wonders whether at that time anyone else had such a comprehensive knowledge of what was going on in the minds of scientists and sociologists, philosophers and authors. But as he reflected on the answer to be given to their questions, he came more and more to the conclusion laid down in these words: 'Either the Christian affirmation holds good, that God has disclosed his nature, his Will, his purpose in Christ, so that those who respond to the revelation are united in a new, divinely-created and divinely-sustained order of life, or man is left to his own vague, uncertain and conflicting intuitions and surmises of the divine.'[5] And he saw that between this Christocentric universality and the new political universal ideologies there was an irreconcilable opposition. It was due to this insight, shared by many others, that the Oxford Conference gave a good witness over against the idolatries of the time and helped mightily to lay the spiritual foundations for the future of the ecumenical movement.

Thus 'Life and Work' and 'Faith and Order' had by 1937 both moved toward a deeper and wider conception of Christian universalism. It was more generally understood that the ecumenical movement would have to be definitely Christocentric, that it would have to be a movement of rediscovery and renewal of the Church, but not of the Church as an aim in itself, rather of the Church as the chosen instrument for the world-embracing saving work of Christ.

Thus it was natural for these movements to decide together the formation of the World Council of Churches. In 1938 at Utrecht the constitution for the new World Council was drawn up and it was decided to take the basis which had so far been that of Faith and Order alone, as the basis for the World Council itself. William Temple explained that decision as follows: 'It (the

Basis) is an affirmation of the Incarnation and the Atonement. The Council desires to be a fellowship of those churches which accept these truths.'[6]

Was this Christian universalism only theory? That was the great question to be answered when the Second World War broke out. The Oxford message had said: 'If war breaks out, then pre-eminently the Church must be the Church, still united as the Body of Christ, though the nations wherein it is planted fight each other.' To a very real extent this promise was fulfilled and the war years, instead of destroying or weakening the ecumenical movement, became the time when the reality of the Christian fellowship transcending all divisions became more clear than ever before. It was a fellowship which found its nurture in the common confession of loyalty to the one Lord over against the lords of the new and idolatrous ideologies.

At the time of the official inauguration of the World Council of Churches this Christocentric view of the Council's character was reaffirmed. The first Assembly in 1948 described 'our given unity' in the words: 'God has given to his people in Jesus Christ a unity which is his creation and not our achievement'[7] And when the Council sought to define its own character in 1950 (Toronto) it added: 'The Basis of the World Council is the acknowledgment of the central fact that "other foundation can no man lay than that is laid, even Jesus Christ". It is the expression of the conviction that the Lord of the Church is God-among-us who continues to gather his children and to build his Church himself.'[8]

In the further development of the Council it has become increasingly clear that this concentration on the central affirmation of the faith was the only right orientation for the ecumenical movement. That is why the Evanston Assembly had as its theme 'Jesus Christ—the Hope of the World', and the New Delhi Assembly the theme 'Jesus Christ, the Light of the World'. And that is why the Lund Conference on Faith and Order found that the central subject for ecumenical discussion had to be: 'Christ and the Church.'

But even this was not yet the complete witness that the churches were called to make. As long as there were two councils, one concerned with the co-operation and unity of the churches, another with missions, the double misunderstanding was possible that unity could mean a unity sought for the sake of the Church alone and that missions were a specialized activity outside the normal life of the Church. The ecumenical movement had to show that the 'one' and 'the many' belonged together. And this could only be done as the World Council of Churches and the International Missionary Council (which had already entered into close association with each other) became fully integrated. It was therefore providential that in recent years in both bodies there had developed a strong conviction that they belonged together. Unity was to be understood as unity for the sake of the universal mission of the Church. Universality was to be understood as the *raison d'être* of unity. And both found their centre in the one divine Lord. So at New Delhi in 1961 the World Council of Churches and the International Missionary Council became one body.

At the New Delhi Assembly two other events took place which have a bearing on the World Council's conception of universalism. The first was that the Basis of the Council was expanded. In the new formula the confession of the Lord Jesus Christ as God and Saviour is clarified by the words 'according to the Scriptures'. It is in the Jesus Christ who came into history and to whom the Scriptures bear witness that the churches find their common foundation. It was also stated that the churches seek to fulfil their common calling to the glory of the one God, Father, Son and Holy Spirit. The Council is Christocentric, but precisely because it is Christocentric it must be Trinitarian.

The other event was the adoption of a statement which defines what the unity is which the churches in the Council seek and which makes clear that that unity is not some vague, intangible unity, but a concrete, visible unity manifested in each place.

Thus by the time of the New Delhi Assembly the Council had been led step by step to work out the full implications of a specifically Christian universalism: the rootage in the common confession of the one Saviour, the concern for the unity and obedience of his people, the calling to bring the word of salvation and the ministry of reconciliation to all men everywhere.

The answer to syncretism is not introversion, a turning away from the world of religions and cultures fearing that they might contaminate the purity of the Christian message. The answer to syncretism is to enter into that world with the Gospel of the one Saviour who has come for all men everywhere and to do this with the faith that that Gospel, if faithfully obeyed, will itself maintain its purity.

What then are the implications of such an answer to syncretism?

(A) IMPLICATIONS FOR THE NATURE OF A TRUE UNIVERSALISM

The Christian Church must make it unmistakably clear that it believes in a universalism which has its one and only centre in the work of Jesus Christ. At this point there must be no compromise of any kind. We cannot participate in the search for a common denominator of all the religions, because the one foundation has been laid and the edifice of humanity comes tumbling down when that foundation is undermined. But that does not mean that the universalism of the Christian Church is a universalism concerned only with the Christian part of humanity. Too often the churches have given that wrong impression. Too often they have defended Christian interests alone. But the Church does not exist for the sake of the Church. It exists for the sake of humanity. Karl Barth[9] has put this truth in a provocative form. He says that we must dare to affirm that while the world would be lost without Jesus Christ, the world would not be lost without the Church. For who would prevent him from going his own direct way to men? But the Church would be lost without humanity. For if the Church should try to be the Church without caring for humanity, it would depart from Jesus Christ who is the Saviour of all men.

It is a strange fact that the Church and the theologians have left it to the humanistic philosophers, to the freemasons, to theosophists or Bahaists to raise the issue of the unity of mankind. Many widely used treatises of Christian ethics deal fully with the problems of the Christian attitude to the family or to the state but, if they deal at all with humanity, it is in order to warn against a romantic humanitarianism. Not so the New Testament. In it the perspective of humanity is always present. The whole New Testament proclamation is characterized by an 'exuberant joy in the universality of Christ'.[10] This finds expression in the very frequent use of the words 'all' and (meaning basically the same) 'many'. Christ has died for all, for the reconciliation of the world. The Lord identifies himself with all his suffering brethren (Matt. 25). The good news is to be carried to all men. On the last day all the nations will be gathered before his glorious throne.

The more seriously the Christian Church takes its centre, the more universal it becomes. The point has been stated clearly by a great servant of humanity, Dag Hammarskjöld, when Secretary General of the United Nations. Speaking to the Evanston Assembly of the World Council of Churches he quoted the following words from the Report on the Main Theme of the Assembly: 'The Cross is that place at the centre of the world's history . . . where all men and all nations without exception stand revealed as enemies of God . . . and yet where all men stand revealed as beloved of God, precious in God's sight.' Mr Hammarskjöld continued: 'So understood, the Cross, although it is the unique fact on which the Christian churches base their hope, should not separate those of the Christian faith from others, but should instead be that element in their lives which enables them to stretch out their hands to peoples of other creeds in the feeling of universal brotherhood which we hope one day to see reflected in a world of nations truly united.'[11]

The alternative between a Christianity so totally preoccupied by the original central revelation that it forgets the concerns and needs of humanity and a Christianity so obsessed with the interests of humanity that it becomes uprooted, is a false alternative. In the Bible we are forced by the dynamism inherent in the centre to go out to the circumference, but our contact with the circumference throws us back on the centre. It is therefore misleading to say, as Floyd H. Ross says, that the great issue of the hour is not Christian ecumenism, but human ecumenism.[12] For ecumenism is not really Christian if it is not concerned with humanity and a human ecumenism which is not rooted in the fact of Christ is not a true ecumenism, but a vague humanitarianism without a centre and without a foundation.

(B) IMPLICATIONS FOR OUR ATTITUDE TO THE RELIGIONS

The attitude of the Christian Church to the religions can therefore only be the attitude of the witness who points to the one Lord Jesus Christ as Lord of all men. Where the Church ceases to give this witness, it ceases to have a *raison d'être*, for it came into being to proclaim this good news and not to add one more form of spiritual experience to the many which existed already.

The Christian Church cannot therefore participate in the search for a synthesis or confluence of the existing religions. Such a combination would not be an enrichment for humanity, for it could only be achieved by treating the religions as human ideologies of which man himself is the centre. And it would mean that the Christian Church had given up its identity and integrity.

The Church does not apologize for the fact that it wants all men to know Jesus Christ and to follow him. Its very calling is to proclaim the Gospel to the ends of the earth. It cannot make any restrictions in this respect. Whether people have a high, a low or a primitive religion, whether they have sublime ideals or a defective morality makes no fundamental difference in this respect. All must hear the Gospel: Greeks with their rich philosophical tradition; yes and even the Jews with whom the Christians have so much in common and to whom they owe so much.

It is difficult to understand that so many philosophers of religion and historians interpret this missionary attitude of the Church in terms of a complex of superiority. No one can deny that Western Christianity has very often given the impression that it looked down on other religions and considered itself as the proud possessor of the truth. And it is therefore understandable that those who know little of the foundations of Christianity consider Christians as arrogant and narrow-minded. But one would expect that serious students of religion and history would discover that the claim which the Church makes for its Lord has its origin, not in any religious or cultural egocentricity, but in the message of the New Testament itself. For the whole New Testament speaks of the Saviour whom we have not chosen, but who has chosen us. It is possible to reject him, but it is not seriously possible to think of him as one of the many prophets or founders of religion. A Christianity which should think of itself as one of many diverse contributions to the religious life of mankind is a Christianity that has lost its foundation in the New Testament.

Does that mean that the Christian Church must always take the attitude of monologue and that there is no place for any form of dialogue between Christians and non-Christians? Our answer would have to be affirmative, if dialogue left no room for witness. But that is not the case. Martin Buber, who has given us what is probably the most profound analysis of the nature of dialogue, has made it very clear that the presupposition of genuine dialogue is not that the partners agree beforehand to relativize their own convictions, but that they accept each other as persons.[13] In order to enter into a deep relationship with a person the essential requirement is not that he agrees with me, that I agree with him or that we both are willing to negotiate a compromise, but rather that, I turn to him with the willingness to listen to him, to understand him, to seek mutual enrichment. I do not impose my personality on him but put myself at his disposal with all that I am. As a Christian I cannot do this without reporting to him what I have come to know about Jesus Christ. I shall make clear that I consider my faith not as an achievement, but as a gift of grace, a gift which excludes all pride, but which obliges me to speak gratefully of this Lord to all who will hear it. I shall be glad also to listen to my partner and may learn much from his account of his spiritual journey. The dialogue will be all the richer, if both of us give ourselves as we are. For the Christian that giving must include witness. It is possible for convinced Christians to enter into true dialogue with convinced Hindus or Muslims or Jews, yes and even syncretists, without giving up their basic conviction. It should be done in the attitude which Hocking has so well defined as 'reverence for reverence'.[14] The fact that Christians believe that they know the source of divine truth does not mean that they have nothing to learn from men of other faiths. Those of us who have had the privilege of participating in such conversations have often found ourselves humbled and challenged by the evidence we have seen of true devotion, of unflinching loyalty to the truth as they see it among adherents of other religions. And on both sides it has often been found more worth while to have conversations with men of definite convictions rather than with men of uncertain and vague opinions.

But does it not remain true that the acceptance of the uniqueness of the Christian Gospel leads to intolerance? That depends on the meaning we attach to that word. If it is intolerance to believe that there is only one Saviour who has come for all men, then Christians must accept the accusation of intolerance. But if it means that the Christian Church does not recognize the right of the various religions to enjoy the same freedom which the Church asks for itself, then the answer must be quite different. It is of course true that during long periods of history (and unfortunately still to-day in some countries) many churches have claimed freedom for themselves without being willing to grant it to others. To-day the situation has changed. Many churches have learned their hard lessons and have come to understand that the use of other than purely spiritual means in the encounter of religions is unworthy of the Gospel. The third Assembly of the World Council of Churches in 1961 has put this in clear language: 'Christians see religious liberty as a consequence of God's creative work, of his redemption of man in Christ and his calling of men into his service. God's redemptive dealing with men is not coercive. Accordingly human attempts by legal enactment or by pressure of social custom to coerce or to eliminate faith are violations of the fundamental ways of God with men. The freedom which God has given in Christ implies a free response to God's love, and the responsibility to serve fellowmen at the point of deepest need. Holding a distinctive Christian basis for religious liberty, we regard this right as fundamental for men everywhere.'[15] This means of course that the basic right of each religion to carry on missionary activity is recognized, and that the answer of the Christian churches to such activity on the part of the religions must not be the recourse to any form of legal, political or social pressure, but only the spiritual answer of their witness. The coming great encounter of the religions must be a purely spiritual encounter.

(C) IMPLICATIONS FOR COLLABORATION IN COMMON TASKS

The structure of modern national and international society is such that many problems of a cultural, social, political and international character can only be solved through large-scale collaboration of all existing organizations, including the churches. So the churches are constantly confronted with the question whether they are ready to co-operate with other bodies, and this raises especially the issue of interreligious co-operation. Such cooperation is possible and desirable on two conditions.

The first is that it be made clear that it is undertaken to achieve specific common purposes and not to render common witness to common religious convictions. There is everything to be said for having bodies representing different faiths take a common stand on great public issues and work together in the fields of social work or international relations. Far more could be done in this field than is yet being done. But there is nothing to be said for giving the mistaken impression that such collaboration implies that the differences between these bodies are in fact of secondary importance. Interreligious co-operation does not necessarily imply the acceptance of syncretism. It will lead to the creation of a syncretistic atmosphere, if the partners concerned by their statements or by their silence create the misunderstanding that the practical tasks on which they agree are the really important matters and that the differences between the various religions have only to do with 'the details of orthodoxy'. But it is also possible to engage together on common tasks with a clear understanding that the co-operating bodies differ in their basic convictions and that their working together does not in any way mean that they relativize their deepest faith.

In most cases this will mean that interreligious co-operation should be concerned with clearly defined and limited tasks. The problem becomes more difficult if the common task to be undertaken has to do with long-range issues of a cultural character including the realm of education and of national and international ethos or ideology. For it is impossible to work out policies in these fields without opting for a certain conception of man, and the question: 'What think ye of man?' is finally based on the question: 'What think ye of God?' It can easily happen that Christians who enter into co-operation with men of other faiths in such areas find that, in spite of their intention to remain completely loyal to their convictions, they are caught in what is in fact an attempt to proclaim a faith above all faiths which embraces and at the same time smothers all historical religions.

But here again it is not impossible to avoid the syncretistic temptation. An important example is the 'Universal Declaration of Human Rights' adopted by the General Assembly of the United Nations in 1948. That declaration was worked out by a commission of which the membership was formed by men of very different religious background. It bears the marks of being a composite document and uses at certain points ambiguous language. A document written from the point of view of one single religion would of course have greater unity and precision. But it has the great advantage of saying no more than what men of so many different faiths can say together without betraying their real convictions and without pretending that they are ultimately agreed in their basic standpoints concerning the destiny of man. Thus it is not a syncretistic document, but a modest attempt to state what the majority of nations can say together about human rights. In this way it is a useful contribution to the creation of an international ethos and deserves, in spite of its obvious weaknesses, to be taken more seriously than it has yet been taken.

The second condition is that such co-operation must not draw an artificial line of demarcation between those who call themselves religious and those who do not. The distinction is artificial because there does not exist a common definition of religion. The temptation is therefore to include all those who call themselves religious and to exclude those who do not. But this leads to a most arbitrary grouping. Christians or Christian churches have no good reason to associate themselves with every group which calls itself religious over against those who do not. There is no point in creating a front in which the churches would find themselves allied with representatives of religion from the most sublime to the most superstitious and idolatrous against idealists, agnostics and humanists who prefer not to call themselves religious. There are forms of modern secularism which in the light of biblical norms mean spiritual advance rather than retrogression. A common front of all religions against the non-religious could only make our present confusion worse. It would on the one hand confirm the wrong impression that what we stand for is a religion within and behind the existing religions. It would on the other hand widen the gulf between the churches and the secular world. If we co-operate with men of other religions it must not be to defend all that is said and done in the name of religion, but rather to defend together with all who are willing to participate the interests of man against his old enemies: hunger, disease, oppression, injustice.

As the dialogue of the religions, the critical importance of which Dr Hendrik Kraemer has described in his *World Cultures and World Religions*, gets under way, the churches will be called upon more and more frequently to co-operate with men of other faiths and of no faith in matters of public life. We will have to accept that new duty. We must become imaginative in discovering how in the pluriform national societies, and in the even more pluriform international society, we may be able to take common action with others in relation to such burning issues as racial justice, family life, rapid social change and the creation of international order. But we will have to make it perfectly plain that our willingness to co-operate does not in any way imply a willingness to compromise on the basic issues of the faith.

(D) IMPLICATIONS FOR THE COMMUNICATION OF THE GOSPEL

Communication always implies the use of concepts, thought-forms and terminology which are comprehensible to those with whom one wants to communicate. There is therefore no effective Christian witness which is not in a certain sense a translation into categories which differ from the categories used in the original kerygma. All missionary witness implies accommodation or transformation.

It has been suggested that we must therefore admit that all theologies are inevitably syncretistic. Thus Professor Russell Chandran says that every Christian theology contains some syncretism and that the West should acknowledge that its theology is also syncretistic, in so far as it arose always and everywhere in a specific framework.[16] It seems to me that in this and similar statements the word syncretism is not used in the right way. A theology is not syncretistic if and when it uses the thought-forms of the environment in which it operates. A theology becomes syncretistic if and when in using such thought-forms it introduces into its structure ideas which change the meaning of biblical truth in its substance.

This distinction is essential. It is one thing to accommodate the Gospel to a specific culture or to translate it in a specific terminology and to do this with real loyalty to the original message. It is another thing to mix the biblical revelation with categories of thought which transform that revelation into something else than it is. And we must not use the same word for these two processes. We can agree with Professor Chandran that every theology contains the danger of syncretism. We must also agree that Western theology has very often, in seeking to accommodate the Christian message to the Western cultural environment, distorted its substance and thus become syncretistic. But that does not mean that we must resign ourselves to the fact that syncretism is inevitable.

The thesis of this book is that syncretism is not inevitable. This has been proved by St Paul and St John. They had to translate the original Gospel into the categories of thought and the terminology of a new environment. They have done so without becoming syncretistic, without changing the nature of the basic witness. They have done so with an astonishing freedom and courage and taken very great risks. But they have remained faithful.

We must try to regain something of the same freedom and courage. We must believe that it is not only possible but absolutely necessary to interpret the Gospel in terms which will bring it closer to the cultures in which up till now it has been generally proclaimed in a Western and therefore foreign form. It is clear that this cannot be done overnight. It is also clear that real risks are involved. But our desire to arrive at a truly adequate communication of the Gospel must be stronger than our fear of syncretism. Where there is a deep loyalty to the revelation, that revelation itself will overcome the hindrances and keep us from falling into the temptation of cheap and false forms of adaptation. The time has come when the 'multi-coloured' wisdom of God must express itself in new Asian and African expressions of Christian thought and life.

(E) IMPLICATIONS FOR THE LIFE OF THE CHURCH

Finally we must once more emphasize that all our affirmations about Christocentric universalism will be meaningless and our rejection of syncretism will be of little avail if we do not practise that universalism in the life of the Church. So far we have practised it very little. Our lack of unity and the slowness of our progress toward unity are precisely due to the fact that we express our faith in the *'Una Sancta'*, but act as if the Church were our holy denominational Church. And our situation is all the more serious since we have now made it so clear to the world and to ourselves that it is in the nature of the Church to be one and universal.

Kraemer's analysis of the coming dialogue of the world religions ends with this sentence: 'The Christian Church . . . should first and foremost set her own house in order, because the greatest service she can render to the world, the Western and the Eastern world, is by being resolutely the Church of Jesus Christ.'[17] Newbigin's discussion of the faith for this one world of ours concludes that 'nothing is more central to the missionary task of the Church today than this—that there should be a recovery of the visible unity of Christians, that men of every race and culture may be able to recognize in the Church the authentic lineaments of the household of God, the home in which every man is invited to be reborn as a child of the one Father and a brother of the Son of Man'.[18] We have been led to the same conclusion.

The ecumenical movement is the expression of a new understanding of the Church as the people of God, Christ-centred and therefore universal. We have also the beginnings of a relationship between the churches which expresses this insight. But the main task of transforming our churches into that Church Universal which they are meant to be lies still before us.

That we really believe that there is a unity in Christ such as nowhere else can only be truly demonstrated by acts of unity, by overcoming our divisions. That we really believe that Christ is the Saviour of all can only become a convincing faith, if the Church breaks out of its too introverted life, shows clearly its concern for the spiritual and physical needs of all men and manifests that it is not a national, an ideological, a racial or a continental church, but the Church Universal which is at home in every nation and yet does not belong to any nation.

The only effective answer to syncretism is the demonstration in word and deed that the quest of humanity for oneness finds its fulfilment in the mystery of the Son of God who came to give his life for all men.

Notes

1. Reprinted in *Ecumenical Review*, April 1955. p. 260.

2. *Faith and Order Pamphlet* No. 30, p. 17.

3. The original of this letter is in the 'Oekumenische Archiv' in Soest (Germany).

4. Letter to Gardiner from the Executive Committee in August 1922.

5. *The Student World*, 1935, p. 376.

6. Explanatory Memorandum of 1938.

7. Official Report. First Assembly of the WCC, p. 51.

8. Workbook for the New Delhi Assembly, p. 65.

9. *Church Dogmatics* IV, 3.2, ET, 1962, p. 826.

10. B. Reicke in *TWNT* V, p. 895 (*pas, hapas*).

11. *Ecumenical Review,* July 1956, p. 402.

12. In *The Theology* of *the Christian Mission*, edited by G. H. Anderson, 1961, p. 214.

13. *Schriften über das dialogische Prinzip*, Heidelberg. 1954, p. 279.

14. *The Coming World Civilisation*, p. 154.

15. *The New Delhi Report*, pp. 159–60.

16. In *Evangelisches Missions-Magazin* 1961, No. 3, p. 98.

17. *World Cultures and World Religions*, 1960.

18. *A Faith for this one World?*, pp. 125f.

"The Significance of the World Council of Churches"

This essay appeared in one of the four volumes written in preparation for the First Assembly of the World Council of Churches, held in Amsterdam in 1948. Visser 't Hooft presented many of the ideas found in this essay as part of his General Secretary's Report to the assembly. In both the essay and the report, he tried to define the nature and mission of this new ecumenical entity, because, as he notes in his Memoirs, *most delegates and observers did not understand "what implications membership in the Council would have for the conception which their church had of its own nature and its relationships with other churches." His reflections are still a useful and stimulating guide for anyone concerned with conciliar ecumenism.*

"The Significance of the World Council of Churches," in The Universal Church in God's Design, *vol. 1 in* Man's Disorder and God's Design, *ed. W. A. Visser 't Hooft, Amsterdam Assembly (New York: Harper, 1948), 182–95. Footnotes have been converted to endnotes and renumbered.*

III. WHAT THE WORLD COUNCIL IS NOT

This short summary of the background of the World Council has shown that it is possible to consider the World Council from two different angles. The emphasis in the title can be placed on *Churches* or on *Council*. By exclusive emphasis on the second, one arrives at the conception of an organization which works for unity, but which does not itself speak or act as an embodiment of the Church Universal. In the first case it is an association which serves the churches without itself representing "the Church".

Now it is quite clear that neither of these views of the Council meets the case. The Council cannot claim to *be* the Una Sancta or a partial embodiment of the Una Sancta, because it lacks the essential *notae ecclesiae*. If one measures the situation within the ecumenical movement by the various definitions of the Church in the confessional standards of the churches, one finds that the World Council does not correspond to any of these definitions. And if one goes back to the Bible and compares the fellowship which the churches have in the World Council with the *koinonia* of the Acts and the Epistles, one finds that essential aspects of that *koinonia* are lacking to-day, namely, the full common witness and full sharing in the sacramental life.

It is true that the ecumenical conferences have been able to give expression to a common mind, but the scope of their witness has been very limited. And the fact remains that the teaching of the churches in the Council is not a common *kerugma* with different aspects or emphases, but in many respects a confusion of tongues. The churches contradict each other on points which they consider, and must consider, as essential parts of their message. In joining with churches of other confessions in the fellowship of the Council they recognize that Christ is at work in these other churches, they accept, therefore, the duty of discussion and co-operation with these churches, but they continue to look upon these other churches as churches whose teaching is incomplete, distorted or even heretical. It is impossible to claim that this provisional and tentative relationship between the churches is itself the Una Sancta.

Moreover, the impossibility of complete fellowship in celebrating the Holy Communion together is a clear sign that the churches in the World Council dare not pretend to be a *koinonia* in the biblical sense of that term. Indeed our inability to meet together at the Lord's Table reminds us more insistently than anything else that the unity which has been granted to us is only a shadow of that full unity which characterizes the Body of Christ.

Again a body representing the Una Sancta would have far greater authority than that which the churches are willing to entrust to the World Council. At the present moment the constitutional limitations of that authority are probably more rigid than those placed on any other representative church body in the world. Now these limitations are inevitable and even desirable under present conditions. To demand greater authority at this stage would be to ask more than the real ecumenical situation warrants. But that fact by itself shows that the World Council is by no means a first preliminary edition of the Una Sancta.

It is, however, not only in the realm of these easily observable conditions of its life, but in the less tangible realm of the spiritual situation that one discovers strong reasons why the Council should not make too exalted claims for itself. The churches are at the moment not able to manifest the Una Sancta in a way which corresponds to the reality of its nature. The unity which would be seen, if the issue of unity were forced now, would be far too much a unity of compromise. There is still in much of our present ecumenism a strong element of relativism and of lack of concern for the truth of God. And so our unity would not be the biblical unity *in truth*. There can be no real representation of the Una Sancta until the churches have turned in a new way to the Word of God, until they have discovered their sickness, until they have found something of that clarity and certainty of preaching and witness which characterized the New Testament Church, until they are truly "becoming the church" and meet each other on the level of that *metanoia*. In the providence of God signs are not wanting that some of these things are beginning to happen. But we are yet far away from the time of harvest. Until that time it will be well for us to be very modest in our claims.

Is the World Council then just an organization? If it cannot be considered as a visible representation of the Una Sancta, must it be considered as a man-made organ which may have a very noble and useful function to perform and which may render great services to the cause of the Church but which is not itself an expression and representation of "the Church"? Should the World Council look upon itself as one of the many Christian organizations which undertake specific tasks on a temporary basis and until such time as the Church can undertake these tasks itself? Is the World Council just a matter of conferences, committees and secretaries, or of information and philanthropy?

It is a fact that the World Council is often presented in such purely organizational terms. Thus, many "practically minded" supporters of the Council speak of it as just an agency of collaboration of concrete tasks. Now the Council is certainly such an agency, but its origins show clearly that it cannot be satisfied with that role. However grateful we may be to the pioneers of Stockholm, we cannot and dare not go back to the "as if" theology which demands that we shall act "as if" we were one in faith. We have discovered that our witness to the common faith is our first and foremost duty to the world and that without that witness our unity in "life and work" is impotent. When churches meet together they cannot leave on one side the question of their common confession of allegiance to their common Lord. It is not by accident that the ecumenical conferences have borne that witness in spite of all canonical obstacles to their doing so. The inner dynamic of the Church forced them to do so.

The same applies to the view that the exclusive purpose of the Council is the fostering of common study. Study is indispensable and common study on an ecumenical level is one of the great needs of the hour, but a Council of Churches cannot possibly consider study as an aim in itself. In the setting of the Church's mission study can have meaning only as a preparation for action, that is, for decisions of faith. When this is forgotten study may even become a danger, for study without decision fosters a theology-for-the-sake-of-theology rather than for the sake of the Church. If the ecumenical movement meant that all possible Christian standpoints were to be set permanently side by side on equal pedestals, it would become a museum and cease to have any relevance for the living Church.

The World Council cannot be content to be a federation of bodies, each of which watches jealously over its own sovereignty. A fellowship of churches which know that there is no sovereignty save that of their common Lord must differ essentially from a pragmatic combination of sovereign states. The gathering together of the churches can have spiritual relevance only if these churches desire in some way to become members of the one Body, and if, even in the early stages of their meeting, they give evidence of that desire. But if they do so, their relationships cannot possibly remain of a purely organizational character.

The World Council cannot be a mere organization simply because it is a Council *of Churches*. For the Church in the churches insists on asserting itself. Wherever two or three churches are gathered together, the Una Sancta is in the midst of them and demands to be manifested.

IV. WHAT THEN IS THE WORLD COUNCIL?

We have seen that the World Council cannot claim to *be* the Una Sancta. We have also seen that it cannot be satisfied to be a more or less permanent conference about church unity or an organization for practical purposes. On the one hand it dare not minimize the very real disunity within its membership; on the other hand it may not refuse the gift of unity which the Lord has actually given and gives to the churches, when He enables them to speak and act together. The Council may not anticipate that unity which belongs only to the truly reunited Church,[1] but neither can it refuse to follow the call to speak with one voice and to act as one body whenever that call is addressed to it. The Council cannot create the Church out of the churches, but neither can it stand aside as an observer when the Church in the churches affirms and expresses itself.

This is the dilemma which dominates the whole existence of the Council. Its member churches are as yet unable to *be* together the one Church of God; but they are no longer able to regard their fellow-members as being outside the Church of God. They cannot unite, but neither can they let each other go. They know that there is no unity outside truth, but they realize also that truth demands unity.

Is there a way out of this dilemma? Only a way of faith. Only a way which takes its point of departure not in man-made syntheses or theoretical schemes, but in the simple truth that the unity of the Church is the work of the Lord of the Church. This truth has been clearly expressed at both the Oxford and Edinburgh Conferences. The Oxford Message says: "The source of unity is not the consenting movement of men's will; it is Jesus Christ whose one life flows through the Body and subdues the many wills of His." And the Edinburgh Affirmation says: "Thus unity does not consist in the agreement of our minds or the consent of our wills. It is founded in Jesus Christ Himself."

In his opening sermon at the Edinburgh Conference, Archbishop Temple said:

> It is not we who can heal the wounds of His Body. We confer and deliberate, and that is right. But it is not by contrivance and adjustment that we can unite the Church of God. It is only by coming closer to Him that we come nearer to one another. . . . Only when God has drawn us closer to Himself shall we be truly united together, and then our task will be, *not to consummate our endeavor, but to register His achievement.*

Karl Barth puts the same truth in a different way. He states that: "all efforts towards unity depend altogether on an act of recognition by the Church", namely, the recognition of the fact that this particular unity is willed by God. When this is really the case "we must obediently do our share so that we do not contradict on earth what is God's will in heaven".[2]

And is not this also the true significance of the basis of the World Council? It means that the living Christ—God and Saviour—alone can create the unity which we seek. Thus it gives the Council the indispensable foundation for its existence.

Unity is *received*, but that does not mean that man's role is purely passive. We are to look out for it and to be constantly ready to receive it. The unity which is given to us must become visible and effective in our midst.

Archbishop Temple wrote in 1939:

> The full unity of the Church is something for which we must still work and pray. But there exists a unity in allegiance to Our Lord, for the manifestation of which we are responsible. We may not pretend that the existing unity among Christians is greater than in fact it is, but we should act upon it so far as it is already a reality. (Letter of Invitation to membership in the World Council.)

The way out of our dilemma is, therefore, to consider the World Council as a means to manifest the unity of the Church, whenever and wherever the Lord of the Church Himself gives that unity: a *means* and a *method* and no more. The World Council is not the Una Sancta, but a means and a method which have no other *raison d'être* than to be used for the building of the Una Sancta. Therefore, it is far more than a movement about unity, and far more than an organizational innovation.

The World Council must, therefore, not pretend that it represents the Una Sancta, but it may and it must claim that it is the body in which and through which, when it pleases God, a foretaste of the Una Sancta is given. As an institution, it has no authority, not even as much authority as its member churches, which can take their stand on the basis of their respective confessions of faith and whose authority within their own sphere of action is unchallenged. From a horizontal viewpoint it remains just a council of dissimilar churches which disagree about important matters of faith, order and ethics. But from a vertical viewpoint, it is the place where the *koinonia* in the one faith may become (and has become) at least partly visible. When that happens, then indeed it has true authority. Then the confusion of tongues ceases for a moment, and the disunity of the many churches is overshadowed by the unity of the one Church of Christ.

Who shall say when this is the case? Certainly not the World Council itself. For as we have seen, it can only try to express the mind of the Una Sancta, but not claim to *be* the Una Sancta. Rather it is open to any member church, and indeed to every church member to decide whether, in each given case, it recognizes in the World Council a manifestation of the one Body which fulfils the will of the Head. The World Council does not claim any authority for itself. But it must realize that it may, *Deo volente*, suddenly take on the formidable authority of an organ of the Holy Spirit.

Its whole life must be a constant counting of that possibility and a constant watching for that intervention from above. If it lives in that attitude, it will not become a mere ecclesiastical bureaucracy and will have true relevance for the life of the churches.

V. THE WITNESS OF THE WORLD COUNCIL

That witness consists first of all in the *fact* of praying, living and working together. The very existence of the World Council proclaims the good news that Jesus Christ unites men of all churches, nations and races. But that witness is incomplete if it does not lead on to a clear common proclamation of the Lordship of Christ in all realms of life. In this sense the original "Stockholm" tradition must remain alive in the World Council. Our basis in which we affirm the Lordship of Christ (for the words "God and Saviour" mean that we acknowledge Him as divine Lord in the radical biblical sense) is not merely a doctrinal formula, but the answer of the Church militant to the decree of mobilization issued by its rightful Head.

The demand that the churches as gathered together in the World Council should speak out and take a clear stand in relation to the idolatries, the crimes and temptations of our chaotic age, comes with all the more insistence now that a number of churches have, after a very long period of silence, realized again that the Church has a prophetic ministry to perform. This insight must permeate the whole ecumenical Church. Such common testimony has an especial significance for minority churches or for churches suffering isolation. But the world also needs to hear a clear united voice which confronts it with the reality of God's judgment and God's grace.

But though it is clear that the churches *ought* to speak together, it is not so clear that they *can* speak together. The particular churches speak on the basis of their confessions and (or) their confessional theologies. Their witness is an application of all that their members have heard and learned in their common effort to live by the revelation of God in Jesus Christ. Within these churches there may be considerable divergences and tensions, but there are nevertheless common "traditions" which enable each of them to speak in one voice.

Now the World Council has no such background. It has

nothing but its basis, which is interpreted in different ways. It has no common spiritual language. The meaning of witness and confession is understood differently by different churches. And while they are all at one in recognizing the authority of Holy Scripture, there are deep divergences between them as to the actual significance of that authority for the life of the Church. Dare the World Council speak as long as it has to stand on so uncertain a foundation?

Before we answer that question we have to look at another aspect of the problem, namely, who is to speak *as* or *for* the World Council? As we have seen, the World Council is not a union, not even a federal union of churches. It is only a *council* for specific purposes and with strictly limited authority. It consists of churches which are opposed to any delegation of power to officers of an ecumenical body, some because they are against all hierarchical forms of church order, others because they believe that such an order can only exist in fullness in a truly reunited church. It is therefore out of the question that one person could speak officially on its behalf.[3]

This is not merely a matter of canon law. It is an inevitable consequence of the present situation. For every one of the officers of the Council is a churchman who stands somewhere in one of the particular churches. Not one of them is a supra-confessional person. Every one of them represents a voice *in* the Council rather than *the* voice *of* the Council. And even if one of them should try to speak for it, no one who knows the realities of the ecumenical situation could possibly regard his voice as being the voice of the fellowship as a whole.

But if the World Council is neither spiritually nor legally entitled to speak out, should it then remain silent? At this point, we have to remember the paradoxical character of the World Council. If the World Council looks inwards as its own situation, it cannot possibly speak. For it will then become obsessed with the difficulties of its own internal life and postpone the day of witness to the Greek kalends. But if it remembers that it is not merely an organization which has to take account of the empirical realities of its own life, but that it is an instrument offered to the Lord of the Church to be used as He wills, then it will hope for and pray for the miracle of its receiving authority from God to speak.

A true miracle! For the World Council can only speak if the very heterogeneous group of its leaders is suddenly transformed into a homogeneous fellowship of witness. The many individual voices which speak from somewhere in the divided Church may become the common voice which speaks from the centre of the one and undivided Church. A miracle—and, therefore, not something to be forced, but something to be received.

What is the weight of such common word? It cannot commit the churches in the World Council. It carries no official character. It is a defenseless utterance which may be challenged from almost any quarter. It is simply the word of men who say: "We have no canonical authority. We have no right to speak for all the Christian churches, not even for all non-Roman Christian churches. But we are leaders of a council in and through which the churches seek to re-establish the *koinonia* which they had lost. We cannot, therefore, refrain from praying and working for the manifestation of that *koinonia*. And we cannot remain silent when God answers our prayer and gives us a word of common witness. It is for each church to decide whether it recognizes in our witness the genuine voice of the Una Sancta."

The World Council must then always be ready to be used as the voice of the Una Sancta. And it must prepare itself for this task by eliminating all conditions which keep it from witnessing and which it is in its power to eliminate. Thus it must get rid of all fear of the political and organizational consequences of a clear witness, and of many other human, all too human, considerations. It must be ready to speak out whenever there arises an issue of decisive moment for the cause of the Church in the world. Very often it will fail. In the future, as on several occasions in the past, it will happen again and again that, though there is a willingness to speak, no agreement can be reached as to the content of the message to be proclaimed. And, if it does speak, it will have to be prepared to meet with severe criticism and to be repudiated as a voice which does not represent the conviction of the churches. All that is inevitable and belongs to the risks of the ecumenical adventure.

Everything depends finally on the fundamental readiness to be used. If the World Council refuses to act as the organ of the Una Sancta, it has no promise. But if it is founded on an absolute willingness to be used, even its failures will finally prove to be blessings.

VI. IMPLICATIONS OF WORLD COUNCIL MEMBERSHIP

What does it mean for a church to become a member of this World Council? What we have said about the Council means that the acceptance of membership is more than a matter of practical strategy. Participation in the Council must be based on a willingness to collaborate with other churches and on a readiness to share in serious common study concerning the witness of the Church to the world and concerning church unity. But there is more. Entrance into the World Council pre-supposes willingness to manifest together with other churches that measure of unity which is now granted to the churches in the Council and to strive with them for the manifestation of the full unity of the Church of Christ.

This does not mean that a church entering into the Council automatically recognizes the claims of all other churches in the Council to be in the full and true sense of that word parts of the Church Universal. Such recognition is most desirable, but it is the goal, not the beginning of the ecumenical process. We need the World Council as an emergency solution just because the churches are not at one in their convictions concerning the true faith and the true order of the Church. It must be, and indeed is, possible to enter the World Council without compromising on any fundamental confessional points of faith and order. Participation in the World Council does not imply a relativistic attitude concerning the essential and indispensable characteristics of the true Church of Christ.

But membership in the World Council implies that each church should recognize as least in its sister churches in the Council the *vestigia ecclesiae*, that is, the fact that in some sense the Church of Christ exists also in them and that the Lord of the

Church is at work in their life. It has been well said (by Professor Herrmann Sasse) that the creation of the World Council of Churches means that for the first time the churches accept the consequences flowing from the classical doctrine, taught by practically all churches in the Council, according to which the Church of Christ includes all those who confess His name, even if their confession is incomplete or mixed with error.

But if it is recognized that Christ is at work in other churches, it is the duty of each church in the fellowship to listen to the witness of these churches, to open itself to the truth of God which it may learn from them, and to be ready to let its own faith and life be enriched or corrected by this fraternal contact.

Churches cannot treat each other as if they were sovereign states which defend the integrity of their rights and territory. They must on the contrary rejoice when the ecumenical situation leads to constructive battles and beneficial invasions. The members of the ecumenical family cannot adopt the principle of non-intervention. They let themselves be questioned by their fellow members. They exhort each other to greater faithfulness and to renewal of life. They call each other back to the Apostolic witness. They are their brothers' keepers, and whatever concerns the churches confessing the same Lord, is their concern. If the World Council should do nothing else but set in motion this process of constructive and mutual challenge, so that the churches cease to be on the defensive towards each other or to behave like rival states, and that they let themselves be transformed in the give and take of a common struggle for the truth of God—that alone will justify its existence.

But the purpose of it all is the healing of the Church. All churches need the same physician. As together they turn to Him, together they will be healed.

VII. INSTITUTION OR MOVEMENT?

All that has been said so far can be summarized in the statement that the World Council has no future. If it does no more than reflect the empirical reality of the *churches as they are*, but that it has a promise, if it is and remains a willing instrument in the hands of the Lord, Who is the power of God. It is specially true in the ecumenical realm that to stand still is to go backward. If the ecumenical movement becomes an ecumenical institution, its days are numbered.

But does the official institution of the World Council at the time of the Assembly not mean that the danger has become much greater? Are we not precisely at the point at which a pioneering movement in the life of the churches is transformed into an official and representative ecclesiastical body? Are we not attempting the impossible, if we make the churches with their immobility and ineradicable conservatism the pillars of an ecumenical fellowship which can only live if it remains on the move?

These are real questions. The risk is indeed considerable. There is a real possibility that a church centred ecumenical body will prove to be so static, so inhibited, that it will tend to "freeze" the ecumenical situation and become an obstacle to advance. Church history is full of examples of movements of the Spirit which have ended up as bureaucratic organizations without true spiritual power.

But we have no choice in this matter. The ecumenical movement has discovered with increasing certainty that its aim is not a unity of individuals, but the unity of the Church. And the Church is not to be found in the realm of abstract ideas or of inward sentiments, but in the historic and visible churches. At the present moment ecumenical advance means precisely the determination to carry the witness to the Una Sancta into the daily life of the churches, to give up the mirage of an ecumenical movement above or outside the existing churches and to make the churches themselves the pillars on which the ecumenical structure rests. The transfer of responsibility to the churches themselves is the direct result of the convictions which have been forced upon us in our ecumenical discussions. The principle that the churches alone will determine the policy of the Council is therefore fundamental in its structure and in its work.

But this principle can be applied in different ways. It might be taken to mean that the Council will be wholly in the hands of the clerical leaders. This interpretation is, however, rejected by the Utrecht Constitution which states that the Assembly and the

Central Committee shall consist of both clerical and lay persons, men and women. For the churches in the Council believe that the laity (men and women) have a creative role to play in church life. None of the functions which the Council sets out to fulfil can be performed unless the whole membership of our churches participates, directly or indirectly, in its life. If this insight is taken seriously, it will go a long way to save the Council from excessive clericalism.

But there is more to be said. As the churches accept their ecumenical responsibility, they should remember that in the carrying out of this task they will need the continued assistance of those forces which the "pioneering" and the "provisional" stages have given the real impetus to the ecumenical movement. Now some of these, although they are *of* the churches and *in* the churches, are not "official" and "representative" in the more technical sense of the term. It must not happen that important groups which are devoted to their churches and to the ecumenical cause suddenly find the doors closed to any active participation in ecumenical life simply because they are not in official positions of church leadership. While it is clear that the governing bodies of the Council must consist of men and women directly chosen by their churches, it is not only desirable but quite indispensable for the healthy development of the Council's life that it should make the fullest possible use of the services, the contributions and also the criticism which come to it from "unofficial" quarters. This is particularly true with regard to those Christian thinkers, theologians and men of many other professions, who have given substance to the programme of ecumenical study and through it to the preparation of the world conferences. It is also true with regard to the workers in the field of interdenominational co-operation, of missions and of inter-church aid. It should become increasingly true of the women of the churches. And the ecumenical youth movement must be given its rightful opportunity. Ways and means should, therefore, be discovered by which in the work of the commissions, the departments, the conferences under the auspices of the Council, the present participation of all such forces is not only maintained but strengthened. Thus alone can we escape the danger of becoming institutionalized, and remain a movement sensitive to the dynamic influences of the Spirit.

Is it possible to build a World Council which is truly rooted in the life of the churches, but which corrects and completes its own official character by welcoming spontaneous contributions from groups and individuals who are in another significant sense members and spokesmen of the Church Universal? Is it possible to give the prophetic voice a place in a priestly structure? Whether it is possible or not, the attempt must be made. For we go forward in the name of a King Who is both prophet and priest. Where His Kingship is acknowledged, and there alone, the priestly and the prophetic are seen to be aspects of the same reality, which is His Church.

Notes

1. One critic, who speaks for many-of similar outlook, wishes to reject the word "*re*-union", holding that, historically, there never has been a wholly united Church, and that the use of this word obscures the fact that something *new* is now being wrought by God.

2. *Evangelische Theologie*, April 1935.

3. An Anglican critic writes, ". . . some churches are opposed to delegation of power to officers of an ecumenical body not for either of the two reasons given, but because they are *supporters* of an hierarchical form of church order and believe that it exists in the churches possessing the apostolic episcopate. I think for completeness, it is important that this third reason should be stated."

Visser 't Hooft at his desk, approximately 1953. Photo credit: WCC Photo.

Visser 't Hooft in 1966, the year he retired as general secretary of the WCC. Photo credit: John P. Taylor / WCC.

Visser 't Hooft at the Bossey Ecumenical Institute in 1955. To his left is the evangelist, Billy Graham. Photo credit: WCC Photo.

Visser 't Hooft with Indian Prime Minister Jawaharlal Nehru at the WCC's assembly in New Delhi, 1961. Photo credit: WCC Photo.

Visser 't Hooft, middle, with his father and brothers in 1928, the year he received his doctoral degree. Photo credit: WCC Photo.

Visser 't Hooft, third from the right, at a Life and Work planning committee in 1936. To his left is the theologian Reinhold Niebuhr. To his right is Archbishop William Temple and, beyond him, the lay ecumenical leader J. H. Oldham. Photo credit: WCC Photo.

Visser 't Hooft at the World Conference of Christian Youth, Amsterdam, 1939. Next to Visser 't Hooft, who is seated on the left, is the ecumenical patriarch John R. Mott. Behind Visser 't Hooft is the Sri Lanka church leader D. T. Niles, and behind him, Visser 't Hooft's wife, Jetty Visser 't Hooft-Boddaert. Photo credit: World Council of Churches.

Visser 't Hooft with the theologian Karl Barth. Photo credit: WCC Photo.

Visser 't Hooft at a meeting of the WCC Central Committee in Nigeria, 1965. Photo credit: John Taylor / WCC.

3.

A Theology of Wholeness

One of the most famous definitions of the word *ecumenical* came from the WCC's Central Committee in 1951: "everything that relates to the whole task of the whole church to bring the gospel to the whole world." Visser 't Hooft picked up on these emphases nearly thirty years later, in an address to the Central Committee on the occasion of his eightieth birthday (my first meeting as a member of the WCC staff). As an octogenarian, he was worried not about the popularity of the movement but about its faithfulness to its calling of biblically grounded wholeness. "It seems to me," he said, "that these three emphases—the whole church, the whole world, the whole gospel—are not only an interesting part of our heritage, but abiding characteristics of the ecumenical movement."[1]

They are also central, and inseparable, foci of his theology. The gospel is the basis of the church, even as the church is an essential dimension of the gospel—all for the sake of the world. And the ecumenical movement is an expression, and an instrument, of this conviction. Or as Visser 't Hooft put it: "[Ecumenism's] significance lies ultimately in the common recapturing of the simple biblical truth that the church as the people of God and body of Christ must exemplify in this world how God gathers men together from the ends of the earth in order to live as a new humanity."[2]

In chapter 1, we saw how Visser 't Hooft embodied this vision, especially through his leadership in the World Council of Churches, and we examined the ideas and events that shaped him as a theologian. In this chapter, we will look more carefully at his own theology, using the concept of wholeness as a framework. The intent here is to describe. Critique of his theological positions will come in chapter 4.

THE WHOLE GOSPEL

One of Visser 't Hooft's successors as WCC general secretary, Emilio Castro, told of how he met "Wim" a few weeks before the older man's death. His main advice, as Castro remembered it: "Keep Jesus Christ at the center of your reflection."[3] Visser 't Hooft had, of course, said the same thing numerous times during the course of his career, frequently quoting the Stockholm conference of 1925: "The nearer we draw to the Crucified, the nearer we come to one another."[4]

It hardly needs to be said that such a statement is not at odds with a fully Trinitarian conception of God. Indeed, the doctrine of the Trinity is the context for a theologically sound understanding of Christ—the One who not only bears the message of God's kingdom but is himself the message by which God, through the power of the Holy Spirit, is revealed. God, as Visser 't Hooft stressed in his debate with advocates of the social gospel, is the transcendent Creator who becomes imminent in gracious and decisive self-disclosure. In Jesus the Son, believers grasp the nature and purpose of God the Father, whose Spirit animates and guides the church.[5]

Our role, writes Castro in his remembrance of Visser 't Hooft, is like that of John the Baptist in the famous Isenheim Altarpiece (a favorite of Barth): to point together toward the incarnate One on the cross as the foundation not only of our lives but of the life of the world. "Behold, the lamb of God who takes away the sins of the world!" The widely studied Faith and Order document *Baptism, Eucharist and Ministry* says that "the eucharist involves the believer in the central event of the world's history."[6] Visser 't Hooft made clear to me during our conversations that he had no doubt this is literally true. The Christ we confess "is the One who is the Savior of all mankind, the Lord of Lords in whom all things hold together."[7]

Visser 't Hooft's concern, however, was not only that people often fail to recognize Christ as the center of human history, but that Christians also fail to confess the whole Christ: prophet, priest, and king.[8] An overemphasis on the prophetic office, with Christ valued primarily as a great teacher and motivator of social change, leads to moralism in the church and a stress on human, rather than divine, initiative. An exclusive focus on the priestly leads to a concentration on the internal life of the church or the believer to the neglect of Christ's victory over sin and death in the world. And a one-sided emphasis on the kingship of Christ leads to utopianism, as if the glory of Easter did not necessarily go through the humiliation and suffering of Good Friday. "The history of theology and of preaching," writes Visser 't Hooft, "is a long series of battles of the full Gospel against the partial and one-sided gospels."[9] The sterile debates of spiritual life versus social action can be overcome by a grasp of the whole ministry of the One we recognize as Lord.

In Visser 't Hooft's estimation, Protestants have been particularly guilty of obscuring the kingly office. Especially in its more pietistic forms, Protestantism has regarded the reign of God as "an invisible reality experienced in the souls of those individuals who have been saved out of this corrupted world."[10] The cosmic dimension of salvation, the world transforming character of the incarnation, is thereby minimized.

Of course, the kingdom of Christ the king is unlike that of Jewish messianic expectations or worldly models. He is a priestly king, revealed (through the eyes of faith) in the cross, and a prophetic king, whose realm gives special attention to the ones society tends to neglect. And—another paradox—this kingdom is both a coming event and a present reality. Christ *has* overcome the world, even as his final victory over the powers and principalities is the object of hope. Not surprisingly, Visser 't Hooft argues that the gospel is truncated by a focus on one at the expense of the other. A purely "realized eschatology" (the kingdom is already present) often leads its defenders to underestimate the continuing reality of evil, to devalue the importance of hope, and, at times, to equate the historical church with the kingdom of God. A purely "futurist eschatology," however, runs the risk of separating the church from the present world, leaving the latter to its unredeemed fate. Both of them, in his judgment, think too much in "quantitative" terms (how much we now have or how much we can expect), rather than in terms of "hiddenness and revelation." Scripture speaks of the movement from that which is veiled to that which is manifest, a movement in which the church has a vital role. The church, to use his language, is an "eschatological fact." It gives evidence of Christ's victory by living as a reconciled people, thereby proclaiming to the world the newness promised by God.[11]

Ecumenism is sometimes disparaged—generally, I think, by those who have little familiarity with it—as an exercise in theological compromise. Nothing could be further from the spirit of Willem Visser 't Hooft! In his history of the ecumenical movement since 1968, Jonas Jonson observes that Barth's "persistent assertion that the church, bound by God's word, could not negotiate its faith . . . was taken over by the ecumenical movement"—especially in the person of Visser 't Hooft.[12] For both Barth and Visser 't Hooft, the future of ecumenism rested on its confession of the gospel—the whole gospel. The early WCC assemblies, in Visser 't Hooft's words, "helped to convince many that the ecumenical movement was not a movement of superficial relativism, avoiding all really important issues, but a movement striving for unity through renewal of the churches by a common rediscovery of the full richness of the faith."[13]

This is why syncretism was, for him, an even bigger threat than atheism. The church, he writes in *No Other Name*, has been concerned with those who think all religions are equally false, when it should be concerned with those who think they are equally true, because this calls into question the nonnegotiable uniqueness—the *particularity*—of God's self-revelation in Jesus Christ.[14] Ecumenism, like Christianity as a whole, is rooted in "the common confession of the one Savior, the concern for the unity and obedience of his people, [and] the calling to bring the word of salvation and the ministry of reconciliation to all men everywhere."[15] This, for Visser 't Hooft, is *the* truth, the gospel Christians proclaim.

THE WHOLE CHURCH

Visser 't Hooft's overwhelming certainty that God's design for humanity is revealed in Jesus Christ, as testified to in Scripture, included another unshakable conviction: that this plan is carried out in history through a God-given, God-inspired community. "A churchless Christ," he argues in a *Student World* article, "is not the real Christ, a churchless Christ is not the Christ who communicates life to the world"[16]—a churchless Christ would be more a revered figure from the past than a present reality. But, in fact, the Lord *is* gathering his people into one body in order that it might be an incarnate witness to God's reconciling grace. The church—when it is, indeed, the church—is an indispensable dimension of the gospel.[17]

The tragedy, from his perspective, is that Christians have generally been content to view the churches in purely human terms—as separated institutions whose purpose is "the maintenance of religious culture," as congregations of "unrelated individuals who attend church services for private reasons," as organizations that basically exist to meet our spiritual needs and can, therefore, be fashioned as we please.[18] He laments in his Oberlin sermon that many Christians are satisfied with the current state of affairs, seeing the variety of denominations as a way of accommodating different preferences and needs.[19] If the church is "ours," a voluntary association of like-minded people, often involved in a competitive scramble for members, then why not have as many as we have sports teams? And like all human institutions, the divided churches are resistant to change. They become ends in themselves, as if the preservation of their particular life is God's will.[20]

Worse, the church often tries to serve two masters: for example, God and nation or Christ and capitalism. It allows the gospel to be compromised by less than ultimate commitments, which is when its mission becomes an agent of cultural colonialism and it forgets its calling as a single, holy people of God.[21] The church, of course, has also been subject to external oppression; but, despite the German church experience, this is not Visser 't Hooft's main concern. Persecution, as he saw it, is the church's normal condition and may be the stimulus for renewal. The real danger is to lose sight of what the church truly is.[22]

What Visser 't Hooft repeatedly insists is that the church, for all its obvious humanness, is also the *Una Sancta*—the one, holy, catholic, and apostolic church (*unam, sanctam, catholicam, et apostolicam ecclesiam*) confessed in the Nicene Creed. The key discovery of the ecumenical movement, in his judgment, is that the *Una Sancta* (a term he often used) is not only an ideal by which the historical church with all its flaws is measured but a God-given reality that demands concrete manifestation.[23]

Once again, the eschatological tension is crucial. We are given in Scripture a vision of the church as God sees it: a coherent whole in which the parts are mutually interdependent. And, as followers of Christ, we are called to participate in God's work of making such wholeness visible, celebrating God's achievement when, from time to time, it appears. Visser 't Hooft frequently underscored that an eschatological orientation does not mean "otherworldly" or "exclusively futurist," because the new age is always breaking into the old. Christian life is, therefore, inherently paradoxical: living in and for the *Una Sancta* within one of the presently divided bodies.[24] One evening, as I was bemoaning the state of the church, Visser 't Hooft told me simply, "You must be part of the church that is for the sake of the church that ought to be."

To come at this another way, the church, if it is to be the church, if it is to express its inherent wholeness, must listen to Christ and be willing to be judged by him.[25] Scattered throughout his writings are indications of what Visser 't Hooft regards as signs that the church is listening to its Lord, including:

When it transcends in its fellowship such human divisions as race, class, and nation.[26] It seems to be a law of human society that birds of a feather flock together; and thus, the church shows that it is not simply a human organization, that it lives by the power of the Holy Spirit, when it breaks that law. "The church of Christ," writes Visser 't Hooft, "is meant to be a clear manifestation of something quite unknown in this world, namely that bodies with very different characteristics instead of making their differences into barriers and reasons for division conceive of these differences as contributions to mutual enrichment and to a fuller common witness."[27]

When it is conscious of living in one global fellowship, including in times of conflict, making intercession for the whole church and offering service to those parts that are in need.[28] A church that is listening to Christ will not live only for itself, but will recognize its responsibility for other Christians, even to the point of suffering with them. A practical expression of this is interchurch aid, not as a temporary task or only in time of crisis, but with an eagerness to give and receive that is always appropriate for members of one body.[29]

When living in the one global church includes full participation in local congregations. There is a danger, he notes in an essay in *Ecumenical Review*, that participants in the movement will grow disillusioned with their local communities of faith, preferring to live in a kind of "utopian ecumenicity" of international community. This reflects a failure to listen to the Christ who walked among us in a very particular place.[30]

When it is not concerned with accumulating worldly power. The church will show that it is listening to its crucified Lord—and, thus, speak with real authority—when it accepts that it, too, must go the way of the cross. Its actual authority is compromised when it confuses authority with political power or worldly status.[31]

When it allows Scripture to be the measure of its faithfulness and the source of its renewal. This, as we have seen, is a theme that runs throughout Visser 't Hooft's career. A church that doesn't give the Bible the last word will lose the capacity for self-criticism and likely be conformed to cultural prejudices.

When it is a "confessing church," speaking "without uncertainty and confusion about the victory of its Lord and the relevance of that victory for the life of men today"[32]—and willing to suffer for the sake of obedience to Christ. Such a church, paradoxically, will also speak with a humility that comes from knowing that the truth it confesses has been given to it and reflects no merit of its own.

When it affirms the wholeness of its mission. The church for Visser 't Hooft is neither a pious huddle nor a social-justice coalition. It is a body charged with the ministry of reconciliation, proclaiming and celebrating the good news that through Jesus Christ people are reconciled to God, and enacting this good news through Spirit-led efforts to reconcile people to each other.[33] However, the church witnesses to God's reconciling love not only by what it *says* and *does* but also by what it *is*—by the way its members live in reconciled community. Which leads to what may be the crucial point:

When the church speaks to the world with one voice. The most obvious sign that the church is listening to Christ, and not simply to its own desires or those of the culture, is when it manifests its inherent unity.

THE UNITY OF THE CHURCH

When Visser 't Hooft speaks about the church's unity, he uses the term in at least three distinct ways.[34] The first is the inherent unity we have already received through faith. "We do not come together," he told the delegates at the New Delhi assembly, "as people who have to begin by finding a common foundation for their relationship. That foundation has been laid. The starting point is given. We seek *koinonia* [communion, fellowship] because there is *koinonia* in our common submission to Christ."[35] The ecumenical task is paradoxical: to become what we are, to make visible the organic, inherent wholeness of the church. He often quoted from the "Affirmation of Unity" produced by the 1937 conference on Faith and Order: "[Our] unity does not consist in the agreement of our minds or the consent of our wills. It is founded in Jesus Christ Himself. . . . We are one because we are all the objects of the love and grace of God and called by Him to witness to all the world to His glorious Gospel."[36] Christians would lack sufficient incentive to undergo the arduous search for deeper union if they didn't already possess such given unity.[37]

Visser 't Hooft also uses the word, however, to designate that "ultimate unity in which Christ is all in all," a unity that "belongs in its fullness to the wholly new life of the Kingdom."[38] Even if all the scattered churches were to unite tomorrow in faith and order, the goal would still be before them, because this unity for which Christians pray is not simply a matter of organization and doctrine. It will be evidenced when Christ's followers love one another as he has loved them.[39]

Between these two conceptions of unity is a third, what he calls "the unity of the road." Because Christians know that they are bound to one another through the gift of the Savior, and because they know that the church belongs to the coming age when all things will be gathered up in him, they seek to manifest such oneness, however inadequately, here and now.[40] William Temple captured Visser 't Hooft's thinking when he wrote, "We may not pretend that the existing unity among Christians is greater than in fact it is; but we should act upon it so far as it is already a reality."[41] It is not appropriate to act "as if" all the human-made obstacles to manifesting God's gift—disputes over faith and worship, divergent mission priorities, seemingly intractable conflicts rooted in history and culture—have been resolved. Indifference to such divisions can actually hinder the quest for more enduring expressions of unity. But it would also be inappropriate, even unfaithful, not to express relationship with other parts of Christ's body whenever, and to the extent, possible. "It is not enough," writes Visser 't Hooft, "to discuss plans of reunion; we must also expose ourselves right now to those forces which make for unity, and that means living and acting together on the basis of convictions which we already have in common."[42] In this way Christians will feel the pressure of their common biblical calling—and the ecumenical movement will move.

His writings contain other assertions about ecclesial unity that, for the most part, have become central elements of ecumenical thinking, ideas he helped shape and by which he was shaped.[43] Some of these have already been touched on, but are worth listing more systematically.

Churches should not seek unity with one another for the sake of organizational efficiency or to effect a common front against others or because of governmental pressure.[44] The ecumenical movement is an act of obedience to Christ and to the biblical affirmation that unity belongs to the church's essence. As Visser 't Hooft suggests in his Oberlin sermon, it is not an option on which Christians get to vote![45]

"Unity at the expense of truth isn't unity at all."[46] This axiom, here expressed in his essay for the second volume of *A History of the Ecumenical Movement*, will be familiar from previous chapters. Ecumenism, contrary to its critics, is not a matter of accepting all differences! His thinking, however, is actually more nuanced. There are obviously times when, for the sake of the gospel, Christians must part company with others who claim the name of Christ, as we saw in the discussion of the German church of the 1930s and the apartheid-supporting churches in South Africa. But these are extreme cases. Generally, it is within the fellowship of the church that Christians engage in a battle for truth, learning more about the meaning of the gospel through their life with one another. The biblical account of the early church, he argues, "is a dialectical story which should warn us against a defense of truth without concern for fellowship, as well as against an idolizing of fellowship without taking the question of truth seriously."[47]

Unity does not mean uniformity but appropriately encompasses "a proper freedom in the various forms of spiritual life and discipline, in the variety of liturgical rites, and even in the theological elaborations of revealed truth."[48] It is fair to say that Visser 't Hooft's appreciation for diversity grew over the years—as, indeed, was true for the ecumenical movement as a whole. At the Amsterdam youth conference of 1939, he contended that "unity will prove to be stronger than diversity," apparently setting them in opposition.[49] Nearly two decades later at Oberlin, however, he affirmed that "unity does not exclude a great and rich variety," and by the time of the Uppsala assembly in 1968, he saw the work of the Holy Spirit in different forms of church order and in differences stemming from diverse cultures.[50] Visser 't Hooft was consistent, however, in his insistence that the task of the ecumenical movement is not to unite diversities but to celebrate and learn from the diversity inherent in the church's oneness. As Paul says in 1 Corinthians, there is one body whose unity includes members as different as an eye and a hand. The ecumenical challenge is to distinguish legitimate diversity, that which builds up the body, from illegitimate, that which tears it apart.[51]

The unity of the church is not an end in itself but is part of God's plan for the healing of the nations. Ecclesial communion is not simply a concern of Christians but has "cosmic significance" as a foretaste, a demonstration project, of what God intends for creation. That is why an invisible spiritual unity alone is insufficient. Such platonic oneness would not be a witness to others of God's power of reconciliation.[52]

Unity is not synonymous with cooperation. There are several reasons why this is true: Cooperation is the result of human decision, not theological imperative. The aim of cooperative activity is the achievement of a particular, immediate purpose, not lasting community. Cooperation is more successful when differences are ignored, not shared for the sake of common growth.[53] But most importantly, churches can cooperate without being changed, as if the occasional cooperation of unrenewed churches is an adequate response to Scripture. In Visser 't Hooft's words, "The theme of the ecumenical movement is not unity as an isolated goal; it is unity as the outcome of a common effort to express the integrity and wholeness of the Church of Christ. It is unity through renewal."[54]

THE RENEWAL OF THE CHURCH

In his 1973 study, François Gérard contends that "the notion of renewal is the central theme of W. A. Visser 't Hooft's thinking."[55] Visser 't Hooft's most creative contribution to ecumenism, wrote Reinhold Niebuhr in a *festschrift* for the general secretary, is the conviction that ecumenical encounter must be based on, and result in, the renewal of the churches. "Without this presupposition and consequence the ecumenical movement will merely result in added ecclesiastical machinery"[56]—a statement Visser 't Hooft surely applauded. Visser 't Hooft himself claimed that the basic motif of the movement is "the rediscovery of the Church as the new people of God." Only a radically transformed church could become the needed conscience of society and harbinger of the world God intends.[57]

As we saw in the excerpt from *The Renewal of the Church*, Visser 't Hooft's book from 1956, unity and renewal have frequently been set in opposition. Leaders who have emphasized Christian unity have often looked with suspicion on renewal movements and the disruption they inevitably create; meanwhile, those who have emphasized renewal of church life have often looked with suspicion on talk of unity as a preservation of the status quo.[58] Part of the reason, Visser 't Hooft suggests, is that renewal has been misunderstood. Some have confused it with ecclesial improvements; but more active congregations, better liturgy, a more responsive bureaucracy, even the addition of ecumenical offices mean little if Christians have not rediscovered the meaning of their own existence as God's people. Some have failed to see that renewal demands repentance, demands confession of the ways we have failed to be the church. Some have seen it as mere innovation, change for the sake of change or for the sake of adapting to current trends. Others have made the mistake of thinking that such adaptation extends even to the content of the faith. Beneath each of these distortions, he argues, is the tendency to secularize both unity and renewal, seeing them as something humans do, not something God does in and for us.[59]

Visser 't Hooft is clear: At its best, the ecumenical movement has seen unity versus renewal as a completely false dichotomy. Renewal is meaningless if it does not enable Christians to live together—to break bread around one table, to take responsibility for one another—beyond the human barriers of race, class, and ideology. And unity is dangerous, either because it turns authoritarian or relativistic, if divorced from the constant pressure to transform the church's life through closer identification with Christ.[60] For Visser 't Hooft, ecumenism is *always* a threat to the churches as they are.

As with unity, renewal, properly understood, is both a reality and an aspiration. Visser 't Hooft turns to Paul when speaking of this paradox. Those who are "in Christ," according to the Apostle, are already "new creations"; yet they are also exhorted to be renewed, even as they are told that their "inner nature is being renewed every day" through the grace of God. Our task is to accept this gift and participate in it, demonstrating the new life in Christ in the midst of the old, orienting our life to the new age inaugurated by him, conforming ourselves increasingly to the newness of the kingdom promised in Scripture.[61]

Of course, the church in history, far from representing the new creation, is often the guardian of ideas and practices that should be consigned to the past.[62] Visser 't Hooft saw the ecumenical movement as a new Reformation, one that hears a calling to perpetual reform.[63] One sign of the church's wholeness is when the now-separated churches begin to experience transformation through the sharing of the spiritual gifts God has given them in trust to be used for the common good. Another is when the churches begin to be attentive to the whole people of God, including women, youth, and laity. These often-neglected voices, Visser 't Hooft firmly believed, can help shake churches free from past-oriented thinking and from outdated alliances with cultural norms, thus contributing to their renewal.[64]

THE WHOLE WORLD

So, the church must be the church, a community manifesting the wholeness given by God; but its fundamental purpose, the reason for its being, is to proclaim to the whole world the re-creation of the world in Christ. "The church," writes Visser 't Hooft, "does not exist for the sake of the Church. It exists for the sake of humanity."[65] Some of his sharpest statements come in his little book, *The Wretchedness and Greatness of the Church*, written in the midst of the Second World War. "In a world which has lost the sense of human solidarity, where hate is made a national duty and whole races are exterminated like vermin, the Church reconstructs, indirectly but in a very profound sense, the fundamental unity of humankind."[66]

The church, of course, should never pretend that *it* can transform society; Visser 't Hooft knew full well how utopian schemes had been deadly for the twentieth century! It trusts, however, that God can, and has already begun to do so through the incarnation. The church's political significance is to participate in God's work of promoting human dignity and, even more importantly, to witness to God's power and God's promise by being a community in which old animosities and barriers give way to a new, shared identity. Visser 't Hooft's reservations and hopes are both captured in the following paragraph from his report to the WCC Central Committee in 1951:

> We need not be ashamed if we fail to find common answers and solutions [to political crises]. For it may well be that this is the very lesson which God desires us to learn in this hour of history, that we are not the lords of history and that we must patiently and expectantly wait for the moment when He shall give us a clear word to speak together. But we fail in our duty when we do not make desperate efforts—even in the midst of the impasse—to *be* the Church of Christ together . . . the greatest contribution we can make to world peace is perhaps not in the realm of statements but in the maintenance of a fellowship which transcends man-made divisions.[67]

Visser 't Hooft's theology, as might be expected from an ecumenical leader, is often characterized by "both-and." "We must get out of that rather primitive oscillating movement of going from one extreme to the other, which is not worthy of a movement which by its nature seeks to embrace the truth of the gospel in its fulness."[68] Or as the Catholic theologian Hans Küng once put it, "Whoever preaches one half of the gospel is no less a heretic than the person who preaches the other half of the gospel."[69] We have already seen, for example, how he argued against those who would split the horizontal and vertical dimensions of Christian life, as if we could split love of neighbor from love of God. Social engagement is the "necessary consequence" of the church's worship and confession.[70]

In the same way, he insisted, the church's horizontal engagement with the world is both social justice and evangelism. This tension, which has so divided US denominations since at least the 1960s, also fractured the ecumenical movement. After the International Missionary Council merged with the WCC in

1961, conservative evangelical Christians began holding separate world mission conferences (what became known as the Lausanne Movement), in large part because they feared that evangelism was becoming simply one mission priority among many—including such things as overcoming racism, reducing poverty, and working for peace.[71]

As we have seen, Visser 't Hooft was a champion of evangelism, the spreading of the gospel, as long as the missionary church took to heart the legitimate concerns of its critics: removing cultural imperialism from its witness, seeking to avoid even the appearance of maintaining control over "younger churches," and avoiding arrogance (as if the possession of the gospel were somehow due to the church's merit!).[72] For Visser 't Hooft, however, evangelism is not just preaching the good news to individuals; it is throwing "the light of the gospel on the great human problems of our time."[73] The church will never convince the world of the truth that God was in Christ, he told the church and society conference in 1966, unless it engages in a radical critique of social attitudes and structures. Prophetic action for social justice *is* evangelism in the truest sense. It witnesses to the reconciling, justice-affirming mission of God, a witness that will draw people to Christ far more surely than verbal proclamation alone.[74]

The language of "vertical and horizontal" is useful for understanding Visser 't Hooft, but even better is the language of "already and not yet." The kingdom that is to come for all the world has been inaugurated with the incarnation, the church being the part of the world that lives in light of this generally unrecognized reality. Better still is the language of "indicative" (what has happened) and "imperative" (what should now happen as a consequence). This dialectic, familiar to readers of the Bible, informs all of Visser 't Hooft's writing. If we, Christians, live in the Spirit (which we do), let us also walk in the Spirit (Gal 5:25). If we are one people (which we are), let us also live and act as a reconciled community. If we participate in the renewed humanity promised by God (which we do), let us give evidence of it by promoting justice and peace. If we are the community that knows of Christ's victory over the powers and principalities (which we are), let us declare that victory with joyful boldness.[75]

Readers of this book may well be familiar with H. Richard Niebuhr's famous study of social ethics, *Christ and Culture*, published in 1951 when Visser 't Hooft was at the height of his career. In it, Niebuhr distinguishes five types of engagement, each with its own theological foundation, between Christians and the societies in which they live. Visser 't Hooft fits, for the most part, into Niebuhr's fifth type, "Christ the Transformer of Culture."[76] Those who see through this lens contend that human culture, on its own, is opposed to Christ, is part of a fallen creation. Visser 't Hooft, for example, argues that the world doesn't just need to be improved, but "overcome." Human society, generally speaking, does not know God and is perpetually trying to work out its own salvation.[77] But unlike the type Niebuhr calls "Christ against Culture" (e.g., the early Anabaptists), the answer for Visser 't Hooft and those who identify with Niebuhr's fifth type is not withdrawal into insular community.[78] Nor is it mere endurance in expectation of a transhistorical salvation, the stance taken by what Niebuhr calls "Christ and Culture in Paradox." Rather, Christ gives humans the power to remove the threat to his kingship and to participate in establishing society on a different basis.

It is probably not surprising that Visser 't Hooft's thought accords with this type, since it was generally characteristic of Calvin and can be seen in much of the Protestant Reformed tradition.[79] But while that tradition's eschatology has, at times, focused heavily on the eternal existence of individual believers, Visser 't Hooft emphasized the eschatological hope for a transformed world—a hope grounded in what Christ has already accomplished, a hope made visible in the church's active anticipation.

In his major book from the 1930s, *None Other Gods*, Visser 't Hooft suggests that the church's relationship to the world is like a pendulum: withdrawing from time to time from active social involvement in order to prepare itself for entering more deeply and effectively into the life of the surrounding society. To put it another way, the church must get its own act together, must be renewed, before it can carry God's promise of wholeness to others.[80]

Such a stance would obviously have paralyzed the World Council of Churches, for who can say when the churches in it are sufficiently ready to make effective witness? Thus, Visser 't Hooft the general secretary encouraged social engagement, along with simultaneous efforts at church renewal—always the two together. And by the 1960s, new voices in ecumenical conversations began to shift the paradigm: The church, by participating in God's mission in the world (promoting racial justice, opposing exploitation and violence), may discover something of its own wholeness.[81] Visser 't Hooft gave at least tacit endorsement to this perspective, acknowledging that the church often has much to learn from, and considerable common cause with, secular leaders. His *Memoirs*, for example, shows deep appreciation for such figures as Hammarskjöld and Nehru, whose promotion of universal community and concern for the poor made them instructive allies in the work of the WCC.[82] In his book on "emancipation," written when he was over eighty, he readily admits that the church has often been an obstacle to emancipation from paternalism in its various forms, and he acknowledges that such movements as feminism, Christian or otherwise, have prodded the church to recover the liberating message of the gospel.[83]

What Visser 't Hooft wanted to avoid, it seems to me, is the world setting the church's agenda.[84] "The point," he writes, "is not whether the churches are too little or much involved with the problems of the world. Basically, they can never be involved deeply enough."[85] The question is whether they are properly involved. If the church simply defines its mission in terms borrowed from politicians and the media, if it runs after political favor, if it is co-opted by the social order (e.g., confusing monetary success with God's blessing), then it will have lost its capacity to speak prophetically. This can even happen with the best of intent. Too often, Christians are first committed to economic development or peacemaking or racial justice, and then turn to the church for resources or theological support. For Visser 't Hooft, Christians must *start* with the agenda God gives to the church: a vision of the kingdom as set forth in Scripture. Human goals must be evaluated in light of this.[86]

This discussion about the "whole world" underscores how Visser 't Hooft was both pragmatic and visionary. Various of his books suggest principles that he believes constitute an emerging ecumenical consensus on church and society. For example, "the church declares that each nation must be assured of an equitable share in the wealth of the earth and that each member of society must be assured of the possibility of worthy employment and protection against social insecurity."[87] The role of the ecumenical Christian community, he argues, is not to take political decisions but, on the basis of Scripture, to declare God's will for human society in order that this might help shape public debate.[88] And, as he notes in the *Memoirs* and elsewhere, this approach *has* produced concrete results: promoting postwar reconciliation with Germany, contributing to the Universal Declaration on Human Rights, supporting the achievement of nuclear weapons treaties, and helping to end conflicts (e.g., between northern and southern Sudan). There is no reason to exalt over such practical accomplishments, he tells his readers, but also no reason to pretend that ecumenical efforts at encouraging social betterment, when guided by the Spirit, have been in vain.[89]

Behind these pragmatic steps, however, is a vision of the unity of the human family. The unity of the church is of great, but only penultimate, importance. An essential part of the biblical revelation is the conviction that people are related as children of one Creator and that there will be no warfare or economic injustice in the *shalom* of God's kingdom. It is this vision, he was convinced, that compels Christians to work for peace and justice here and now and sustains them in the face of inevitable setbacks.[90]

Does this mean that Visser 't Hooft envisions the day when the whole world will recognize Christ as Lord? His answer is an emphatic "Yes!" Christian faith, he contends, is presented in Scripture as "a universal faith, which will unite rather than divide humanity and provide a foundation for that common life which the nations and races must learn to live, if there is to be a future for mankind."[91] An individualistic understanding of Christianity (i.e., a focus on my relationship with Jesus and my salvation) obscures the gospel's universal message, which is that only the cross of Christ opens the way for overcoming the forces that divide humans one from another.[92] The ecumenical movement, he argues, is based on this "Christocentric universalism," a claim we will examine more closely in the next chapter.

I don't think Visser 't Hooft believed that human community could transcend its painful divisions by being incorporated into the church.[93] He was too Barthian to think that Christian religion, with its all-too-human structures, is the final answer to the human dilemma. And, as we saw in chapter 1, he also did not believe, contrary to the dream of the nineteenth-century missionary movement and many ecumenical pioneers, that Christ's lordship will be recognized anytime soon. Christians now live in a pluralistic world, which is a "temptation" to relativism and syncretism but also an "opportunity" to collaborate in addressing human need and to be the church rather than a societal buttress. Pluralism cannot be a goal for Christianity, but in the current situation it can be embraced.[94] This means a commitment not only to common service but to dialogue—deep communication "that is impossible when one party considers the other simply as an object or as a victim."[95] But for Visser 't Hooft, such dialogue is also, always, an occasion to tell the story of Jesus Christ, the One who is Savior of the whole world.

THE WHOLE ECUMENICAL MOVEMENT

The ecumenical movement, with its vision of global Christian fellowship, was born at a time conducive to efforts aimed at realizing international concord. Two world wars provoked, particularly in Europe, a longing for what some called "ethical internationalism," manifest in such forms as the League of Nations; the United Nations; the International Fellowship of Reconciliation; the plethora of international bodies dealing with trade, labor, and economic development—and the Christian ecumenical movement, especially as expressed in the World Council of Churches. Visser 't Hooft did not deny the impact of broader historical forces in the shaping of the movement, but he vigorously insisted that ecumenism is, first and foremost, the outcome of a theological imperative: God's gathering of a people to be a light to the world. The movement, he contended, has shown it is capable of transcending social-political pressures—including war, both hot and cold—that could have destroyed or co-opted it. This is a sure indication, as he saw it, that ecumenism is grounded in a theological vision, not political calculation or sociological necessity.[96]

Visser 't Hooft repeatedly emphasizes in his writings that the ecumenical movement is not the church, let alone the "super-church" feared by its critics.[97] It is, rather, a multifaceted effort "to liberate the Church from her captivity in the churches" by confronting them with the church as spoken of in Scripture.[98] Ecumenism is based on the conviction that this church really exists, through the grace of God, and that the gospel has the power to call the churches away from self-interested sectarianism into wholeness.

In his published works, he describes ecumenism in various ways. It is

- an attempt to manifest "the economy of the *charismata*" (i.e., the mutual sharing of spiritual gifts).[99] The movement, by bringing formerly distant churches into structured contact, enables them to learn from one another and to "discover that in ecumenical life receiving is often more blessed than giving."[100]

- "a disturber of the peace of self-sufficiency" in the churches.[101] The very existence of other churches raises—or, at least, should raise—questions that require ecclesial self-examination, even self-criticism.

- a "rediscovery of the universal dimension of Christian faith."[102] Churches used to living and thinking provincially are called, through the movement, to affirm their intrinsic connection with Christians of other confessions, cultures, and countries.

- "liberation of the churches from an idolatrous attachment to outdated values and patterns of life."[103] This includes the pattern of colonialism, of domination and dependence, as churches in the Pacific, Asia, Africa, and Latin America claim their voice as equal participants in the movement.

It is also a shared struggle for truth through the most important of ecumenical disciplines: dialogue, theologically grounded conversation among Christians. Visser 't Hooft stressed that dialogue about matters of Christian faith is not diplomacy or negotiation, as if revealed truth could be compromised for the sake of "getting along." It does start, however, with the assumption that no partner possesses a full grasp of God's will and, therefore, that each should listen carefully to the others, should take the others seriously as potential bearers of gifts, should try to see themselves as others see them.[104] Since dialogue is not diplomacy, it can and must involve "a frank and penetrating confrontation of our convictions";[105] excessive politeness indicates that the dialogue participants have not grasped that this is a struggle to understand God's self-revelation more fully.[106] It should aim at concrete results but, at the same time, not be overly concerned with immediate outcome. Ecumenical conversation is itself an act of obedience to the One who calls us to ever deeper relationship.[107]

There is, of course, a perennial tension between charismatic movements and the institutions they almost inevitably spawn.[108] This is certainly true of ecumenism, which in its early years was driven by visionary individuals (whose memory Visser 't Hooft tried to keep alive) but quickly took institutional form, especially with the establishment of the WCC. More than anyone else, Visser 't Hooft was the bridge between these periods of ecumenical history, leading the WCC but always insisting that the churches should be focused more on their "common calling" than on their membership in an organization, on the end rather than the means. "If the ecumenical movement becomes an ecumenical institution," he writes in his paper for the council's first assembly, "its days are numbered"[109]—a surprisingly strong statement from the person charged with guiding this new institution.

This tension is visible in his claim that the World Council is both an instrument of the churches and of the movement. On the one hand, the WCC, if it is fulfilling its intended role, is a force for renewal, pushing the churches beyond what they may initially identify as their common agenda. If the churches cling to marks of division, then it is surely the duty of the staff and council leaders, as servants of the movement, to challenge the churches to deeper, costlier ecumenical commitment.[110] Councils, in the words of Lukas Vischer, are "the thorn in the flesh of the churches. They are a constant reminder to the churches of the anomalous situation in which we live. They prod the churches to expose themselves continually to the power of the Holy Spirit. They constitute the setting, *created by the churches themselves*, within which the promise of renewal may be heard."[111] The worst thing, Visser 't Hooft often claimed, would be for the WCC, or any council of churches, to become simply a cog in the ecclesiastical machinery, an organization that enables its members to feel righteously ecumenical without actually changing the way they do mission or relate to other churches.[112]

On the other hand, the WCC *is* the churches in fellowship with one another. To quote the general secretary, "It has no being apart from the churches."[113] It would be contrary to the self-understanding of the council for ideas or programs to be imposed on the members. The WCC, he told the first assembly in Amsterdam, is not simply a cooperative agency that does things for the churches. It is not simply a study circle that fosters relationship without action. Nor is it a mere federation based on minimal commitments. It is a council *of the churches*, a structured expression of their growing relationship to one another.[114]

One way to preserve some of the movement character, in Visser 't Hooft's view, is to make sure there is room in the WCC for those who aren't in official leadership positions in the churches.[115] This, too, is a tension. The WCC's governing bodies must consist of persons chosen by their churches (historically, older men), but the council must never become "the victim of a self-centered institutionalism which suppresses prophetic voices."[116] Its health depends on the capacity to hear fresh insights, including criticisms, from unofficial quarters.

Another way is to see the council as that place where churches are held accountable to commitments that they, in their better moments, have made to one another. There is no external entity called the World Council of Churches that can force its members to accept theological agreement or engage in cutting-edge mission. But when representatives of the churches reach agreements or authorize actions, when they make commitments by virtue of becoming members, then it is the responsibility of the council, in the form of its staff and elected leaders, to weave these into the fabric of the council's fellowship—to hold the churches accountable to the promises they have made to each other.[117]

Visser 't Hooft's speeches and writings suggest numerous implications of membership in the WCC, including

- a willingness to manifest the unity now possible and to strive for ever fuller unity in Christ;[118]

- a willingness to acknowledge, at the very least, that elements of the church exist in the other members, and that the Lord is at work in their life;[119]

- a willingness to learn from, even be corrected by, contact with other churches through a "process of constructive and mutual challenge";[120]

- a willingness to engage in common study concerning the unity and witness of the church, and to give serious consideration to the results of such study;[121]

- a willingness to act on decisions made together in the life of the Council;[122] and

- a willingness to support other members in their joys and struggles, including prayer for and with the others.

From a horizontal (human) perspective, the WCC is an organization made up of disparate, often divergent, churches, without intrinsic authority. From a vertical viewpoint, however, "it is the place where the *koinonia* in the one faith may become (and has become) at least partly visible."[123] In such moments, it is possible to glimpse the wholeness of the church. And when this happens, writes Visser 't Hooft, the council has true authority.

In 1983, less than two years before his death, Visser 't Hooft spoke to students at the Ecumenical Institute at Chateau de

Bossey about the future of the WCC.[124] He began by telling them that three convictions, foundational to the ecumenical movement (and his own theology) were now being called into question: that it is Christ-centered, Bible-centered, and church-centered. With regard to the first, voices within the movement itself were calling for a focus on interfaith relations—"wider ecumenism"—thus setting aside the decisive finality of what God has done for the world's salvation in Jesus Christ. With regard to the second, many Christians were suggesting that the Bible so reflects the thought of a patriarchal culture that large parts of it cannot be normative for our age. And with regard to the third, there were many who believed that the institutional church has a paralyzing effect on prophetic, Spirit-led community.

Visser 't Hooft, though a representative of earlier generations of ecumenists, did not dispute the cogency of these critiques. However, it is possible, he told the students, (1) to eschew Christian triumphalism—which, after all, exalts humans rather than Christ—and to enter into dialogue and cooperation with other religions, without denying the universality of the incarnation; (2) to disavow one-sided masculine interpretations of the Bible, lifting up the role of women in early Christianity without denying the authority of Scripture; and (3) to safeguard against institutional petrification in the church, encouraging the contribution of prophetic voices.

Is this true? Does Visser 't Hooft's vision of the ecumenical church make sense in this century? We turn to these questions in the following chapter.

Notes

1. W. A. Visser 't Hooft, "Pan-Christians Yesterday and Today," *Ecumenical Review* 32, no. 4 (1980): 391. The importance of this address for understanding Visser 't Hooft is highlighted by Philip Potter, introduction to *Voices of Unity: Essays in Honour of Willem Adolf Visser 't Hooft on the Occasion of His 80th Birthday*, ed. Ans. J. van der Bent (Geneva: WCC, 1981), vi.

2. Visser 't Hooft, "General Ecumenical Development," 6.

3. Emilio Castro, "Editorial," *Ecumenical Review* 38, no. 2 (1986): 122.

4. The "Message" from the Stockholm conference, which contains this sentence, is in Kinnamon, *Ecumenical Movement*, 2nd ed., 186.

5. Castro makes this point in "Editorial," 123. Visser 't Hooft made it frequently. See, e.g., Visser 't Hooft, *None Other Gods*, 57.

6. Paragraph 20 of the Eucharist section.

7. W. A. Visser 't Hooft, "The Calling of the World Council of Churches," *Ecumenical Review* 14, no. 2 (1962): 224.

8. Visser 't Hooft, *Kingship of Christ*, 17.

9. Visser 't Hooft, *Kingship of Christ*, 18.

10. This apt wording comes from an analysis of Visser 't Hooft's theology in Gérard, *Future of the Church*, 48.

11. Material in this paragraph is drawn from Visser 't Hooft, *Kingship of Christ*, 73, 86, 96, 97. See also Gérard, *Future of the Church*, 48, 61.

12. Jonson, *Wounded Visions*, 9.

13. Visser 't Hooft, *Memoirs*, 248.

14. Visser 't Hooft, *No Other Name*, 49.

15. Visser 't Hooft, *No Other Name*, 113.

16. Quoted in Gérard, *Future of the Church*, 42. The original article appeared in *Student World* 51, no. 3 (1958).

17. See Visser 't Hooft, *Wretchedness and Greatness*, 30.

18. Visser 't Hooft, *Wretchedness and Greatness*, 30; Visser 't Hooft, *Kingship of Christ*, 112.

19. W. A. Visser 't Hooft, "The Ground of Our Unity," in *The Nature of the Unity We Seek: Official Report of the North American Conference on Faith and Order*, ed. Paul S. Minear (St. Louis: Bethany, 1958), 121.

20. Willem A. Visser 't Hooft, "The Task of the Churches in the New Ecumenical Situation," in Bea and Visser 't Hooft, *Peace among Christians*, 197; Visser 't Hooft, *Has the Ecumenical Movement a Future?*, 36.

21. Visser 't Hooft, *None Other Gods*, 76. The point is reinforced in Newbigin, "Legacy of W. A. Visser 't Hooft," 78–82.

22. This idea is forcefully advanced in his book written during World War II. See Visser 't Hooft, *Wretchedness and Greatness*, 5–6.

23. Visser 't Hooft, "Mandate of the Ecumenical Movement," 320.

24. W. A. Visser 't Hooft, "Renewal and Wholeness," *Ecumenical Review* 4, no. 4 (1952): 385–86; W. A. Visser 't Hooft, "The Una Sancta and the Local Church," *Ecumenical Review* 13, no. 1 (1960): 5.

25. Visser 't Hooft, *Kingship of Christ*, 100.

26. Visser 't Hooft, *Kingship of Christ*, 111.

27. Visser 't Hooft, "Renewal and Wholeness," 387. My formulation of this point owes much to the work of Jürgen Moltmann, a participant in Faith and Order dialogue. See, e.g., Jürgen Moltmann, *The Future of Creation: Collected Essays*, trans. Margaret Kohl (Philadelphia: Fortress Press, 1979), 54.

28. Visser 't Hooft, *Wretchedness and Greatness*, 58.

29. Visser 't Hooft, *None Other Gods*, 77; Visser 't Hooft, *Pressure of Our Common Calling*, 57–59.

30. Visser 't Hooft, "Una Sancta and the Local Church," 4.

31. Visser 't Hooft, *Kingship of Christ*, 130.

32. Visser 't Hooft, *Kingship of Christ*, 106.

33. Visser 't Hooft, "Ground of Our Unity," 124–25.

34. Visser 't Hooft actually speaks of four meanings of unity, but I have combined two of the meanings for the sake of clarity. See Visser 't Hooft, *Pressure of Our Common Calling*, 87–90.

35. Visser 't Hooft, *Pressure of Our Common Calling*, 73.

36. See, e.g., Visser 't Hooft, *Pressure of Our Common Calling*, 87. The "Affirmation of Union in Allegiance to Our Lord Jesus Christ," produced by the 1937 World Conference on Faith and Order, is in Kinnamon, *The Ecumenical Movement*, 2nd ed., 76–77.

37. For a discussion of "given unity," see Kinnamon, *Vision of the Ecumenical Movement*, ch. 1. A classic expression of the point made in this sentence comes from William Temple in his opening sermon at the Faith and Order conference in 1937. See Kinnamon, *The Ecumenical Movement*, 2nd ed., 14.

38. Visser 't Hooft, *Pressure of Our Common Calling*, 85.

39. Visser 't Hooft, *Pressure of Our Common Calling*, 90. Visser 't Hooft is borrowing here from Lesslie Newbigin.

40. See, e.g., Visser 't Hooft, *Pressure of Our Common Calling*, 21; Visser 't Hooft, *Wretchedness and Greatness*, 15; and Visser 't Hooft, "Faith and Order and the Second Assembly," 136.

41. Quoted in Visser 't Hooft, *Pressure of Our Common Calling*, 22.

42. Visser 't Hooft, *Pressure of Our Common Calling*, 21.

43. For his first—and, in some ways, fullest—attempt to summarize the growing ecumenical consensus regarding the shape of Christian unity, see W. A. Visser 't Hooft, "Various Meanings of Unity and the Unity Which the World Council of Churches Seeks to Promote," *Ecumenical Review* 8, no. 1 (1955): esp. 21–22.

44. Visser 't Hooft, *Kingship of Christ*, 113; W. A. Visser 't Hooft, "The Super-Church and the Ecumenical Movement," *Ecumenical Review* 10, no. 4 (1958): 375.

45. Visser 't Hooft, "Ground of Our Unity," 123.

46. Visser 't Hooft, "General Ecumenical Development," 19.

47. Visser 't Hooft, *Pressure of Our Common Calling*, 69. See Kinnamon, *Truth and Community*, ch. 1.

48. The quotation is from the "Decree on Ecumenism" of the Second Vatican Council, par. 4.

49. W. A. Visser 't Hooft, "Opening Address," in *Christus Victor: The Report of the World Conference of Christian Youth*, ed. Denzil G. M. Patrick (Geneva: Conference Headquarters, 1939), 148.

50. Visser 't Hooft, "Ground of Our Unity," 123; Visser 't Hooft, "Mandate of the Ecumenical Movement," 321–22.

51. Visser 't Hooft, "Ground of Our Unity," 123. For a fuller discussion of this point, see Kinnamon, *Vision of the Ecumenical Movement*, ch. 4.

52. Visser 't Hooft, *Pressure of Our Common Calling*, 83–84; Visser 't Hooft, "Pan-Christians," 391.

53. Visser 't Hooft, *Pressure of Our Common Calling*, 18. This issue is discussed more fully in Kinnamon, *Vision of the Ecumenical Movement*, ch. 2.

54. Visser 't Hooft, *Pressure of Our Common Calling*, 27.

55. Gérard, *Future of the Church*, 2.

56. Reinhold Niebuhr, "The Development of a Social Ethic in the Ecumenical Movement," in Mackie and West, *Sufficiency of God*, 111.

57. W. A. Visser 't Hooft, *The Renewal of the Church* (London: SCM, 1956), 11; Visser 't Hooft, "Mandate of the Ecumenical Movement," 315.

58. Visser 't Hooft, *Renewal of the Church*, 117.

59. The ideas in this paragraph are scattered throughout Visser 't Hooft's Dale lectures at Mansfield College, Oxford. See Visser 't Hooft, *Renewal of the Church*, 12, 86–92, 95, 119–22. See also Visser 't Hooft, *Wretchedness and Greatness*, 25.

60. Visser 't Hooft, *Renewal of the Church*, 119–20.

61. Visser 't Hooft, *Renewal of the Church*, 34–35. The biblical quotations are from 1 Cor 5:6–8, Col 3:9, Rom 7:6, and 2 Cor 4:16.

62. Visser 't Hooft, *Renewal of the Church*, 103.

63. Visser 't Hooft, "Faith and Order and the Second Assembly," 136.

64. Visser 't Hooft, "General Ecumenical Development," 9; Visser 't Hooft, *Renewal of the Church*, 123.

65. Visser 't Hooft, *No Other Name*, 114. See also Visser 't Hooft, *Wretchedness and Greatness*, 70–71.

66. Visser 't Hooft, *Wretchedness and Greatness*, 75.

67. Quoted in Bilheimer, *Breakthrough*, 161.

68. Visser 't Hooft, "Mandate of the Ecumenical Movement," 318.

69. Quoted in Arie R. Brouwer, *Ecumenical Testimony* (Grand Rapids: Eerdmans, 1991), 110.

70. Visser 't Hooft, "Mandate of the Ecumenical Movement," 317–18. See also Visser 't Hooft, *Has the Ecumenical Movement a Future?*, 97.

71. Beginning in the early 1950s, world mission conferences spoke less of the church's mission than of God's mission (*missio Dei*) in which the church participates. This suggests that the purpose of mission is not simply the planting of churches but participation in all that God is doing to promote peace and justice in human community. For a brief discussion of this transition and the resulting division between "liberals" and "conservatives," see Kinnamon, *The Ecumenical Movement*, 2nd ed., 263–65.

72. See Visser 't Hooft, "Missions as the Test of Faith," 27.

73. Visser 't Hooft, "General Ecumenical Development," 19.

74. A brief summary of Visser 't Hooft's address to the conference is in M. M. Thomas and Paul Abrecht, eds., *World Conference on Church and Society: Christians in the Technical and Social Revolutions of Our Time* (Geneva: WCC, 1967), 13.

75. This paragraph is informed by Harding Meyer, *That All May Be One: Perceptions and Models of Ecumenicity*, trans. William G. Rusch (Grand Rapids: Eerdmans, 1999), 9–13.

76. H. Richard Niebuhr, *Christ and Culture* (New York: Harper & Row, 1951), ch. 6.

77. See, e.g., Visser 't Hooft, "I Have Overcome," 231–32.

78. Visser 't Hooft, "Pluralism," 217–19.

79. Niebuhr, *Christ and Culture*, 217–18.

80. Visser 't Hooft, *None Other Gods*, 78–79, 76–77.

81. See Kinnamon, *Vision of the Ecumenical Movement*, 42.

82. Visser 't Hooft, *Memoirs*, 251. See also Visser 't Hooft, *Has the Ecumenical Movement a Future?*, 64–65.

83. Visser 't Hooft, *Fatherhood of God*, 143–44, 54–59.

84. Visser 't Hooft, *Has the Ecumenical Movement a Future?*, ch. 4.

85. Visser 't Hooft, *Has the Ecumenical Movement a Future?*, 95.

86. Visser 't Hooft, *Has the Ecumenical Movement a Future?*, 88; Visser 't Hooft, *Memoirs*, 367.

87. Visser 't Hooft, *Wretchedness and Greatness*, 86.

88. Visser 't Hooft, *Wretchedness and Greatness*, 77.

89. See, e.g., Visser 't Hooft, *Has the Ecumenical Movement a Future?*, 87–88. See also Visser 't Hooft, "Pan-Christians," 393, where he argues that triumphalism confuses the church of the present with the church that is to come but defeatism is a form of ingratitude.

90. See Visser 't Hooft, "Mandate of the Ecumenical Movement," 319. It is telling that a *festschrift* in honor of Visser 't Hooft is subtitled "Essays on the Unity of Mankind." J. Robert Nelson, ed., *No Man is an Alien: Essays on the Unity of Mankind* (Leiden: Brill, 1971).

91. Visser 't Hooft, *No Other Name*, 92.

92. Visser 't Hooft, *No Other Name*, 102–3.

93. This charge was made by S. Wesley Ariarajah, to whom I will refer more extensively in chapter 4, in an unpublished paper from 2003.

94. See Visser 't Hooft, "Pluralism," 211, 226–27.

95. Visser 't Hooft, *Has the Ecumenical Movement a Future?*, 66.

96. Visser 't Hooft, "General Ecumenical Development," 5.

97. Visser 't Hooft, "Significance of the World Council of Churches," 181–82.

98. Visser 't Hooft, *Wretchedness and Greatness*, 63.

99. Quoted in H. R. Weber, "The Laity: Its Gifts and Ministry," in Mackie and West, *Sufficiency of God*, 187.

100. Visser 't Hooft, *Memoirs*, 211.

101. Visser 't Hooft, *Anglo-Catholicism and Orthodoxy*, 150. See also Bea and Visser 't Hooft, *Peace among Christians*, 79.

102. Visser 't Hooft, "General Ecumenical Development," 4.

103. M. M. Thomas, "Ecumenism in Asia: An Assessment," in van der Bent, *Voices of Unity*, 92. Thomas is summarizing lectures Visser 't Hooft delivered in 1959 at the inauguration of the East Asia Christian Conference.

104. See Visser 't Hooft, *Pressure of Our Common Calling*, 73–75; Visser 't Hooft, *Anglo-Catholicism*, 151. Ecumenical dialogue, dialogue between or among churches that can appeal to shared sources of authority, should be distinguished from interfaith (interreligious) dialogue, which is between or among different religions (e.g., Christianity, Judaism, Islam, Buddhism, Hinduism) that, generally

speaking, have different sources of authority for their claims.

105.   Visser 't Hooft, "Faith and Order and the Second Assembly," 129.

106.   See Visser 't Hooft, *Teachers and the Teaching Authorities*, 63.

107.   See Visser 't Hooft, *Pressure of Our Common Calling*, 75; Visser 't Hooft, *Anglo-Catholicism*, 10, 174.

108.   Visser 't Hooft, "General Ecumenical Development," 20.

109.   Visser 't Hooft, "Significance of the World Council of Churches," 193.

110.   Visser 't Hooft, *Memoirs*, 345. See also Kinnamon, *Vision of the Ecumenical Movement*, 94–95. For the report of a seminal study of the WCC, relevant to this issue, see José Míguez Bonino, "The Concern for a Vital and Coherent Theology," *Ecumenical Review* 41, no. 2 (1989): esp. 172.

111.   Lukas Vischer, "Christian Councils—Instruments of Ecclesial Communion," in Kinnamon, *The Ecumenical Movement*, 2nd ed., 428.

112.   Visser 't Hooft, *Memoirs*, 345. See also Visser 't Hooft, *Has the Ecumenical Movement a Future?*, 40–41.

113.   Visser 't Hooft, "Significance of the World Council of Churches," 181.

114.   Visser 't Hooft, "Significance of the World Council of Churches," 184–85. There are times when Visser 't Hooft seems to say that the WCC is an entity alongside the churches, as if the WCC holds the churches accountable rather than the churches holding each other accountable in conciliar fellowship. See, e.g., Visser 't Hooft, *Has the Ecumenical Movement a Future?*, 75. This, I take it, is because he sees the council both as an instrument of the churches and of the ecumenical movement.

115.   Visser 't Hooft, "Significance of the World Council of Churches", 194.

116.   Visser 't Hooft, "Super-Church," 23.

117.   Visser 't Hooft, *Has the Ecumenical Movement a Future?*, 43. See Kinnamon, *Vision of the Ecumenical Movement*, 49.

118.   Visser 't Hooft, "Significance of the World Council of Churches," 191.

119.   Visser 't Hooft, "Significance of the World Council of Churches," 192. Many Protestant ecumenists were concerned that the

Toronto Statement allowed members of the WCC to refuse to recognize other members as "churches." This was not Visser 't Hooft's concern! He would not have favored an ecclesiological relativism that precluded normative statements, even if they were exclusive.

120. Visser 't Hooft, "Significance of the World Council of Churches," 192.

121. Visser 't Hooft, "Significance of the World Council of Churches," 191; Visser 't Hooft, *Has the Ecumenical Movement a Future?*, 46.

122. Visser 't Hooft, "Significance of the World Council of Churches," 184–85.

123. Visser 't Hooft, "Significance of the World Council of Churches," 187.

124. W. A. Visser 't Hooft, "Questions about the Future of the World Council of Churches," *Ecumenical Review* 38, no. 2 (1986): 133–39.

4.

A Theology for Today?

PROPHETIC IN HIS TIME

The assessment of Visser 't Hooft's close associate Robert Bilheimer seems accurate: the three persons who did the most to shape modern ecumenism are John R. Mott, the driving force behind the missionary stream of the movement; Pope John XXIII, whose calling of the Second Vatican Council launched the Roman Catholic Church on an ecumenical trajectory; and W. A. Visser 't Hooft, the chief architect of the World Council of Churches.[1]

The word Bilheimer uses to describe Visser 't Hooft is *prophetic*. He had a capacity, perhaps unparalleled among his contemporaries in church leadership, to discern the essence of historical developments and to bring scriptural insight to bear on them. He also "attacked ecclesiasticism in a manner worthy of Amos";[2] and he was fearless in calling the often-timid churches to address injustice and division in international affairs. He was certainly not afraid to think outside the box. I recall him, near the end of his life, outlining to me a novel eight-week cycle of worship in congregations. Perhaps above all, Visser 't Hooft communicated an infectious, biblically grounded vision of the whole church acting as an ambassador of God's reconciliation that was in the best prophetic tradition. His life reflected the conviction that he was doing God's work.[3]

Any list of Visser 't Hooft's accomplishments is bound to be partial. His holistic vision of ecumenism helped integrate the disparate strands of the movement. He insisted that the WCC have a solid, theological grounding, and he helped give content to its claim to be a "fellowship of churches." He was the person most responsible for the council's commitment to grapple with social issues,[4] even as he challenged the churches to resist idolatrous entanglements with the wider society. He stressed the importance of education for ecumenism and did more than anyone else of his era to expand the range of ecumenical participants. Another person who worked closely with him, Ans van der Bent, has written that Visser 't Hooft was one of those rare leaders who "manifestly matched the need of the hour."[5]

Having said that, it is also important to point out that the historical context—the "hour"—changed dramatically during his lifetime.

When Visser 't Hooft was born in 1900, the missionary movement was at high tide, and Christian leaders such as Mott spoke of "the evangelization of the world in this generation." As late as the 1930s, when Visser 't Hooft was preparing for leadership in the WCC, eminent mission scholars could write of Christianity's rapid spread and the "stationary" condition of other world religions.[6] By the time of his death in 1985, however, these religions were experiencing new vitality and growth, including in Western countries once thought of as "Christendom."

When Visser 't Hooft was a boy, the world, in the words of Samuel Huntington, "was more one politically and economically than at any other time in human history."[7] After all, European and North American nations controlled 84 percent of the earth's land surface and most of its economic output. The push for "internationalism," especially manifest in the call to abolish war, reached its peak when Visser 't Hooft was a young adult, making it only natural that Christian leaders would dream of the oneness of the church.[8] By the time he was an ecumenical elder statesman, however, nations in the South had gained independence, the center of the church's gravity had shifted in that direction, and there was growing appreciation for cultural, and even confessional, distinctiveness.

At the time of the WCC's formal inauguration in 1948, many of the historic Protestant churches in the West, pillars of the emerging ecumenical movement, were socially-politically influential and growing. A 1951 policy statement of the US National Council of Churches exudes confidence that the denominations, acting as council, would help shape public debate on major issues of the day.[9] But by the time of Visser 't Hooft's retirement, less than twenty years later, these churches were already losing members and influence, with consequent diminishment of the councils they founded. As one of my predecessors as NCC general secretary, Joan Campbell, was fond of saying, "When the churches catch a cold, the councils get pneumonia."

At the time of Visser 't Hooft's retirement in the mid-1960s, his dialogue with Cardinal Bea, published as *Peace among Christians*, could be described as "a record of the most important religious event [i.e., ecumenical *rapprochement*] since the Reformation and a prophetic account of the future of Christianity."[10] By the time of his death in the mid-1980s, however, ecumenical claims and expectations were far more chastened.

A SHIFT IN PARADIGMS

This raises the central question of this study: Does the voice of Visser 't Hooft, prophetic in its time, still speak to us today? Clearly, he warrants historical study, but can such examination be of service to current church leaders?

One way of approaching an answer is to examine critiques of Visser 't Hooft's theology offered by more recent ecumenists who, while expressing appreciation for his achievements, have challenged some of his assumptions. The work of Konrad Raiser, fourth general secretary of the WCC, and Wesley Ariarajah, former deputy general secretary of the council, seems especially important in this regard. Neither of these ecumenical leaders criticizes Visser 't Hooft in an *ad hominem* way. Their concern is with a paradigm they think has outlived its usefulness, a paradigm for which Visser 't Hooft is the dominant, most representative figure. As we have seen, Visser 't Hooft himself called it "Christocentric universalism." He came too late to champion "the evangelization of the world in this generation," and he experienced too much of the church's failure "to be the church" to regard it as a ready instrument of God's plan to unite all things in heaven and earth. He had no doubt, however, that "the Christ event is . . . the key to the unity, renewal and eventual redemption of the whole universe" and that "the ecumenical movement of our time is an attempt to realize this specific Christian universalism."[11]

Raiser outlines what he takes to be the essential elements of the old paradigm: (1) the confession of Jesus Christ as the One who on the cross has confronted the powers of evil and overcome them, and who, therefore, is Lord of all realms of life; (2) the centrality in God's salvific plan of the church, a community whose unity is (to be) an embodiment of the divine-human union; and (3) God's universal mission to reconcile those who are estranged from God and from one another. The church's task, as Visser 't Hooft and his colleagues saw it, is far greater than calling individuals to confess Christ and join the church. It is pointing to the meaning of history under the lordship of Christ.[12] To use one of Visser 't Hooft's favorite images, Jesus is the Good Shepherd who gathers the members of his flock in order that through them he may draw all people to himself.

As Raiser sees it, a key passage for understanding Visser 't Hooft comes in *No Other Name*.

> New Testament universalism is . . . characterized by the fact that in it the central figure, the body which he creates, and the humanity for whom he has given his life belong together and are inseparable. Uniqueness, unity and universality are all indispensable and mutually interdependent. There is no universality if there is no unique event. But the unique event is not realized in its significance where there is no movement forward and outward toward universality. And the link between the two is in the body which in its unity, transcending all divisions, is the first fruit of the new humanity.[13]

Humanity, on its own, cannot realize its longing for true, universal oneness and peace. Only when it accepts Christ is the way opened for humanity to overcome the forces of division that so distort it.

Both Ariarajah and Raiser fully acknowledge that the old paradigm gave the ecumenical movement, after World War II, "a fresh, clear sense of direction."[14] It gave energy to Christian mission; it encouraged the churches to undertake prophetic social ministries; it helped churches in the West grow beyond provincialism into a more global perspective; it provided a theological foundation for efforts to overcome centuries of Christian division and to engage in fruitful collaboration.

The movement, however, has also experienced great disappointments that underscore its limitations. Ariarajah highlights three of them.[15] First, the Faith and Order stream of ecumenism, despite producing significant theological consensus documents, has not led to the tangible results for which so many Christians have worked and prayed. This is not to discount the significance of the church unions and full communion agreements that have taken place, but it seems that divisions are more entrenched than earlier generations of ecumenists had imagined. In the old paradigm, argues Ariarajah, the church was idealized, with too little attention paid to continuing tensions rooted in differences of race, class, and culture—not to mention bureaucratic intransigence and a desire to preserve cherished identity markers.

Second, large segments of the world have heard the gospel, have been recipients of Christian compassion, and yet chosen to remain in their own religious tradition (or lack of one). Far from witnessing the evangelization of the world (the animating impulse of the mission stream of the movement), recent generations have experienced the revival of other religions, part of the reclaiming of cultural and national identity after the colonial period.

Third, Christocentric universalism not only set unrealistic expectations for mission, it also devalued other religious traditions, thus keeping the church from entering into faith-based partnerships when dealing with public issues. The ministries carried out by the Life and Work stream of ecumenism were hampered because the old paradigm allowed no recognition that Christians are only one of the communities bringing healing and wholeness to the world.

Raiser takes a somewhat different approach to the same set of issues. The old paradigm, he argues in his book *Ecumenism in Transition: A Paradigm Shift in the Ecumenical Movement?*, is an example of "Christology from above"—the kingship of Christ over the church and human society. The paradigm he sees emerging puts far more emphasis on Jesus of Nazareth, who in his solidarity with the poor and his death at the hands of imperial power is the embodiment of God's promised reign and the model for our own struggle against endemic poverty, war, and oppression.[16]

A focus on the second person of the Trinity can also be problematic because it suggests that God's redemptive activity is limited to human history, with nature as merely a stage on which the human drama of redemption is played out. The Orthodox, with their fully Trinitarian theology, have long emphasized that human life is part of the whole created order; but it was an address by the Lutheran theologian Joseph Sittler, at the New Delhi assembly in 1961, as Visser 't Hooft entered his last years as general secretary, that really placed the theme on the movement's radar. The commanding task of the moment, said Sittler, is "to fashion a theology catholic enough to affirm redemption's force enfolding nature, as we have affirmed redemption's force enfolding history."[17] It took a while for this to sink in, but by the 1970s, the image dominating discussion of the WCC's public ministry shifted from "the responsible society" to "a just, participatory and *sustainable* society." And the council's agenda became even less anthropocentric and more ecologically oriented in the 1980s with its study program "Justice, Peace and the Integrity of Creation."

The emerging paradigm, in Raiser's judgment, is also more aware of the seemingly intractable character of historical conflicts: structural racism, the lust for power, greed inherent in the global economic system. Viewed from this perspective, any unity of the human family will not arise out of existing structures but can only be spoken of as a future hope toward which we struggle in the present.[18] As a result, ecumenical programming has shifted from development to liberation, from speaking truth to power to standing with the powerless. The WCC's

Program to Combat Racism, in particular, signified that ecumenical leaders now believe racism will not be abandoned as a result of education or persuasion but must in some way be "combated"—and will likely never be fully overcome this side of God's promised kingdom.

Visser 't Hooft's fight was with false forms of universalism, especially totalitarian hegemony, but his vision of human unity never wavered. Soon after his retirement, however, transnational corporations and other forms of economic globalization were making universal claims less appealing; ecclesial efforts at global solidarity seemed increasingly illusory when set alongside the power of dominating global systems. And by the time of his death, less and less emphasis was placed on "one world" (the title of a now-defunct WCC magazine) and more on particular local cultures.[19]

An equally momentous shift has to do with the relationship between unity and diversity. The ecumenical movement, including Visser 't Hooft, long insisted that unity does not mean uniformity; but, in fact, argues Raiser, the old paradigm thought of diversity as a problem to be dealt with and resolved. Particular confessional identities needed to die as part of the cost of church union. Particular racial and ethnic groups needed to be included (i.e., blended in) for the church to experience wholeness. Theological differences needed to be eliminated—or, at least, resolved—through dialogue aimed at reaching consensus. The old paradigm, exemplified by Visser 't Hooft's life-long battle against relativism, talked about the limits of diversity. The emerging paradigm, with Raiser as a key representative, speaks about the limits of unity. His primary concern is that forms of faith and order will be foisted off as universal by those with power, thereby suppressing life-giving diversity. The new paradigm speaks less of unity and more of fellowship or communion marked by the abiding difference of the other.[20]

Raiser's fundamental criticism—shared, I think, by Ariarajah—is that the old paradigm is too dogmatic, too willing to pronounce theological judgments in the abstract. Other churches, he contends, should be experienced through actual relationship before judging whether the Spirit is in them, whether their way of living the faith and structuring the community can be encompassed in any future communion. The flaws of the church in history need to be taken fully into account before declaring the church to be the primary, even sole, instrument of God's mission. Other religions should be experienced "from the inside"—as living communities, not just static systems of belief—rather than judged on the basis of predetermined doctrine. Barthian theology, so influential for Visser 't Hooft and his generation in Europe, had, in effect, relegated other religions to the realm of unbelief as a matter of doctrine. It is this approach that ecumenists of later generations find so troubling.[21]

What Ariarajah calls "wider ecumenism"[22] shifts the model from God-church-world (God works through the church for the sake of the world) to God-world-church. The church is in the world "because God is there bringing about its healing with and without us. Wider ecumenism is participation with God in God's mission in the world."[23] The theological issue, writes Ariarajah, has to do with discernment: Where and how is God at work for the transformation of societies that are not predominantly Christian? What is the scope of God's saving work, and who are the agents of God's mission?[24]

As Ariarajah sees it, the claim that Christ alone is the author of the world's salvation makes God a prisoner of God's own actions in Jesus Christ. Surely, the God of all creation is active in and through other faith traditions. Division of the world into the saved and unsaved belies the actual experience of God's unconditional, generous love in other places, other communities. Christians need to become, and are becoming, less sectarian, seeing themselves less as outsiders entrusted with a saving message and more as insiders who are partners with others in discerning and doing God's will.[25]

It should be noted that Visser 't Hooft's emphasis on the universal saving ministry of Christ did not arise out of a confrontation with other world religions. Rather, it was a response to liberal Protestantism, with its accommodation to culture, and to totalitarian ideologies that demanded complete allegiance.[26] The problem, say his critics, is that he universalized his mid-twentieth-century European experience. In our own era, when religious pluralism is practically everyone's experience, when claiming God's favor for our group alone has been the cause of great suffering, the old paradigm no longer seems to fit.

A CONTINUING LEGACY?

One doesn't have to agree fully with Raiser's "paradigm shift" in ecumenism or Ariarajah's "wider ecumenism" to acknowledge that there is cogency in their challenges. In my judgment, it is not possible or desirable to hold fast to Visser 't Hooft's entire theological agenda in this era. As a longtime participant in the ecumenical movement, I am also convinced, however, that there are elements of Visser 't Hooft's vision that are essential for Christians, then and now.

THE IMPORTANCE OF A SOLID
THEOLOGICAL FOUNDATION

Anyone familiar with churches will recognize the temptation, resisted by some better than others, to substitute ideologically driven assertions for the hard work of wrestling with Scripture, the temptation to use the Bible and church tradition to bolster predetermined conclusions instead of allowing them to challenge culturally informed assumptions. I am tempted to cite examples of this in recent ecumenical documents, but a more constructive approach is to highlight Visser 't Hooft's theological rigor.

A good example is his little book from 1954, *The Ecumenical Movement and the Racial Problem*. Visser 't Hooft begins with a careful examination of the problem—How should the church deal with race relations?—historically and sociologically, concentrating on three situations with which he has firsthand experience: the United States, South Africa, and Germany under Nazi rule. This historical study includes, of course, a review of what major ecumenical conferences have said about the subject. Visser 't Hooft never fails to acknowledge that he stands on the shoulders of others, even as he points out that ecumenical statements about race have too infrequently led to ecumenical action against racism.

The heart of the book, however, is his attempt to deal with the issue theologically. Drawing on Scripture, he argues for the fundamental unity of humankind, but his real focus, characteristically, is ecclesiology. Ecumenical appropriation of biblical scholarship and systematic theology have resulted, he contends, in substantial agreement: "The Church is the people of God, gathered together by Jesus Christ, so as to represent the new humanity."[27] And in this new fellowship, all racial barriers have been torn away. "This basic principle of the supra-racial character of the Christian Church belongs then to its very nature."[28]

Until the late 1970s, racism was generally regarded within the ecumenical movement as a problem of mission (i.e., it undermines the church's witness), and it only came to be seen as an issue of ecclesiology (i.e., racial inclusiveness is a basic mark of the church) once the churches declared apartheid a heresy. Visser 't Hooft anticipated this shift a quarter century earlier. Responding to the "racial problem" is not simply a matter of Christians doing what they ought to do but being what they ought to be. There can be no strategic compromise when the very nature of the church is at stake.

I also appreciate, however, that Visser 't Hooft does not shy away from the hardest questions, ones that demand nuance. In this case, the question is one familiar to US Christians: Is there a place for separate "ethnic churches" within the one supraracial church of Christ? To ask it another way, is it defensible to have denominations or congregations that are structured along racial or ethnic lines? Visser 't Hooft lays out the various arguments without caricature, before stating what he believes to be the slowly emerging consensus, grounded in Scripture and the hard-won lessons of experience: that the formation of such churches must never be more than provisional, that enforced segregation can never be justified, and that where racially distinctive churches exist, for linguistic or other reasons, responsibility rests with these churches to demonstrate that they are members of the one body.[29] And he ends by identifying the task that confronts the churches if they are true to these theological convictions—always aware that racial prejudice, a deeply rooted form of sin, "can only be cured by the discovery of that deep security which is the gift of faith in God's sovereign rule."[30]

In short, Visser 't Hooft exemplifies rigorous theological reflection that is biblical, historical, and pragmatically aimed at changing behavior. I can only hope that this part of his legacy will not be lost.

THE NECESSITY OF THE CHURCH

For Visser 't Hooft, individual Christian is an oxymoron. To be a follower of Jesus Christ is to be incorporated into the fellowship that confesses him as Lord and Savior.[31] The church isn't simply a community in which the gospel of God's reconciling love is taught and through which it is proclaimed. The church, if it is truly the church, is a visible expression of the gospel, a witness to the world of God's power and intention to heal estrangement.

But while the primary reason for Visser 't Hooft's insistence on the necessity of the church is theological, there also is a practical one: Only the church—the whole, universal church—can stand up to the idolatries of the surrounding culture. Desmond Tutu once famously declared that "Apartheid is too strong for a divided church."[32] The German church experience convinced Visser 't Hooft that Nazism was too strong for a divided church, let alone for individuals of good will. The problem, of course, is that the church has itself so often succumbed to idolatry, giving allegiance to worldly powers, providing a religious veneer for dominant values of the society.[33] Thus, as we have seen, the church for Visser 't Hooft is always the *renewing* church, always striving to become what, by God's grace, it is.

A good example of Visser 't Hooft's high, yet clearly Protestant, understanding of the church can be found in his book *The Kingship of Christ*. Drawing on the Pauline Epistles, as well as Ephesians, he argues that "the Church is the concrete, visible manifestation of the crucified and risen Christ in the world. . . . The risen Lord continues to work in the world and the way in which he is present is in and through the Church."[34] He is its head, the source of its growth and measure of its faithfulness. Whenever the church refuses or forgets to listen to him, to be guided by him, it becomes merely a human association of little lasting value to others.[35]

Visser 't Hooft resists the idea, however, of a mystical identification of Christ and the church. "He is the King and the members of the church remain the King's people."[36] In the same way, he resists any blurring of the boundary between the church and the kingdom of God, a blurring he identifies with Roman Catholic ecclesiology. The church is not an end in itself. Its task, a provisional one, is to announce and serve the coming kingdom. It manifests the "already" of Christ's kingship over the world, while pointing to the "not yet realized" day when all things will be united in him.[37]

There are parts of Visser 't Hooft's ecclesiology that I find problematic, especially his supersessionist claim that "the great promises once given to the nation of Israel are now passed on to the spiritual nation, the Church of God . . . the new 'edition' of Israel will accomplish the mission which the old Israel refuses to accomplish."[38] However, his passionate emphasis on the necessity of the church is a counter to the current penchant for isolated spirituality (as if Christianity could be reduced to a matter of private, and often subjective, convictions). In *Has the Ecumenical Movement a Future?*, Visser 't Hooft names three "falsifications of religious life" that keep the church from playing its proper role. One is an institutionalism for which continuity of traditional structures and patterns is a primary concern. Another is the idolatry that treats secondary things as absolutes. And the third is a private piety that unscripturally focuses on the individual soul.[39] For Visser 't Hooft, Christianity is not about "using" Christ for our own salvation but about allowing ourselves to be used by Christ, through the church, for the salvation of the world. I hope this part of his legacy will not be lost.

THE CONTINUING RELEVANCE OF
CONCILIAR ECUMENISM

A more obvious heading would be "the continuing relevance of the ecumenical movement," but Visser 't Hooft's special contribution was to insist on, and provide intellectual foundation for, the particular expression of ecumenism in councils of churches. Bilateral dialogues are certainly important and can address issues that are particularly pertinent to the churches involved; but the multilateral discussions that can take place in a conciliar body open its members to a greater variety of theological perspectives. Any service in the name of Christ is laudable; but when service is done through a council, it also gives witness to the church's unity. Moreover, conciliar ecumenism demonstrates that theological dialogue and service, Faith and Order and Life and Work, belong together in the life of the church.

Visser 't Hooft spoke and wrote often about the nature and purpose of councils of churches, including in his report to the 1963 meeting of the WCC's Central Committee.[40] Nineteen sixty-three marked the twenty-fifth year since the Utrecht conference set up the WCC "in process of formation" and the fifteenth year since the council was formally launched at the assembly in Amsterdam. Looking back over this period, the general secretary makes three points that clarify the nature, and underscore the continuing relevance, of conciliar ecumenism.

1. The essence and ecclesiological significance of a council of churches is the relationship of the members to one another, not their relationship to the structure of the council—not just what they *do* together but what they *are* together. There are many organizations that provide services on behalf of churches. These should not be confused, however, with a council, a fellowship or community, of the churches themselves. Whenever the church speaks of "that council" rather than "our fellowship," it is likely to avoid the mutual accountability that should be a hallmark of ecumenical life.[41]

2. Because of this mutual accountability, a council of churches should be a place, unlike any other, where churches engage in "profound self-examination."[42] Conciliar life, if taken seriously, demands that members grow beyond what he elsewhere calls "ecclesiastical introversion." Visser 't Hooft is convinced that spiritual renewal is possible if churches use the oppor-

tunity of conciliar fellowship to engage in both affirmation and admonition.[43]

3. Councils of churches must not be regarded as ends in themselves. They are by their very nature provisional, always prepared to die in favor of fuller manifestations of communion. To say it another way, they are steps toward richer fellowship *as the church*, which is why councils must not become service agencies aimed at self-perpetuation.[44]

It probably could go without saying that councils of churches have not lived up to this vision! Nearly a half century ago, a member of the WCC staff, after visiting national councils around the world, reached this conclusion: "The key issue is that most churches show only partial commitment to what is involved in being a fellowship of churches. Where there is commitment, it is often to the council as an institution and not to the other churches that comprise its membership. Most councils, thus, are an ecumenical facade behind which churches remain as unecumenical as ever."[45] The current scene is even more troubling. Across the United States, state councils are dying or morphing into interfaith bodies. The National Council of Churches has seen its staff and agenda drastically pared, and Visser 't Hooft would no doubt bemoan the present diminishment of the WCC. While all of this suggests that old *models* of conciliar organization have run their course, I hope it doesn't mean that we lose sight of Visser 't Hooft's insights regarding the continuing relevance of councils of churches in some form.

THE VALUE OF PATIENT IMPATIENCE AND
IMPATIENT PATIENCE

In *Has the Ecumenical Movement a Future?*, Visser 't Hooft laments "the torpidity and the resistance to real renewal so often encountered in the Church."[46] And this, naturally, has infected the movement, which, it certainly can be argued, has been domesticated by the churches it was intended to help reform.

Those that are ecumenically engaged generally refrain from past polemics and cooperate, with prudent moderation, but they seem satisfied with modest gains and, thus, feel no urgent passion for unity. I agree (as would Visser 't Hooft) with the head of the Vatican's Pontifical Council for Promoting Christian Unity, Cardinal Kurt Koch, when he says that what pains him most is that so many Christians are no longer pained by divisions in the body of Christ.[47] Churches have set up offices to take care of ecumenical business, to foster good neighborliness and occasional cooperation, but without internalizing the vision—the passionate, urgent vision—that once made ecumenism, in Temple's words, "the great new fact of our era."[48]

This is where Visser 't Hooft is most prophetic, constantly urging the churches to submit themselves to the pressure of their common calling. "We need impatient people," he writes, "who call for boldness, imagination and forward-looking hope in action."[49] The churches need laypersons who refuse to leave ecumenism to the "professional ecumenists" and their often glacially slow agenda. The movement needs youth who refuse to be content with the ecumenical status quo.[50] "But," he adds, "there is an impatience which gives up and an impatience which builds up."[51] Old models and priorities must be reexamined. New ideas should be welcomed and tested. It would be "sheer ingratitude," however, to discard the lessons of the past, to minimize what God *has* done to heal estrangement or, most importantly, to fail through impatience to trust in God's promise of fuller reconciliation.

I love this tension in Visser 't Hooft—patient impatience, impatient patience—a tension that was not unique to him. In the *Decree on Ecumenism*, Roman Catholic bishops at Vatican II warned of an "imprudent zeal" that can harm ecumenical advance.[52] They are commending, I think, a holy patience that refuses to cut corners in the pursuit of unity grounded in truth (a key Visser 't Hooft theme), a patience that insists that the unity we seek must be the unity God wills and not simply schemes of our devising.

At the same time, however, the bishops declare that present disunity "openly contradicts the will of Christ, scandalizes the world, and damages that most holy cause, the preaching of the gospel to every creature."[53] There is good reason, therefore, to speak also of a holy impatience that deplores the constant, subtle pressure to tame, through prudent moderation, the Spirit's call to greater oneness in Christ. The gospel imperative "that all may be one" allows no self-congratulation or compromise or delay. I am reminded of Visser 't Hooft's statement not long after the end of the ecumenically electrifying Second Vatican Council: "Everything, or nearly everything, still remains to be done." This is truly a theology of *semper reformanda*—and yet, Christians must also live patiently in the gospel-informed hope that it is God's will that matters and that God's will *will* be done.[54]

The well-known missiologist David Bosch, in his classic volume, *Transforming Mission*, suggests that the proper attitude for mission-minded Christians is "bold humility or humble boldness"—boldly declaring a faith they believe is true and just, while humbly confessing the limitations of their perspective, their consequent need for others, and their trust in the One who guides them into fuller understanding.[55] The knowledge that Christians have a word from God makes them bold and impatient. The knowledge that it is *God's* makes them humble and patient. This part of Visser 't Hooft's legacy I hope is never lost.

MAINTAINING NECESSARY TENSIONS

Even where the paradigm of Visser 't Hooft's era seems dated, we can be instructed, I am convinced, by keeping his emphases in tension with more current perspectives.

UNITY AND JUSTICE

Visser 't Hooft's *Memoirs* includes a two-page chapter, "Is This Really War?," that is both agonizing and insightful.[56] He and his colleagues at the WCC (then "in process of formation") had been insisting to the churches that the impending battle against Nazi Germany should not be regarded as a crusade. The church, knowing itself to be the one body of Christ, should not so identify with any political cause or ideology that it fragments the body. But now he is having second thoughts. Unity is central to the gospel, but so is opposing radical injustice and military aggression. Can the church really remain silent when faced with such idolatrous nihilism? Unless the answer to this question is a clear "No," he concludes, the church is in danger of "living in the clouds," of little use to its members who need guidance in the face of conflict here and now.

This tension between unity and justice was Visser 't Hooft's constant companion in his role as ecumenical leader. It surfaced during the Cold War when the WCC could neither write off churches in Communist countries (the church's unity included them) nor refrain from bearing witness against violations of basic rights perpetrated on both sides of the Iron Curtain—even though council statements periodically threatened the tenuous connection. We must, he writes in his *Memoirs*, "accept the full spiritual tension in which God has placed us."[57] The tension surfaced again in the struggle against apartheid. As we have seen, Visser 't Hooft considered apartheid a heresy long before it was declared to be such by various churches. But his *Memoirs* details the extraordinary lengths to which he went in attempting to keep churches on both sides of this divide in the council.[58]

Visser 't Hooft, as noted in chapter 1, participated in both Faith and Order and Life and Work, maintaining throughout his ministry that their integration is essential for any adequate understanding of conciliar ecumenism. The tension between them, however, never really abated and, arguably, has become more acute in the years since his death. The voices of the oppressed have grown louder, the appreciation for unity-in-diversity has grown greater—and the more diverse the church, the harder it is to pursue justice issues together.[59]

In my own writings, I have drawn on Visser 't Hooft to help me articulate principles for addressing this tension:[60]

- The church *is* one. If this were taken to heart, Christians should be able to bring disagreements over social and environmental questions to the table without fearing division.

- In the last analysis, the church's capacity to demonstrate unity, even when its members disagree, may be its greatest contribution to peace and justice—especially in an era when civil discourse is in such short supply.

- The same divisive issues that plague human society are obviously in the church. It simply isn't possible to work for ecclesial unity without, at the same time, addressing such matters as racism, poverty, and war.

- The unity of the church, while it can be glimpsed in the present, is finally an eschatological goal. Christians may at times need to disrupt present partial "unities" for the sake of the greater wholeness promised by God.

- Just as Bonhoeffer warned against a "cheap grace," so ecumenists should warn against a "cheap unity" that avoids contentious issues for fear of disruption. Costly unity means a refusal to withdraw from the ambiguities of historical actions in order to preserve shallow harmony in the church.

In the early years of the ecumenical movement, the emphasis in the unity-justice dialectic was on the former; in recent years, the pendulum has clearly swung in the other direction. A rereading of Visser 't Hooft may help us find a better balance.

UNIVERSAL AND PARTICULAR

As we have seen, Visser 't Hooft's insistence on the universality of the church, as a sign of human unity, was shaped, in large part, by the struggle against the German Christian Movement, which opposed the very ideas of a universal church and "world citizenship." Visser 't Hooft's response was unequivocal: A focus on national sovereignty can easily become, as it did in 1930s Germany, an idolatrous distortion of Christian identity.[61] The followers of Christ should not think of themselves as Christian *Germans* or Christian *Americans*, but German *Christians* or American *Christians*, connected to brothers and sisters in Christ from other countries by bonds deeper than nationality. The acid test of an ecumenical sensibility is whether Christians, in times of war, can affirm their solidarity with members of the church in nations their own nation calls enemies.

Of course, the gospel's call to oppose injustice may well lead Christians to side with their nation in times of conflict. Visser 't Hooft was certainly not neutral in the fight against National Socialism. But the basis of his stance was the gospel, not national affiliation; and, in any case, he insisted, the bonds of prayer must not be broken. If the church cannot demonstrate such universality, then people will surely look elsewhere for a solution to the problem of global fragmentation.[62]

Today the picture looks different. We now see that what Visser 't Hooft and his contemporary colleagues thought of as universal was often just European Christianity in other settings. "Christian universalism" can feel like code for practices destructive of particular local cultures. Isn't it possible, however, that both perspectives are needed, and that the ecumenical movement is stronger when it holds them in tension? As I write this, political leaders in the United States, including its president, take pride in the slogan "America First," use language that demonizes those of different nations and ethnicities, and propose policies that would literally and figuratively wall this country off from other parts of the human family. Don't Christians need, once again, to lift up a vision of universal solidarity, a vision grounded in the faith of the church?

When thinking of this, I find it useful to recall a statement attributed to the Supreme Court Justice Oliver Wendell Holmes Jr.: "I wouldn't give a fig for simplicity this side of complexity, but I would give my right arm for simplicity on the far side of complexity." Christians shouldn't give a fig for a vision of the universal church that doesn't take full account of diverse local contexts. But isn't it possible to envision a universal church on the "far side" of a genuine encounter with such particularity? A rereading of Visser 't Hooft may help us ask this question.

CHRISTIAN WITNESS AND INTERFAITH RELATIONS

Since Visser 't Hooft's rejection of syncretism is such a core principle of his theology, it needs to be examined more carefully than we have yet done. Syncretism, as Visser 't Hooft understood it, is "essentially a revolt against the uniqueness of revelation in history."[63] It is the view that holds that there are many ways to touch divine reality, that all expressions of religious truth are inadequate, and, therefore, "that it is necessary to harmonize as much as possible all religious ideas and experiences so as to create one universal religion for mankind."[64]

There is real tension within Visser 't Hooft's thinking on this topic. He laments that Western Christianity has often looked down on other religions, as if it alone were the possessor of truth. It has promoted a kind of universalism that seems only or primarily concerned with the Christian part of humanity. It has often been, as others charge, arrogant and narrow-minded.[65] Still, he argues that Christianity must never see itself as one of many diverse contributions to the religious life of humanity. Jesus Christ is *the* definitive revelation of God in history. "The attitude of the Christian Church to the religions can therefore only be the attitude of the witness who [humbly] points to the one Lord Jesus Christ as Lord of all men."[66]

Visser 't Hooft was convinced that it is possible to make such claims while also entering into dialogue with other religions—dialogue that seeks to listen, understand, and provide mutual enrichment. In his writings, he affirms what W. E. Hocking called "reverence for reverence," preferring conversation with people who have definite convictions to those of "uncertain and vague opinions." "The fact that Christians believe that they know the source of divine truth does not mean that they have nothing to learn from men of other faiths."[67] He frequently encouraged fellow Christians to cooperate with people of other religions in matters of public life. His language, however, is telling: "We will have to accept that new *duty*. . . . But we will have to make it perfectly plain that our willingness to cooperate does not in any way imply a willingness to compromise on the basic issues of faith."[68] As far as I can tell, Visser 't Hooft never addressed the question "Can non-Christians be saved?"—likely because he would have seen the question as too individualistic. The primary issue is the salvation of the world, and that is being accomplished by God through Jesus Christ.

This position raises several obvious questions: Is it really the case that Christianity is threatened by a clamor for a single world religion? In my experience, active Muslims, Jews, Buddhists, and Hindus generally value the spiritual integrity of their religious traditions, even if they affirm that truth may also reside with others. Isn't it possible to defend the uniqueness, the particularity, of God's revelation in Christ and still be open to the possibility that God may be known, may even act salvifically, in other ways? Are dialogue and cooperation simply "duties" Christians must perform in a pluralistic era? Aren't they better understood as a privilege through which Christians may participate in God's mission of service and reconciliation? Is conversation truly "dialogue" if Christians enter into it with the certainty that they already know the truth about God and God's will for creation?[69]

Having raised these questions, however, I also want to agree with Visser 't Hooft that syncretism *is* a problem. In his words, "Western theology has very often, in seeking to accommodate the Christian message to the Western cultural environment, distorted its substance and thus become syncretistic."[70] When the society attempts to co-opt Christian faith in order to make it a bolster for financial prosperity or military defense of national interests or the cult of personality, there is surely a need for the church to assert its own identity and integrity.

It is interesting to note that Visser 't Hooft's sharpest critique is not aimed at other world religions[71] but at such figures as Rousseau and Goethe, for promoting a universal religion without revelation; Whitman and Lawrence, for reviving a pagan religiosity of nature and fertility; Jung, for claiming the existence of a universal religious unconscious; and Toynbee, for reducing religion to supposedly universal philosophical teachings.[72] Isn't it possible to distinguish between neighbors who worship the Divine as part of major religious traditions and those who promote more individual quests—taking their religion à la carte, picking and choosing from a variety of beliefs and practices? A rereading of Visser 't Hooft may help us sort through these questions.

LIBERAL AND CONSERVATIVE

All biblically grounded Christians recognize the prayer of Jesus in John 17 that his followers may all be one. In the contemporary church, however, many Christians (often called "conservative" or "evangelical") are suspicious of the ecumenical movement, often fearing that it involves a compromise of gospel truth. Meanwhile, other Christians (often called "liberal" or "progressive") are suspicious of evangelism, often fearing that it leads to intolerance. It's not that they are not committed to Christ, but they are little concerned with whether others are committed to him. Visser 't Hooft defies such labeling and bridges any such divide.[73] He was conservative in his fervent rejection of relativism. The center of the church is Jesus Christ as witnessed to in Scripture! In the words of the Barmen Declaration, he is "the one Word of God which we have to hear and which we have to trust and obey in life and in death." It is also the common calling of Scripture, however, to manifest the church's given unity as a visible testimony to the gospel. Yes to unity. Yes to evangelism. And yes to the proclamation of the gospel through ministries of charity and justice. There are those, he writes in *No Other Name,* who are so preoccupied with preserving the core revelation that they forget the needs of humanity, and those who are so focused on human need that they become uprooted from the original message.[74] It is, for Visser 't Hooft, an utterly false alternative.

The church historian Martin Marty once characterized the split in the contemporary church this way: "The civil people are not committed and the committed people aren't civil!"[75] Visser 't Hooft was evangelical about an ecumenical faith. He passionately believed that Christians, in the words of Paul's Letter to the Romans, are to "welcome one another just as Christ has welcomed us" and thereby call others to trust in God's welcoming grace. I am convinced that a rereading of Visser 't Hooft, a man both committed and civil on the basis of Scripture, can help us move beyond the liberal-conservative divide.

THE TASK OF OUR GENERATION

In his *Memoirs*, Visser 't Hooft notes that the early 1930s was a period of great uncertainty and confusion for the emerging ecumenical movement. Great leaders had passed from the scene. There was a multiplicity of ecumenical organizations, all of them under financial constraint. Those whose priority was *rapprochement* in the realm of ethics and service, and those who gave priority to *rapprochement* in the realm of doctrine and church order, were practically in separate movements. Perhaps most importantly, ecumenism had not really taken root in the churches.[76] I could have drawn up the same list of challenges when I became general secretary of the National Council of Churches in 2008!

There are also similarities of social context. Visser 't Hooft and colleagues pursued their vision of wholeness in the midst of growing nationalism and xenophobia, of political polarization and social fragmentation. The world needed an embodied word of reconciliation from the church! Who can deny that the same is true today?

And yet, as noted at the beginning of this chapter, there are also significant differences between Visser 't Hooft's era and our own. "Each generation," he wrote in 1955, "has its specific task. That is as true in the ecumenical movement as it is in other realms. . . . In order to know our next assignment we must know what assignments were given to previous generations."[77] My hope is that this examination of how Willem Visser 't Hooft saw his task will help this generation see its own more clearly.

Notes

1. Bilheimer, *Breakthrough*, 75.

2. Bilheimer, *Breakthrough*, 75.

3. See Müller-Fahrenholz, "No Communion without Compassion," 167.

4. This claim is made by the WCC's longtime director of Church and Society. See Paul Abrecht, "Ecumenical Social Thinking in a Changing World," in Mackie and West, *Sufficiency of God*, 148.

5. van der Bent, *W. A. Visser 't Hooft*, 41.

6. Cited in Douglas John Hall, *The End of Christendom and the Future of Christianity* (Valley Forge, PN: Trinity Press International, 1997), 13. Hall is referring to a work by E. Stanley Jones, Kenneth Scott Latourette, and John Mackay published in 1934.

7. Samuel P. Huntington, *The Clash of Civilizations and the Remaking of World Order* (New York: Simon & Schuster, 1996), 51.

8. Visser 't Hooft, *Memoirs*, ch. 5.

9. See National Council of Churches of Christ in the USA, "The Authority of the Church in the World," in Kinnamon, *The Ecumenical Movement*, 2nd ed., 168.

10. Bea and Visser 't Hooft, *Peace among Christians*, dust jacket.

11. Visser 't Hooft, *No Other Name*, 102–3.

12. Konrad Raiser, *Ecumenism in Transition: A Paradigm Shift in the Ecumenical Movement?* (Geneva: WCC Publications, 1991), 41–46. Raiser names a fourth component of the "classical understanding"—"history as the central category of thought"—which I incorporate in other parts of this discussion. See, e.g., Visser 't Hooft, *No Other Name*, 107–8.

13. Visser 't Hooft, *No Other Name*, 102.

14. Raiser, *Ecumenism in Transition*, 52. "The basic insights of the former paradigm," writes Raiser, "must be incorporated into the new paradigm" (77). Ariarajah offers a glowing tribute to the pioneer generations of ecumenists, including (especially) Visser 't Hooft, in S. Wesley Ariarajah, "Wider Ecumenism: A Threat or a Promise?," *Ecumenical Review* 50, no. 3 (1998): 322–25.

15. S. Wesley Ariarajah, "Wider Ecumenism: Some Theological Perspectives" (paper presented at the Ecumenical Institute, Chateau de Bossey, July 2003).

16. Raiser, *Ecumenism in Transition*, 58–59, 62.

17. Joseph Sittler, "Called to Unity," in Kinnamon, ed., *The Ecumenical Movement*, 2nd ed., 255. For a fuller discussion, see Kinnamon, *Can A Renewal Movement Be Renewed?*, 47–48.

18. Raiser, *Ecumenism in Transition*, 60, 66.

19. Raiser, *Ecumenism in Transition*, 65–66.

20. Raiser, *Ecumenism in Transition*, 76. For a fuller discussion of this dimension of Raiser's argument, see Michael Kinnamon, "Conflicting World Views and the Ecumenical Quest," in *The Vision of Christian Unity: Essays in Honor of Paul A. Crow, Jr.*, ed. Thomas F. Best and Theodore J. Nottingham (Indianapolis, IN: Oikoumene Publications, 1997), 105–19.

21. Raiser, *Ecumenism in Transition*, 57, 78. Ariarajah makes this point clearly in the unpublished paper, "Wider Ecumenism: Some Theological Perspectives."

22. In "Wider Ecumenism: A Threat or a Promise?," Ariarajah recounts an exchange in which Visser 't Hooft expressed strong opposition to the term *wider ecumenism*. Visser 't Hooft's concern has merit, writes Ariarajah, if its use suggests that Visser 't Hooft and his contemporaries were oblivious to the oneness of the whole human family in God's salvific plan, or if those who use it fail to appreciate the commitment and daring of the earlier generations of ecumenists (321, 324).

23. Ariarajah, "Wider Ecumenism: Some Theological Perspectives."

24. Ariarajah, "Wider Ecumenism: A Threat or a Promise?," 327–28.

25. Ariarajah, "Wider Ecumenism: Some Theological Perspectives."

26. See Raiser, *Ecumenism in Transition*, 55–56.

27. Visser 't Hooft, *Ecumenical Movement and the Racial Problem*, 50.

28. Visser 't Hooft, *Ecumenical Movement and the Racial Problem*, 53.

29. Visser 't Hooft, *Ecumenical Movement and the Racial Problem*, 8, 62.

30. Visser 't Hooft, *Ecumenical Movement and the Racial Problem*, 67.

31. See, e. g., Visser 't Hooft, *Kingship of Christ*, 90.

32. Desmond Tutu, "Towards *Koinonia* in Faith, Life, and Witness,"

in Kinnamon, *The Ecumenical Movement*, 2nd ed., 55.

33. Visser 't Hooft, *Kingship of Christ*, 111.

34. Visser 't Hooft, *Kingship of Christ*, 94–95.

35. Visser 't Hooft, *Kingship of Christ*, 95–96, 100.

36. Visser 't Hooft, *Kingship of Christ*, 96.

37. Visser 't Hooft, *Kingship of Christ*, 99.

38. Visser 't Hooft, *Kingship of Christ*, 91–92, 90.

39. Visser 't Hooft, *Has the Ecumenical Movement a Future?*, 93.

40. Bea and Visser 't Hooft, *Peace among Christians*, 78–81.

41. For a fuller discussion, see Kinnamon, *Vision of the Ecumenical Movement*, ch. 7.

42. Bea and Visser 't Hooft, *Peace among Christians*, 80.

43. Visser 't Hooft, *Pressure of Our Common Calling*, 37. The principle of our "mutual affirmation and admonition" was made prominent in ecumenical dialogue by the Lutheran-Reformed theological conversations in the United States. See Keith F. Nickle and Timothy F. Lull, eds., *A Common Calling: The Witness of Our Reformation Churches in North America Today* (Minneapolis: Augsburg Fortress, 1993). The title of the report echoes one of Visser 't Hooft's favorite phrases.

44. See, e.g., Bea and Visser 't Hooft, *Peace among Christians,* 80.

45. Quoted in Kinnamon, *Vision of the Ecumenical Movement*, 91.

46. Visser 't Hooft, *Has the Ecumenical Movement a Future?*, 34.

47. Kurt Koch, "Fundamental Aspects of Ecumenism and Future Perspectives," (paper presented at Catholic University of America, November 2011).

48. Visser 't Hooft, *Has the Ecumenical Movement a Future?*, 40–41. See also Kinnamon, *Vision of the Ecumenical Movement*, 84.

49. Visser 't Hooft, *Has the Ecumenical Movement a Future?*, 52–53.

50. Visser 't Hooft made the point in his address to the Ecumenical Youth Assembly in 1960. An excerpt from his remarks is quoted in Philip Potter, "Youth and the Ecumenical Movement," in Mackie and West, *Sufficiency of God*, 219.

51. Visser 't Hooft, *Has the Ecumenical Movement a Future?*, 53. Bilheimer calls for more of this second kind of impatience in *Break-*

through, 223.

52. Second Vatican Council, "Decree on Ecumenism," par. 4.

53. "Decree on Ecumenism," par. 1.

54. Visser 't Hooft, "Task of the Churches," 183.

55. David J. Bosch, *Transforming Mission: Paradigm Shifts in Theology of Mission* (Maryknoll, NY: Orbis, 1991), 489.

56. Visser 't Hooft, *Memoirs*, 113–15.

57. Visser 't Hooft, *Memoirs*, 223; for a focus on Cold War tensions, see ch. 35.

58. Visser 't Hooft, *Memoirs*, ch. 34.

59. See Kinnamon, *Can a Renewal Movement Be Renewed?*, 57.

60. For a fuller discussion, see Kinnamon, *Can a Renewal Movement Be Renewed?*, 59–62.

61. See Müller-Fahrenholz, "No Communion without Compassion," 170.

62. Visser 't Hooft, *No Other Name*, 94.

63. Visser 't Hooft, *No Other Name*, 48.

64. Visser 't Hooft, *No Other Name*, 11.

65. Visser 't Hooft, *No Other Name*, 116. See van der Bent, *W. A. Visser 't Hooft*, 52–54.

66. Visser 't Hooft, *No Other Name*, 116; see also 95, 117.

67. Visser 't Hooft, *No Other Name*, 117–18.

68. Visser 't Hooft, *No Other Name*, 122.

69. For a similar argument, see van der Bent, *W. A. Visser 't Hooft*, 53–54.

70. Visser 't Hooft, *No Other Name*, 123.

71. He does contend, however, that the Bahá'í religion is an example of syncretism, as is the modern Hindu reform movement associated with Ramakrishna, Vivekananda, Radhakrishnan, and Gandhi. Visser 't Hooft, *No Other Name*, 43, 36–40.

72. Visser 't Hooft, *No Other Name*, 29–35. As early as the 1930s, Visser 't Hooft attacked what he called "the worship of life," as exemplified by Nietzsche, Freud, and D. H. Lawrence. See Visser 't Hooft, *None Other Gods*, 140–48.

73. If I had to choose a single passage from Visser 't Hooft's writings as a summary of his theological vision, it might be in *No Other Name*, p. 101. There he argues that the church has a double function: (1) to manifest in its own life the universality of the new reconciled humanity, and (2) to be the messenger of God's universal offer of reconciliation—unity and evangelistic witness, which can include service and ministries of justice. In this way, he bridged the liberal (ecumenical) / conservative (evangelical) divide.

74. Visser 't Hooft, *No Other Name*, 115.

75. Quoted in Robert Jewett, *Christian Tolerance: Paul's Message to the Modern Church* (Philadelphia: Westminster, 1982), 9.

76. Visser 't Hooft, *Memoirs*, 76.

77. Visser 't Hooft, "Our Ecumenical Task," 310.

Bibliography

PRIMARY SOURCES

Bea, Augustin Cardinal, and W. A. Visser 't Hooft. *Peace among Christians.* Translated by Judith Moses. New York: Association Press, 1967.

Visser 't Hooft, W. A. "Accommodation, True or False?" *South East Asia Journal of Theology* 8, no. 3 (1967): 5–18.

———. *Anglo-Catholicism and Orthodoxy: A Protestant View.* London: SCM, 1933.

———. *The Background of the Social Gospel in America.* St. Louis: Bethany, 1963.

———. "The Calling of the World Council of Churches." *Ecumenical Review* 14, no. 2 (1962): 216–26.

———. "The Church as an Oecumenical Society." In *The Church and Its Function in Society*, by Willem A. Visser 't Hooft and J. H. Oldham, 88–100. London: George Allen & Unwin, 1937.

———. "Dietrich Bonhoeffer and the Self-Understanding of the Ecumenical Movement." *Ecumenical Review* 28, no. 2 (1976): 198–203.

———. *The Ecumenical Movement and the Racial Problem.* Paris: UNESCO, 1954.

———. "Faith and Order and the Second Assembly of the World Council of Churches." In *The Third World Conference on Faith and Order*, edited by Oliver S. Tomkins, 128–38. London: SCM, 1953.

———. *The Fatherhood of God in an Age of Emancipation.* Geneva: WCC, 1982.

———. "The General Ecumenical Development since 1948." In *The Ecumenical Advance: A History of the Ecumenical Movement*, edited by Harold E. Fey, vol. 2, 1–26. 2nd ed. Geneva: WCC, 1970.

———. *The Genesis and Formation of the World Council of Churches.* Geneva: WCC, 1982.

———. "The Ground of Our Unity." In *The Nature of the Unity We Seek: Official Report of the North American Conference on Faith and Order*, edited by Paul S. Minear, 121–26. St. Louis: Bethany, 1958.

———. *Has the Ecumenical Movement a Future?* Belfast: Christian Journals, 1974.

———. "The Historical Significance of Stockholm 1925." In *The Gospel for All Realms of Life*, 1–16. Geneva: WCC, 1975.

———. "I Have Overcome the World." In *Christus Victor: The Report of the World Conference of Christian Youth*, edited by Denzil G. M. Patrick, 230–35. Geneva: Conference Headquarters, 1939.

———. "Jesus Christ the Reconciler." *Student World* 50, no. 1 (1957): 22–30.

———. "Karl Barth and the Ecumenical Movement." *Ecumenical Review* 32 no. 2 (1980): 129–51.

———. *The Kingship of Christ: An Interpretation of Recent European Theology.* New York: Harper, 1948.

———. "Life through the Church." *Student World* 51, no. 3 (1958): 1237–45.

———. "The Mandate of the Ecumenical Movement," In *The Uppsala Report 1968: Official Report of the Fourth Assembly of the World Council of Churches*, edited by Norman Goodall, 313–23. Geneva: WCC, 1968.

———. *Memoirs.* London: SCM, 1973.

———. "Missions as the Test of Faith." In *Witness in Six Continents: Records of the Meeting of the Commission on World Mission and Evangelism of the World Council of Churches*, edited by Ronald K. Orchard, 20–28. London: Edinburgh House, 1964.

———. *The New Delhi Report: The Third Assembly of the World Council of Churches.* New York: Association Press, 1962.

———. *New Delhi Speaks.* London: SCM, 1962.

———. *None Other Gods.* New York: Harper, 1937.

———. *No Other Name: The Choice between Syncretism and Christian Universalism.* London: SCM, 1963.

———. "Opening Address." In *Christus Victor: The Report of the World Conference of Christian Youth,* edited by Denzil G. M. Patrick, 146–49. Geneva: Conference Headquarters, 1939.

———. "Our Ecumenical Task in the Light of History." *Ecumenical Review* 7, no. 4 (1955): 309–20.

———. "Pan-Christians Yesterday and Today." *Ecumenical Review* 32, no. 4 (1980): 387–95.

———. "Pluralism—Temptation or Opportunity." In *Peace among Christians,* by Augustin Cardinal Bea and W. A. Visser 't Hooft, 205–34. Translated by Judith Moses. New York: Association Press, 1967.

———. *The Pressure of Our Common Calling.* Garden City, NY: Doubleday, 1959.

———. "Renewal and Wholeness." *Ecumenical Review* 4, no. 4 (1952): 385–92.

———. "Questions about the Future of the World Council of Churches." *Ecumenical Review* 38, no. 2 (1986): 133–39.

———. *Rembrandt and the Gospel.* Translated by Gregor K. Smith. New York: Meridian, 1960.

———. *The Renewal of the Church.* London: SCM, 1956.

———. "The Significance of the World Council of Churches." In *Man's Disorder and God's Design,* edited by W. A. Visser 't Hooft, 182–95. The Universal Church in God's Design 1. New York: Harper, 1948.

———. "The Super-Church and the Ecumenical Movement." *Ecumenical Review* 10, no. 4 (1958): 365–85.

———. "The Task of the Churches in the New Ecumenical Situation." In *Peace among Christians,* by Augustin Cardinal Bea and W. A. Visser 't Hooft, 181–98. Translated by Judith Moses. New York: Association Press, 1967.

———. "The Task of the Christian Community Today." *Student World* 33, no. 1 (1940): 77–86.

———. *Teachers and the Teaching Authorities.* Geneva: WCC Publications, 2000.

———. "The Una Sancta and the Local Church." *Ecumenical Review* 13, no. 1. (1960): 2–13.

218   BIBLIOGRAPHY

———. "Various Meanings of Unity and the Unity Which the World Council of Churches Seeks to Promote." *Ecumenical Review* 8, no. 1 (1955): 18–29.

———. "Weakness and Strength of the Christian Community." *Student World* 30, no. 4 (1937).

———. "World Conference on Church and Society." *Ecumenical Review* 18, no. 4 (1966): 417–25.

———. "The Word 'Ecumenical'—Its History and Use." In *A History of the Ecumenical Movement 1517–1948*, edited by Ruth Rouse and Stephen Charles Neill, 735–40. 2nd ed. Philadelphia: Westminster, 1967.

———. *The Wretchedness and Greatness of the Church.* Translated by Dorothy Mackie and Hugh Martin. London: SCM, 1944.

SELECTED SECONDARY SOURCES

Abrecht, Paul. "Ecumenical Social Thinking in a Changing World." In *The Sufficiency of God: Essays on the Ecumenical Hope in Honor of W. A. Visser 't Hooft*, edited by Robert C. Mackie and Charles C. West, 148–58. Philadelphia: Westminster, 1963.

———. Review of *Memoirs* by W. A. Visser 't Hooft. *Ecumenical Review* 40, nos. 3–4 (1988): 539–43.

Ariarajah, S. Wesley. "Wider Ecumenism: A Threat or a Promise?" *Ecumenical Review* 50, no. 3 (1998): 321–29.

———. "Wider Ecumenism: Some Theological Perspectives." Paper presented at the Ecumenical Institute, Chateau de Bossey, July 2003.

Barth, Karl. *Against the Stream: Shorter Post-War Writings.* London: SCM, 1954.

———. *The Church and the Churches.* Grand Rapids: Eerdmans, 2005.

Berkhof, Hendrikus. "Visser 't Hooft as Ecumenical Theologian." *Ecumenical Review* 38, no. 2 (1986): 203–8.

Bilheimer, Robert A. *Breakthrough: The Emergence of the Ecumenical Tradition.* Grand Rapids: Eerdmans, 1989.

Bonhoeffer, Dietrich. "The Confessing Church and the Ecumenical Movement." In *The Ecumenical Movement: An Anthology of Key*

Texts and Voices, edited by Michael Kinnamon, 7–12. Geneva: WCC Publications, 2016.

Bonino, José Míguez. "The Concern for a Vital and Coherent Theology." *Ecumenical Review* 41, no. 2 (1989): 160–76.

Bosch, David J. *Transforming Mission: Paradigm Shifts in Theology of Mission*. Maryknoll, NY: Orbis, 1991.

Bria, Ion. "The Eastern Orthodox in the Ecumenical Movement." *Ecumenical Review* 38, no. 2 (1986): 216–27.

Brouwer, Arie R. *Ecumenical Testimony*. Grand Rapids: Eerdmans, 1991.

Castro, Emilio. "Editorial." *Ecumenical Review* 38, no. 2 (1986): 121–26.

Chirgwin, A. M. *These I Have Known*. London: London Missionary Society, 1964.

Clements, Keith. *Ecumenical Dynamic: Living in More Than One Place at Once*. Geneva: WCC Publications, 2013.

Cochrane, Arthur C. *The Church's Confession under Hitler*. Philadelphia: Westminster, 1962.

Fischer, Martin. "The Confessing Church and the Ecumenical Movement." In *The Sufficiency of God: Essays on the Ecumenical Hope in Honor of W. A. Visser 't Hooft*, edited by Robert C. Mackie and Charles C. West, 129–47. Philadelphia: Westminster, 1963.

Gérard, François C. *The Future of the Church: The Theology of Renewal of Willem Adolf Visser 't Hooft*. Pittsburg: Pickwick, 1974.

Hall, Douglas John. *The End of Christendom and the Future of Christianity*. Valley Forge, PN: Trinity Press International, 1997.

Hromadka, Josef L. "Biblical Theology in the Ecumenical Struggle." In *The Sufficiency of God: Essays on the Ecumenical Hope in Honor of W. A. Visser 't Hooft*, edited by Robert C. Mackie and Charles C. West, 17–23. Philadelphia: Westminster, 1963.

Huntington, Samuel P. *The Clash of Civilizations and the Remaking of World Order*. New York: Simon & Schuster, 1996.

Jewett, Robert. *Christian Tolerance: Paul's Message to the Modern Church*. Philadelphia: Westminster, 1982.

Jonson, Jonas. *Wounded Visions: Unity, Justice, and Peace in the World Church after 1968*. Translated by Norman A. Hjelm. Grand Rapids: Eerdmans, 2013.

Kessler, Diane, and Michael Kinnamon. *Councils of Churches and the Ecumenical Vision*. Geneva: WCC Publications, 2000.

Kinnamon, Michael. *Can a Renewal Movement Be Renewed? Questions for the Future of Ecumenism.* Grand Rapids: Eerdmans, 2014.

———. "Conflicting Worldviews and the Ecumenical Quest." In *The Vision of Christian Unity: Essays in Honor of Paul A. Crow, Jr.*, edited by Thomas F. Best and Theodore J. Nottingham, 105–19. Indianapolis, IN: Oikoumene Publications, 1997.

———, ed. *The Ecumenical Movement: An Anthology of Key Texts and Voices.* 2nd ed. Geneva: WCC Publications, 2016.

———, ed. *Signs of the Spirit: Official Report of the Seventh Assembly.* Geneva: WCC Publications, 1991.

———. *Truth and Community: Diversity and Its Limits in the Ecumenical Movement.* Grand Rapids: Eerdmans, 1988.

———. *The Vision of the Ecumenical Movement: And How It Has Been Impoverished by Its Friends.* St. Louis: Chalice, 2003.

Kinnamon, Michael, and Brian E. Cope, eds. *The Ecumenical Movement: An Anthology of Key Texts and Voices.* Grand Rapids: Eerdmans, 1997.

Koch, Kurt. "Fundamental Aspects of Ecumenism and Future Perspectives." Paper presented at Catholic University of America, November 2011.

Mackie, Robert C. "W. A. Visser 't Hooft: An Appreciation." In *The Sufficiency of God: Essays on the Ecumenical Hope in Honor of W. A. Visser 't Hooft*, edited by Robert C. Mackie and Charles C. West, 7–16. Philadelphia: Westminster, 1963.

Mackie, Robert C., and Charles C. West, eds. *The Sufficiency of God: Essays on the Ecumenical Hope in Honor of W. A. Visser 't Hooft.* Philadelphia: Westminster, 1963.

McAfee Brown, Robert. *The Ecumenical Revolution.* New York: Doubleday, 1969.

Meyer, Harding. *That All May Be One: Perceptions and Models of Ecumenicity.* Translated by William G. Rusch. Grand Rapids: Eerdmans, 1999.

Moltmann, Jürgen, *The Future of Creation: Collected Essays.* Translated by Margaret Kohl. Philadelphia: Fortress Press, 1979.

Mulder, D. C. "'None Other Gods'—'No Other Name.'" *Ecumenical Review* 38, no. 2 (1986): 209–15.

Müller-Fahrenholz, Geiko. "No Communion without Compassion: Visser 't Hooft." *Christian Century*, February 15, 1984, 166–70.

Nelson, J. Robert, ed. *No Man Is Alien: Essays on the Unity of Mankind.* Leiden: Brill, 1971.

Newbigin, Lesslie. "The Legacy of W. A. Visser 't Hooft." *International Bulletin of Missionary Research* 16, no. 2 (April 1992): 78–82.

———. *Unfinished Agenda: An Autobiography.* Grand Rapids: Eerdmans, 1985.

———. "W. A. Visser 't Hooft 1900–1985." In *Mission Legacies: Biographical Studies of Leaders of the Modern Missionary Movement*, edited by Gerald H. Anderson et al., 117–22. Maryknoll, NY: Orbis, 1994.

Nickle, Keith F., and Timothy F. Lull, eds. *A Common Calling: The Witness of Our Reformation Churches in North America Today.* Minneapolis: Augsburg Fortress, 1993.

Niebuhr, H. Richard. *Christ and Culture.* New York: Harper & Row, 1951.

Niebuhr, Reinhold. "The Development of a Social Ethic in the Ecumenical Movement." In *The Sufficiency of God: Essays on the Ecumenical Hope in Honor of W. A. Visser 't Hooft*, edited by Robert C. Mackie and Charles C. West, 111–28. Philadelphia: Westminster, 1963.

Oldham, J. H. *The Oxford Conference: Official Report.* Chicago: Willett, Clark, 1937.

Papaderos, Alexandros. "The 'Gadfly' on Trial: The 'Political' Commitment of the World Council of Churches." In *Voices of Unity: Essays in Honour of Willem Adolf Visser 't Hooft on the Occasion of His 80th Birthday*, edited by Ans J. van der Bent, 78–91. Geneva: WCC, 1981.

Parrott, Bob. *Albert C. Outler: The Gifted Dilettante.* Anderson, IN: Bristol Books, 1999.

Potter, Philip. "But Still It Moves: A Review of the *Memoirs* of W. A. Visser 't Hooft." *Ecumenical Review* 25, no. 3 (1973): 377–81.

———. "Youth and the Ecumenical Movement." In *The Sufficiency of God: Essays on the Ecumenical Hope in Honor of W. A. Visser 't Hooft*, edited by Robert C. Mackie and Charles C. West, 207–19. Philadelphia: Westminster, 1963.

Raiser, Konrad. *Ecumenism in Transition: A Paradigm Shift in the Ecumenical Movement?* Geneva: WCC Publications, 1991.

Rouse, Ruth, and Stephen Charles Neil, eds. *A History of the Ecumenical Movement 1517–1948.* 2nd ed. Philadelphia: Westminster, 1967.

Thomas, M. M. "Ecumenism in Asia: An Assessment." In *Voices of Unity Essays in Honour of Willem Adolf Visser 't Hooft on the Occasion of His 80th Birthday*, edited by Ans J. van der Bent, 92–101. Geneva: WCC, 1981.

Thomas, M. M., and Paul Abrecht, eds. *World Conference on Church and Society: Christians in the Technical and Social Revolutions of Our Time.* Geneva: WCC, 1967.

van der Bent, Ans J. "Visser 't Hooft, Willem Adolf." In *Dictionary of the Ecumenical Movement*, edited by Nicholas Lossky et al., 1195–97. 2nd ed. Geneva: WCC Publications, 2002.

———, ed. *Voices of Unity: Essays in Honour of Willem Adolf Visser 't Hooft on the Occasion of His 80th Birthday.* Geneva: WCC, 1981.

———. *W. A. Visser 't Hooft 1900–1985: Fisherman of the Ecumenical Movement.* Geneva: WCC Publications, 2000.

Weber, H. R. "The Laity: Its Gifts and Ministry." In *The Sufficiency of God: Essays on the Ecumenical Hope in Honor of W. A. Visser 't Hooft*, edited by Robert C. Mackie and Charles C. West, 187–206. Philadelphia: Westminster, 1963.

Index

Ingram Content Group UK Ltd.
Milton Keynes UK
UKHW020629290323
419341UK00009B/189